WHO COUNTS?

Ghanaian academic publishing and global science

David Mills, Patricia Kingori,
Abigail Branford, Samuel Tamti Chatio,
Natasha Robinson and Paulina Tindana

**AFRICAN
MINDS**

Critical and up-to-date studies of African journal publishing are rare. This situation does little to help challenge the reality that African researchers rely heavily on journals owned and published outside the continent, that they have little control over or stake in, often to the detriment of the proper appraisal or validation of their research.

This book gives a great sense of the vibrant and energetic research culture at institutions in Ghana. Researchers are doing their best to engage with 'international' publishing, citation metrics and requirements of their own institutions, sometimes against the odds, but not without successes, all the while sustaining an embattled and under-resourced regional publishing ecology.

Importantly, the book also documents newer developments, such as the emergence of African-owned, commercial open-access journal publishing enterprises across the continent and in the diaspora that may not entirely follow models established in the West but are nevertheless proving sustainable and productive.

A great strength of the study is that it investigates publishing strategies in Ghana from both the researchers' and the journals' viewpoints across humanities and (social) sciences fields, thus bringing together author and publisher, who are too often seen as working at cross-purposes.

Refreshingly undogmatic, the authors reject 'easy answers' – such as tech-utopias, 'open science', expensive or unequal open access, the proliferating writing workshops favoured by funders and, most of all, the regime of (commercially-dominated) journal metrics. Instead, they take the continent's own researchers and journals seriously, elucidating the complex landscape of old and new, commercial and institutional, regional and international publishing.

This careful study makes for important reading for all those involved in the funding, management and policy-making of higher education and research in the African continent and beyond. After all, the very infrastructure of the continent's publishing – its researchers, journals, university presses and commercial publishing houses – is at stake.

– Stephanie Kitchen, International African Institute, London

Who Counts? revisits important questions regarding the past and future of academic publishing in African universities and research centres. The authors interrogate the adverse implications to African universities and research centres of global research and publication cultures that are marked by various contradicting binaries. The privileging of quantity over quality; business models over a focus on better knowledge production frameworks; encouragement of academics to publish more papers as opposed to better papers as an indicator of academic excellence; the proliferation of open access publishing journals based outside Africa that target submissions from African academics against the spirited denunciation of the emergence of similar journals within African as predatory; the promotion of individual academic and professional growth as opposed to nurturing a vibrant, self-sustaining and sovereign publishing industry anchored in the culture of African countries and institution; and the onslaught by multinational publishers to capture struggling independent publishing outfits in Africa in the context of the new digital economies.

Based on primary data from two universities in Ghana, *Who Counts?* bravely invites its reader to a new intellectual engagement of an old problem in research and academic publishing in Africa that has kept mutating with little change in its original design. In showing how global research and publishing economies continue to influence individual research and academic careers in Africa at the expense of investing in truly African publishing cultures that echo African interests in the global knowledge production and consumption ecosystems, the authors caution the readership that academic perishing arises from a culture of non-publishing as much as it does from too much publishing that is not anchored in a sovereign agenda.

– Ibrahim Oanda, CODESRIA, Dakar

Published in 2023 by African Minds
4 Eccleston Place, Somerset West, 7130, Cape Town, South Africa
info@africanminds.org.za
www.africanminds.org.za

The views expressed in this publication are those of the authors.
When quoting from any of the chapters, readers are requested to acknowledge all of the authors.

ISBN (paper): 978-1-928502-64-7
eBook edition: 978-1-928502-65-4
ePub edition: 978-1-928502-66-1

Copies of this book are available for free download at:
www.africanminds.org.za

ORDERS:
African Minds
Email: info@africanminds.org.za

To order printed books from outside Africa, please contact:
African Books Collective
PO Box 721, Oxford OX1 9EN, UK
Email: orders@africanbookscollective.com

Contents

Frequently used acronyms and abbreviations

AAAS Open	African Academy of Science Open (an 'open access' journal platform)
AAS	African Academy of Science
ABDC	Australian Business Deans Council
ADRRI	Africa Development and Resources Research Institute
AJFAND	*African Journal of Food, Agriculture, Nutrition and Development*
AJOL	African Journals Online
APC	article processing charges
APNET	African Publishers Network
AREF	*African Review of Economics and Finance*
ASSAf	Academy of Science of South Africa
ASSCAT	Africa Scholarly Science Communications Trust
BANGA-Africa	Building a New Generation of Academics in Africa
BMC	BioMed Central
BMJ	*British Medical Journal*
CJAS	*Contemporary Journal of African Studies*
CODESRIA	Council for the Development of Social Science Research in Africa
COPE	Committee on Publication Ethics
CPD	continual professional development
CSIR	Council for Scientific and Industrial Research
DHET	Department for Higher Education and Training
DOAJ	Directory of Open Access Journals
DORA	Declaration on Research Assessment
EAPH	East African Publishing House
ECR	early career researcher

ERI	Education Research International
GhanJOL	Ghana Journals Online
GhIH	Ghana Institute of Horticulture
GJDS	*Ghana Journal of Development Studies*
GJE	*Ghanaian Journal of Economics*
GJS	*Ghana Journal of Science*
HERANA	Higher Education Research and Advocacy Network in Africa
HoD	Head of Department
IBSS	International Bibliography of the Social Sciences
ICT	Information Communication Technology
IJOPPIE	*International Journal of Pedagogy, Policy, and ICT in Education*
INASP	International Network for the Availability of Scientific Publications
ISBN	international standard book number
JHORT	*Ghana Journal of Horticulture*
JIF	journal impact factor
JPPS	Journal Publishing Practices and Standards
KNUST	Kwame Nkrumah University of Science and Technology
NGO	Non-Governmental Organisation
NSB	National Standards Board (Ghana)
OA	open access
OASPA	Open Access Scholarly Publishers Association
OJS	Open Journal Software
PhD	Doctor of Philosophy
PloS	Public Library of Science
REdalyc	*Red de Revistas Científicas de América Latina y El Caribe, España y Portugal*
SAJE	Society of African Journal Editors
SciELO	Scientific Electronic Library Online
SIDA	Swedish International Development Cooperation Agency
STM	Science, Technology and Medicine
TD	*Journal for Transdisciplinary Research*
UCT	University of Cape Town
UDS	University of Development Studies
UG	University of Ghana

UK	United Kingdom
Unisa	University of South Africa
US	United States
USD	United States Dollar
VC	vice-chancellor
WoS	Web of Science
ZAR	South African Rand

Acknowledgements

We would like to thank all our Ghanaian interviewees for sparing precious academic time to talk about their research journeys and publishing experiences. African journal editors and publishers were equally generous, allowing us to develop detailed case studies of their journals and companies. Covid-19 forced us to redefine this project, and we are grateful for this support, given the consequences of the pandemic for African higher education systems and researchers. We look forward to sharing the insights of this book with all those who helped make it possible.

Our team made a range of contributions over the course of almost three years. These different tasks of researching and writing are best acknowledged using the CRediT (Contributor Roles Taxonomy) framework. These include David: conceptualisation, analysis, funding, investigation, methodology, project administration, supervision, writing, review and editing. Patricia: conceptualisation, analysis, supervision, funding, methodology. Abigail: data curation, formal analysis, investigation, writing, review and editing. Samuel: data curation, investigation, methodology, project administration. Natasha: investigation, writing. Paulina: conceptualisation, data curation, analysis, methodology, project administration, supervision, review and editing. An appendix offers a detailed account of the research design, along with reflections on data collection and ethics.

This research was supported by Research England GCRF (Global Challenges Research Fund) QR funding for Oxford University. We are grateful to African Minds for the opportunity of being able to publish this book open access, for the insights of our two anonymous reviewers, and the careful reading and detailed feedback offered by Ibrahim Oanda.

By capturing the hopes and frustrations of our many respondents, we describe how Ghanaian researchers and African publishers are getting by in a highly unequal global research economy. Academic publishing is dominated by a small handful of global companies and structured by what one could describe as bibliometric coloniality. A powerful set of social and technical infrastructures allocate and gatekeep academic credibility. The rules of the game continue to be defined outside the continent. We hope that, in some small way, this book contributes to the renaissance and renewal of African-centred research and publishing infrastructures.

David, Patricia, Abigail, Samuel, Natasha and Paulina
December 2022

Chapter 1

Introduction:
'You don't want to perish'

If someone brings his CV and I am looking at it and all their publications are in journals that are in volume one, volume two, volume three then I am thinking, 'you don't know how to publish in an old journal'. As one of my friends said regarding church, you should go to a church that is older than you. Similarly, you publish in journals that are older than you are. (Akosua, Associate Professor, Social Sciences)

The conversation had taken an unexpected turn. It is not often that people compare academic publishing and churchgoing. Nor would many think of using age as a measure of the credibility of an academic journal. Yet Akosua's witty apercu, offered in an interview about academic publishing practices in Ghana, reveals an important truth. A scholarly journal's reputation is hard-won, and can take many years to acquire. A senior social scientist at the University of Ghana, with professorial rank, Akosua knew that publishing in the 'right' journals was critical to building a scholarly career. She understood the subtle intertwining of journal reputation and scholarly credibility. Academics constantly evaluate each other's ideas, primarily through the quality of their research and ideas, but also through the status of the journals in which they publish.

Kwame Nkrumah, Ghana's first leader, understood the vital importance of Africa-centred academic knowledge 'free from the propositions and prepositions of the colonial epoch' (Nkrumah 1963, 2). Nkrumah's optimistic vision for an African Studies that studied Africa 'in its widest possible sense – Africa in all its complexity and diversity' (Nkrumah 1963, 9) coincided with the post-war expansion of higher education, the development of a global science system, and the professionalisation of academic publishing (Gray 2020). In the early years of the postcolonial era, a vibrant set of research cultures flourished in Africa's new universities and indigenous publishing houses. Decolonising research and academic publishing and policies of indigenisation went hand in hand. From the 1970s onwards, political and financial crises undermined African university research ecosystems, and European commercial publishers once again dominated.

Since the 1990s, the global publishing landscape has been transformed by digitisation, consolidation and the rise of the internet. The original goal of knowledge dissemination now sits alongside opportunities for individual academics to garner career capital and for businesses to extract financial profit (Fyfe et al. 2017). Governments around the world have begun to measure the research performance of public universities, developing ever more elaborate mechanisms for assessing the quality and quantity of research. Influential numerical proxies – such as the 'impact factor' generated by citation indexes – are used to rank the academic prestige of journals. Publication in 'high impact' journals can be traded for academic promotions, tenure and job security. There is an increasing hierarchy of journal prestige, and 'credibility' (Mills and Robinson 2021) has become the symbolic currency of a global research economy.

As the number of academic publications and journals continues to increase, many African researchers find themselves at the margins of this economy, negotiating a global knowledge system dominated by 'Northern' journals and global publishing conglomerates. Bibliometric data on Africa's share of global scientific publishing shows a slow increase to just over 3% of all indexed articles, but this is mostly dominated by South Africa, Egypt and Tunisia. Despite being

Africa's eighth largest economy (with a GDP of USD 58 billion in 2021) Ghanaian academics authored under 5,000 indexed articles in the years 2011 to 2015, or just 1.8% of Africa's total (Mouton and Blanckenberg 2018). The continent's academic publishers similarly labour in the global shadows of this digital publishing infrastructure.

This book looks beyond bibliometric data to understand the logics and meanings that shape publishing decisions. How, where and when are Ghana's researchers disseminating their academic work, and what do their experiences reveal about an unequal global science system (Marginson 2021)? The story it tells is about the Ghanaian academy, and African academic publishing, but it has resonances for researchers across the 'majority world', where most of the world's population live.

Global science continues to expand, with ever more academic journals. Digital publishing opportunities have accelerated the shift online, leading to rival digital publishing platforms (Mirowski 2019) and the vertical 'integration' of research tools (Posada and Chen 2019). At the same time, the open access movement, championing the democratisation of access to research, has led publishers to adopt profitable new 'author-pays' business models. Publishers such as Elsevier are increasingly 'data analytics' companies, owning citation indexes that provide detailed metrics on the performance of scholarly journals. African universities have adopted promotion criteria that assess staff on the quality and quantity of their research 'outputs', including journal articles and books. The reputation – and visibility – of these journals depends on their inclusion within the main global citation indexes, such as Scopus and Web of Science, making publishing within 'accredited' and 'international' journals ever more important.

Little is heard from those most vulnerable and exposed to the geographical inequalities and hierarchies of this global research economy and its publishing infrastructures. A major study of Africa's young scientists (Beaudry et al. 2018) is one recent exception. It uses bibliometric data, a web-based survey and 250 qualitative interviews to understand the challenges African researchers face in developing academic careers through research and publishing. Its strength – an Africa-wide remit – is also its limitation. By contrast, this book focuses specifically on African academic publishing, offering a richly detailed account of the voices and perspectives of Ghanaian applied scientists and social science researchers. It asks about how they balance recognition and relevance, the need to be both internationally 'visible' and to be engaged in creating knowledge and shaping national policy and practice. It draws on the insights of almost 50 academics in two Ghanaian public universities, bringing them into dialogue with journal editors and publishers from across the continent, with case studies from Ghana, Nigeria, Kenya and South Africa.

For Ghana's academics, research and publication strategies have very real material consequences for their careers and professional reputations. The book explores the expectations of them to publish in 'reputable' international journals, their preparation for this process, and the importance of supervision, collaboration and mentoring. It also asks about the emotional demands of trying to research and publish when time and resources are scarce. The book investigates Ghana's place within an increasingly hierarchical global science system, and how a new geography of credibility, mediated by citation metrics, is reshaping the fortunes of long-established West African scholarly journals and disciplinary associations. Can existing journals and presses adapt? How will they deal with competition from commercially-orientated open-access publishing models?

In the 1920s, a little-known Californian sociologist Clarence Marsh Case distilled the challenge facing US universities (Case 1927). He was worried about the 'inverse relation' between the quality and quantity of published research. Case blamed this on 'the system of promotion used in our universities (that) amounts to the warning 'publish or perish' (Case 1927, 355). Whether or not he invented – or simply borrowed – the phrase, it quickly became an academic commonplace (Wilson 1942; Garfield 1996; Cabanac 2018). All the Ghanaian researchers interviewed were asked why publishing was important in an academic career. Almost half – 19 of 43 researchers – immediately invoked Case's precise phrase 'publish or perish'. Many could recall exactly when they had heard this truism: some from their supervisor, others from faculty deans or university rectors. One called it a 'guiding principle'. None doubted its veracity or staying power, making it an important logic to understand and appreciate.

Akosua, like most of the Ghanaian scholars interviewed for this book, negotiated her own way through the publication maze. Unlike most of her compatriots, she was successful in winning a graduate scholarship at an elite US university. This then opened up opportunities to present her work at US-based African Studies conferences. One event, chaired by an eminent Yale historian, provided her with detailed feedback and suggestions, and an invitation to submit her paper to the highly-regarded *Ghana Studies* journal. She described her reliance on the advice, support and guidance of the journal editor as she revised her work in response to extensive reviewer comments.

She reflected on these early experiences, and the insights they gave her into the importance of connecting different academic spaces and communities. 'I am not interested in just being called a professor in Ghana, but in being connected globally.' Her ideal was to publish not just in 'locally-based journals, but in locally-based journals that are referenced internationally'. She acknowledged the rewards of international scholarly recognition. 'Invited to all manner of conferences, all manner of places, your ticket is bought, your hotel, you go and they take you on a trip, they take you to dinner.'

Akosua was also unusual among her peers for another reason. She insisted that she was not ambitious, or in a rush to be promoted. She admitted that 'in the academic enterprise this is what you were supposed to do' and that some of her friends had 'a 5-year plan, a 10-year plan, a 15-year plan, a 20-year plan'. Currently an associate professor, she felt that she would probably make full professor by the time she was 60. In the meantime, 'when I am interested in a topic, I write it, it gets published'.

Akosua vividly expressed the emotional timescapes and rhythms of academic life: the endorphin-fuelled rush to meet grant deadlines, the painstakingly slow process of writing and revising, and the suspense-laden wait for editorial decisions. As the interviews in this book reveal, many scholars saw time as precious. Some valued the care that went into rigorous peer review, others were frustrated at how long it took to get work accepted and published. Akosua's insights into strategising rang true: all of the Ghanaian interviewees knew precisely how many publications they had authored. Above all others, this metric measured progress towards the magical number required for promotion.

Akosua was perceptive about the challenge of making time to write, especially as a woman in an academic culture with strongly gendered attitudes towards caring responsibilities. When asked if training on publishing would be useful for staff, Akosua was bluntly dismissive. 'The head of department has to speak, then the chair, then the vice-chancellor, I don't have time for all of that'. For Akosua, the culture of lengthy workshops and the assumption that 'African scholars need these things' was a patronising waste of time. Worse, 'if we don't sign up you think we are lazy'. She was blunt about the pressures her colleagues faced. 'The crisis is not that they don't know where to publish. Or how to choose the journal. The crisis is you have to develop your course material to teach, and you also have to publish your own research, you have young children, and you have to balance all of that.' She had a refreshingly honest view of the role of publishing in an academic career.

Akosua is just one of many Ghanaian academics whose voices fill this book. The changing nature of African academic publishing is best understood through the experiences and perceptions of researchers and publishers themselves. Their decisions and rationales offer insights into the influence of a global research economy on African universities, and different ways to respond.

This book builds on these personal perspectives to explore a series of interlinked questions about the changing nature of academic publishing in sub-Saharan Africa (Zell 2018), and the skewed geographies of academic credibility that structure a global research economy (Shapin 1995; Powell 2007). Why are some journals and outlets, published in and from certain places, seen as more credible than others? What are the implications of university expectations on researchers to publish 'internationally', ideally in 'highly ranked' journals, for the Ghanaian research ecosystem? How are African publishers and journals affected by their exclusion from the elite global journal databases and citation indexes? Is the global science system, with its increasing use of citation metrics as a proxy for credibility, undermining the reputation of existing West African academic journals? And how is this in turn redefining national and regional 'credibility economies'?

This project partly emerged from a series of conversations about academic fakery (see Kingori 2021). The authors became interested in why Africa was increasingly seen as the source of illegitimate and 'fake' forms of academic work (Allman 2019; Kingori 2018). Some of this can be traced to the powerful influence of the Colorado data librarian Jeffrey Beall who coined the concept of 'predatory publishing' (2012). Beall's 'list' began as a review of nine commercial open-access publishers (2009). Beall then launched a blog, called 'Scholarly Open Access'. By the time his blog was suddenly taken down from the internet in 2016, the list included almost 1,700 publishers.

Beall's lists had many unintended consequences. They swept a diverse set of open-access journals into one judgemental net. Beall's ire was particularly directed at those journals that charged APCs (article processing charges). For several Ghanian researchers, realising that they had published in a journal that had subsequently been classified as problematic by Beall became a source of embarrassment. Publishing in what might be viewed as the 'wrong' place meant that new journals were increasingly treated with suspicion. Disparaging jokes about academics whose CVs contained long lists of 'vol. 1, no. 1' publications began to circulate. A new journal was no longer seen as an intellectual innovation: it was more likely to be viewed as a vanity project designed to bolster an individual's career. Any new initiative struggles to acquire credibility, accreditation and recognition. The emotive and dehumanising discourse around journal 'fakery' and 'predation' reinforced the power and influence of the dominant science publishers, and they continue to promote these terms (Inouye and Mills 2021). It is in this context that African journals and publishing presses struggle to sustain their credibility and reputation.

Going beyond this emotive rhetoric about fakery, how was the notion of so-called 'predatory' publishers viewed and experienced, by both researchers and publishers themselves? The best way to understand how the perceived risk of 'publish *and* perish' was reshaping research culture was to talk to researchers themselves.

This book is being published at a time when calls to decolonise academic knowledge have renewed prominence (Mbembe 2016; Ndlovu-Gatsheni 2017; Sarr 2022). Many ask what it will take to strengthen Africa-based research ecosystems and develop more diverse publishing infrastructures (Berger 2021; Meagher 2021; Okune et al. 2021). Latin American scholars have highlighted the importance of regional infrastructures and publication circuits for resisting the dominance of the global publishers (Beigel 2018). Are similar models possible in Africa? Will strong regional publishing ecosystems be sustained in Ghana and across West Africa? If not, how will a diverse and pluriversal set of African academic knowledge cultures be protected? In a highly politicised debate about the coloniality of knowledge infrastructures, these questions reward careful analysis.

Researching publishing

Researching academic publishing requires a range of skills. Many journals have long histories and were often founded by particular universities or scholarly associations. The growing influence of commercial publishers has been driven by the changing political economy of university research, and, more recently, the emergence of digital publishing technologies and the open access movement. Understanding how these developments shaped the African academy requires close attention to postcolonial history, geopolitics and an increasingly transnational research economy.

The research was carried out in several stages. The first involved interviewing Ghanaian academics in a range of applied fields across the sciences and social sciences – from public health to education, from agriculture to sociology – in two Ghanaian public universities. The aim was to understand participants' publishing rationales, logics, and experiences, but also to tease out how differences in publishing practices were mediated by gender, age, career stage, discipline and university. It was important to understand perceptions of journal quality, as well as the role of mentors, project leaders and collaborative publishing. The perspectives of senior academic leaders – including heads of department and faculty – helped make sense of the institutional expectations placed on academic faculty, as well as the support and mentoring that they were given.

The second stage involved interviewing journal editors, reviewers, and publishers from Ghana and across the continent, given their insights into the African research and publishing ecosystem. The third stage was to situate both sets of empirical material within a broader history of African academic publishing.

Why Ghanaian universities?

In making sense of academic publishing cultures in postcolonial anglophone Africa, the University of Ghana (UG) was a good place to start. It traces its roots back to University College Ghana which was set up as an elite 'Asquith College' by the British colonial government in the late 1940s (Agbodeka 1998). It is now regarded as Ghana's 'flagship' public university (Acquah and Budu 2017) and has the ambition to be a 'research-intensive world-class' institution. It faces many challenges, not least of rapid growth, with undergraduate numbers more than tripling between 2001 and 2015, from 10,000 to almost 35,000 (Cloete et al. 2018).

The university was part of a ten-year African higher education advocacy network (called HERANA, the Higher Education Research and Advocacy Network in Africa). Each of the eight participating universities established a set of performance indicators by which they could measure progress in developing research capacity. By 2017, UG's research 'inputs' and outputs were still some way behind Nairobi and Makerere, and the final analysis (Cloete et al. 2018) classified it as an 'emerging research-intensive university', trailing well behind the research 'benchmark' set by the University of Cape Town.

In juxtaposition to the University of Ghana, the second case study focused on the publishing expectations placed on academic colleagues at a newer public university – the University of Development Studies

(UDS) – in the north of Ghana. Set up in the 1980s as a multi-campus university for the Northern region, its original vision was to 'demystify the myth between academic work and the concerns of rural peoples' (Bening 2005). The ambition was to take up Kwame Nkrumah's challenge that a 'university must relate its activity to the needs of the society in which it exists, taking root amidst African traditions and cultures' (Nkrumah, cited in Ashby 1966). UDS pioneered a unique pedagogy whereby students spent one term each year living and working in a rural community on a participatory research project. One academic at UDS described his work as having a triple mandate – teaching, research, and community extension. Did the UDS ethos of teaching and public engagement lead to a different set of expectations around publishing and research outputs? As with UG, research access depended on the team's academic contacts and personal connections. A comparison of two Ghanaian public universities offers insights into the influence of different institutional and research cultures on research and publishing practices.

Publishing practices vary widely between disciplines, and disciplinary 'insider' knowledge can help make sense of these cultures. With backgrounds in public health, anthropology and education, the team was less familiar with research and publishing cultures in maths, 'pure' sciences or arts-based disciplines. Investigating fields such as health and agriculture in both universities also made sense because most researchers at UDS were working in the applied disciplines, making for more direct comparisons. One hypothesis was that researchers working in these applied science fields would be more likely to publish in outlets that shaped science policy and practice in Ghana. Publishing in 'prestigious' international journals may have been balanced against these national needs. The importance and significance of African research in agriculture, public health and the applied sciences is visible in the way that African research makes up more than 6% of global research in agronomy and related fields (Mouton and Blanckenberg 2018).

Interviews focused on junior and senior faculty in the health sciences, social sciences, applied sciences and agriculture. With the support of faculty deans and heads of departments, the sample was designed to represent the gender, seniority and age diversity of academic faculty. Staff at different career stages offered insight into how publishing cultures had changed over time. Heads of department explained how they were managing and supporting their faculty. Gender was a key variable, as publishing pressures are experienced differently by female faculty, especially those with childcare responsibilities. Ensuring gender diversity amongst the interviewees was easier at UG than at UDS, where there were markedly fewer female research staff.

Table 1: Academic faculty interviewed by institution

	UG	UDS
Senior academic faculty	5 men, 5 female	5 men, 1 female
Early career academic faculty	6 men, 5 female	12 men, 4 female
Total	21	22

Table 2: Age range (and average) of faculty by institution

	UG	UDS
Senior academic faculty	40–54 (47)	36–56 (48)
Early career academic faculty	36–59 (43)	28–55 (44)

Table 3: Range (and average) of individuals' scholarly publication 'outputs'

	UG	UDS
Publications by senior academic faculty	9–75 (36)	8–35 (18)
Publications by early career academic faculty	5–22 (10)	0–20 (8)

Access involved careful diplomacy and often relied on personal connections. We needed the support of faculty deans to approach heads of department, gaining their permission in turn to approach individual faculty. Being interviewed was never top of busy academics' 'to-do' lists. Appointments were repeatedly cancelled and rearranged as people postponed or double-booked. This meant repeated visits and waiting outside office doors hoping to catch the relevant academic.

Interviews were often interrupted by meetings with supervisees and students. One set of fieldnotes captures this vividly:

> I called this participant on the phone and introduced myself and the study to her. She asked me to see her in the office the next day. I went to her office the following day and I did not meet her. I called her again to find out whether she was coming. She told me she was not going to come to the office that day as well and rather asked me to come the next day. It was the same story when I went to her office the third day. It continued like that for quite some time.

Once interviews began, many enjoyed the chance to talk and reflect on their own publication journeys. Some lasted more than an hour and were rich in biographical detail. All were asked if they knew their current number of publications. Everyone provided this number with precision and without hesitation, even if with a modicum of modesty: 'about 27' or 'over 70'. This is perhaps no surprise. Ghana's public universities have enumerated clear publication requirements for promotion. Parpicipants' answers ranged from none (for an assistant lecturer) to 70 (for one senior lecturer). Perhaps because they had begun their careers before these guidelines were introduced, two senior lecturers had fewer than 10 publications; on the other hand, one prolific junior lecturer had 20 publications.

Given the sensitivities of discussing an academic's publication record, questions sought to elicit interviewees' research and publishing experiences in a non-judgemental way. The aim was to put people at ease, and to reflect on their choices, attending to successes and failures, rewards and regrets. Interviews explored the all-important 'why', 'where', 'when' and 'how' questions. Why did publishing matter to them? Where had they started publishing and how had first experiences shaped their subsequent decisions? Had they published individually, with their supervisor, or with other authors? How had they decided on which journal to send their paper to? Had they had a difficult experience liaising with an editor, or dealing with conflicting peer-review comments? How long had it taken, and what had they learnt about journals and publishers as a result? Did they feel that it had been a formative journey, or just a frustrating one? The chapters exploring these questions offer a distinctly Ghanaian perspective on universal academic experiences. Their strategies, experiences and reflections offer important insights into the institutional contexts in which they are working, and their mediation by discipline, gender, age and seniority.

Interviewing African journal editors and publishers

Academics can tell only one side of the publishing story. Many recount the pressure on them to publish in certain places, or acknowledge the frustrations of slow peer-review decisions or editorial responses. What would journal editors and publishers say in response? Does the increasing expectation that researchers publish in 'reputable' journals with impact factors affect African editors? It felt important to get publishers and journal editors in Ghana and across anglophone Africa (including journals based in Nigeria, Kenya and South Africa) to tell their side of the story. All agreed to speak on the record, and have had several chances to comment on the case studies developed about their journals and organisations

Many of the editors profiled have spent years running highly regarded journals, and are driven by a strong sense of academic service or individual commitment. A few of these are faculty or university journals, surviving on a shoestring, relying on volunteer editorial labour or a small stipend from a hosting institution or research centre. A second group of journals – sampled from across the continent – were independently owned and more commercially orientated. They ranged in scale from bootstrap start-ups to established companies. A couple were emulating the major global publishers, developing sophisticated publishing platforms, and hosting a suite of new online journals. Some of these journals were explicitly mentioned by interviewees as places they had published, others had influential international profiles, and a few had been accused by Beall of 'predatory' publishing. With a range of publishing models, all faced the similar challenge of sustaining and building a scholarly reputation and academic credibility. The case studies in this book retain – with permission – the names of editors and journals, as the details and specificities are key to the analysis. Where appropriate, the interviews were complemented with historical research to help understand the institutional emergence and longer-term trajectories of these journals.

Chapter overview

This book offers a holistic account of African academic publishing, its histories and its potential futures. The experiences of academics and journal editors speak to the broader political economy of research across the West African and sub-Saharan region. The book's argument is that writing and publishing have become key for African academic careers, and that these practices are being transformed within a global research economy. The task is to understand how the digital and data infrastructures that underpin field-specific research ecosystems in Ghana and across the African continent are reshaping academic lives and scholarly writing. The book unfolds across ten chapters, combining empirical insights with history and sociology to make a fresh contribution to a vital topic. Quotes, stories and vignettes help craft an attentive, African-centred understanding of these academic publishing ecosystems and their relationship to global science.

Chapter 2 offers a historical perspective on the links between global developments and African publishing cultures. It begins by describing the emergence of new journals and university presses in postcolonial West Africa. After the heady early years of post-independence research and publishing, the financial and political crises of the 1970s and 1980s hit African university presses hard. Many closed or became dormant (Zell 2018). Only small publishing cooperatives remained, working on a shoestring and reliant on international donations. A few scholar-led journals kept publishing throughout, supported by national scientific research institutions or regional networks such as CODESRIA. Meanwhile the global academic publishing landscape continued to expand and evolve, and the five largest commercial publishers (Wiley, Informa, Elsevier, Springer-Nature, Sage) consolidated their market positions by acquiring more journals. The post-2000 digital revolution, the rise of open-access publishing, and the emergence of non-mainstream and 'entrepreneurial' publishers created new disruptions, opportunities, and challenges. Postcolonial histories and economic geographies are the backdrop for the publishing challenges facing Ghanaian academics and Africa's journals today.

Chapter 3 asks what might seem an obvious question 'why publish?'. What motivates or drives Ghana's academics to spend time on research and writing papers, given the demands of teaching, supervision, and service, of caring and family responsibilities, and the struggle to make ends meet on an academic salary. This chapter, like several in this book, is full of rich quotes and personal insights, offering a Ghanaian perspective on existing literatures on academic work.

Again and again, people resorted to the aphorism 'publish or perish': they felt they had little choice if they were to move forward in their academic careers. In the same breath, many also insisted that doing research made them better teachers, and they felt a duty to share knowledge and contribute to scholarship. Theirs was a vision of research and teaching as symbiotic. Others spoke of the intrinsic and affective rewards that came from research and publishing, espousing a Weberian commitment to the scientific vocation. Through their reflections and perspectives, a complex tapestry of personal motivations and professional values emerges.

Chapter 4 goes on to examine the all-important 'where' question. How do Ghanaian researchers decide where to send their manuscript for peer-review and, hopefully, timely publication? To what extent do formal institutional expectations and informal disciplinary cultures shape individual publishing decisions, ambitions, and expectations? The University of Ghana promotes Elsevier's Scopus citation index as a reliable guide to 'reputable' journals, even though Scopus contains very few African journals. Meanwhile UDS regularly circulates Beall's list of so-called 'predatory' journals. Exploring how university expectations to publish in 'reputable peer-reviewed journals' get interpreted, the chapter describes how Ghana's researchers adopt and even internalise publishing metrics – including the numbers of articles written, and journal impact factors – as part of their academic identities. The chapter introduces the heated debates that have surrounded so-called 'predatory' publishing and the ways in which publishers such as Elsevier market proprietary citation indexes.

The chapter also discusses scholarly perceptions of 'international' as compared to 'local' journals. Many respondents complained about the delays in getting peer-review comments from long-established national journals, and the slow pace at which these journals make editorial decisions. The interviews reveal how individual scholars carefully weigh up journal reputation, 'impact', perceived accessibility, time to publication, and cost when choosing where to submit their manuscripts. A final section explores other avenues for disseminating research, including blogging, and writing for the general media.

Chapter 5 addresses the 'how' and 'who' of Ghanaian academic publishing in the applied sciences and social sciences. How important and formative are first publishing experiences, personal relationships, and academic networks in shaping people's publishing strategies? The literature on collaborative academic publishing has highlighted its growth, posing new ethical and logistical challenges. Interviewees talked about the influential intellectual and academic roles played by supervisors, mentors, and other collaborators and co-authors. They also spoke of how these mentoring and writing relationships changed over time. The chapter highlights disciplinary and institutional differences, the rise of team-based publishing, the motivations for working together, and the hierarchies and exploitation that can result.

Chapter 6 turns to the time and resource economies of scarcity, and how this shapes academic writing and publishing in a Ghanaian context. There is a growing global literature on the precarity of academic work within the research economy, and the emotional and affective pressures it creates, including a pervading sense of competition and rivalry with one's colleagues. These pressures are acutely felt in a resource-constrained setting. Ghana's researchers measure their progress as scholars through their publication profile, and this chapter also explores the frustration or resentment felt towards younger scholars who seek to progress their careers too quickly, or who have not 'served' their time. The importance of patience contrasts with the time pressure respondents are under to publish in order to qualify for promotion or tenure. Informed by research into academic temporality and 'waithood', this chapter reflects on these different time economies. It also explores the emotional costs, especially for female researchers, of trying to carve out space and time to research and publish whilst teaching and being involved in administration, within universities that devote very little funding and resources to research.

Chapter 7 takes a different perspective to understand this changing publishing landscape: that of Ghanaian journal editors and publishers. Informed by interviews with editors and publishers, it compares a range of Ghanaian scholarly journals, describing their history, reputation, status, and publishing models. Editors vividly depict the demands of maintaining the publication cycle, garnering submissions, dealing with peer review, seeking institutional support, and sustaining scholarly standards. For journals run on a largely voluntary basis, funding is a constant concern. These portraits describe how they have survived, and their plans for an uncertain future. Many have benefitted from support and training offered by African Journals Online (AJOL), and the last part of this chapter explores AJOL's role in building capacity within the African publishing ecosystem.

Chapter 8 changes scale, and maps the rise of independent academic publishing houses across Anglophone Africa: with examples from Ghana, Nigeria, Kenya and South Africa. It documents their adoption of 'open-access' business models and digital publishing technologies. The case studies reveal very different philosophies, business models, publishing profiles and editorial approaches. The chapter compares the founding visions of the publishers, the challenges of sustaining growth and quality, and different approaches to accumulating scholarly credibility. Not all are for-profit, but all have to balance the rival demands of academic credibility, global visibility and financial viability (Mills and Robinson 2021). Given the growing pressure to publish in 'accredited' international journals, some have sought to strengthen their legitimacy and reputation through applying for inclusion in the main citation indexes. Others face having that accreditation removed or called into question.

Chapter 9 returns to the question of how Ghana's researchers and African academic journals are negotiating a global research economy that measures knowledge quantitatively. It starts with a vignette from an Elsevier training webinar, where Elsevier faculty were promoting their indexing and research 'solutions' products – including Scopus – to respondents from a range of African universities. The metricisation of scholarly production has led to numbers – of publications, citations, and impact – becoming proxies for academic credibility and reputation. The institutional expectation to publish in globally 'reputable' journals, defined increasingly as those listed in the Scopus or Web of Science indexes, threatens long-standing scholarly journals that have not managed to meet these technical and quality thresholds. The increasing control exerted by these digital publishing infrastructures (Eve and Gray 2020) presents difficult questions for African knowledge systems.

The chapter looks at possible futures for Ghana's journals and the West African research ecosystem. Beyond calls for sustainable models of open access and open science (Weingart and Taubert 2018), can reimagined socio-technical infrastructures foster greater diversity in African-centred scholarly knowledge (Meagher 2021; Okune et al. 2021)? Whilst digital open access creates new opportunities, it also puts existing African journals at risk. The technical and infrastructural demands of building robust regional research ecosystems will take time and resources to solve. Despite advocacy from the African Union for more state support for research, there is little funding for research infrastructures. Many African countries devote far less than 1% of GDP to R&D. Without policy commitments towards research strategy, systems are reliant on short-term donor funding. There are no easy answers.

A short concluding chapter weaves the different themes of this book together, combining history and sociology, along with perspectives from researchers and publishers, both in Ghana and across the continent. It asks what it might take to move beyond bibliometric coloniality, and the potential the potential for democratising, de-commoditising and diversifying knowledge flows.

Chapter 2

The rise, fall and future
of African academic publishing

To establish an indigenous publishing house is an act of liberation, and therefore a necessity, because it breaks the control, indeed the monopoly which the white races have over the world literature, for which reason they have controlled the mind of the African. (Dodson and Dodson 1972, 62)

Recentring the imagination

The 1960s was a time of intellectual effervescence and publishing creativity in universities across newly independent anglophone Africa. In November 1961, the Ugandan Rajat Neogy launched *Transition*, an innovative and outspoken journal, styling it as a space for East African public intellectuals. Building on the precedent set four years earlier by the Nigerian literary journal *Black Orpheus*, Neogy published politicians, academics, and poets alike, attracting submissions from Naipaul and Achebe. A year later, Kwame Nkrumah addressed the first internationalist congress of Africanists in Accra, attracting 600 scholars. In 1963 he opened the University of Ghana's new Institute of African Studies, with a speech entitled 'The African genius', advocating the 'study of Africa in its complexity, and diversity, and underlying unity' (Nkrumah 1963, 9). Inspired by the vision of Kojo

Botsio, Ghana's first minister of education, and Thomas Hodgkin, the institute offered a radical interdisciplinary vision for Africa-focused research and teaching. Its flagship journal, *Research Review*, was launched in 1964 and continues today as the *Contemporary Journal of African Studies*.

In South Africa Randolphe Vigne and James Currey launched *The New African: The radical review*. Two years later *The New African* was closed down by the apartheid government, forcing the editor to flee from the country (Vigne and Currey 2014). In 1963 Bethwell Ogot launched the East African Institute of Social and Cultural Affairs, which published the *East Africa Journal*, and the East African Publishing House (EAPH), the first indigenous publisher in Kenya (Ogot 1965). The 1960s also saw a lively intellectual rivalry between Makerere and Dar es Salaam (Mamdani 2018), whilst Tanzanian scholars like Issa Shivji and Walter Rodney sought to recentre the geographical imagination on Africa, and to 'provincialise' Europe (Sharp 2019). If one starts from Nigeria, as Craggs and Neate put it, one can tell very different histories of the metropolitan social sciences (Craggs and Neate 2019). Like Tanzania, many sub-Saharan African countries developed their own scholarly communities and debates, forging cosmopolitan communities of African and European researchers.

During that period, most African researchers still saw writing as integral to their academic careers. Some universities introduced what Barbour (1984, 96) calls a 'generous policy of publish and be promoted' (see also Van den Berghe 1973). Scholars of publishing acknowledged how 'an independent intellectual life' and 'self-sufficiency in the scientific realm', depended on 'building the structures for knowledge dissemination' across the 'Third World' (Altbach 1978, 489). For Altbach, universities 'stood in the centre of scientific and intellectual process' in many nations. He saw that publishing within an intellectual system was 'complicated and required considerable infrastructure', given the challenges of translation, distribution and the financial power of international publishers. Despite the 'seemingly insurmountable challenges', Altbach felt that creating an 'adequate means of scientific and academic communication' was neither 'very costly nor overwhelmingly difficult' (Altbach 1978, 502). Looking back, Allman (2013, 183) describes the 1970s as a moment when it was possible to imagine 'forms of academic knowledge production about Africa that challenged colonial categories' and 'was Africa-centred, Africa-based and globally engaged'.

Astride this academic tumult, West African university departments launched scholarly journals, fostering local cultures of research and knowledge. *Nature* regularly published updates from the 'British Colonial Territories' and reported at length on the conferences of the Nigeria Science Association, founded in 1959, and the Ghanaian Science Association, founded in 1961 (Yanney-Wilson 1961, 1962). Craggs and Neate (2019) depict the vibrancy of geography at Ibadan in the 1960s, with researchers editing important national journals, including the *Nigerian Journal of Geography* (founded in 1957). The University of Ghana Press launched in 1962 (Ganu 1999). The same year, Makerere hosted the first African Writers Conference. Sichermann (2005) tracks the rise of research cultures across the disciplines at Makerere during this period. Africa's first academic journals, established during the colonial period by museums, missionary societies, and medical services were joined by many more in the 1960s and 1970s (Murray and Clobridge 2014).

African academics and writers also established independent publishing presses. Abigailola Irele, the one-time editor of *Black Orpheus*, set up the influential Ethiopian publishing company in Nigeria in 1970, and went on to support a range of university presses (Irele 1973). Chakava (1993) records that close to thirty academic journals were being published by Kenyan-owned publishing houses in the mid-1970s. A pioneering Unesco-sponsored conference on publishing at the University of Ife marked the launch of several Nigerian presses (Oluwasanami et al. 1975; Zell 2017). African universities paid better salaries than UK universities in the 1960s, and new fields of African Studies flourished. An analysis of article citations in four fields (Botany, Zoology, Mathematics and Physics) from 1963–1975 found that research from the University of Ibadan and Nairobi was cited 550 and 736 times respectively, with work in fields 'presumed to be locally orientated' – namely Botany and Zoology – being more visible internationally than that published by researchers at Victoria University Wellington in New Zealand (Rabkin et al. 1979).

For all the optimism that surrounded Africa's 'university age' (Livsey 2017), the finances of this research economy, and of African academic publishing in particular, were far from secure. Altbach (1978) highlighted how British publishers had developed profitable African subsidiaries selling school textbooks and dominated the African markets. However, there was little profit to be made from publishing African journals. Smith (1975) tells the story of a meeting between Kwame Nkrumah and Harold Macmillan in 1964, as Ghana's president asked the ex-prime minister's advice on how to build an efficient and profitable state publishing house. The Macmillan publishing house made the most of the opportunity, creating a state–private partnership. Subsequent deals with Tanzania, Uganda, Zambia and Nigeria gave the publisher a lucrative monopoly.

Under pressure to Africanise their operations, the six dominant British publishers created local subsidiaries, but publication decisions were still made in London. These companies continued to import books and export profits. The African intellectual community was still largely dependent on international networks and Western publishers for prestige, publicity, and financial recompense. Like other critics of neo-colonialism, Smith and others blamed 'the intellectual and bureaucratic elites in African countries' for having 'entrenched multinational control' and thereby retarding the emergence of a vigorous indigenous publishing industry (Smith 1975, 150). There were similar calls to 'Africanise' universities that were dominated by expatriate academic faculty (Ashby 1964; Awori 1967).

By the early 1980s, the political and financial situation in many African countries was deteriorating rapidly. Rajat Neogy, *Transition*'s editor, had been arrested for sedition in 1968 by Obote's government. His attempt to restart the journal in Ghana in the 1970s foundered due to a lack of support. In country after country, political instability was compounded by financial crises, with first the 'oil shock' of 1973 and then the impact of World Bank structural adjustment policies.

As publishing sales plummeted and the multinational publishers were accused of profit extraction, most pulled out. A few, such as Macmillan, handed over their business to local agents. The hopes for an East African economic community collapsed in acrimony, and the closure of the Tanzanian border meant that Kenyan publishers could no longer export books across East Africa. This led to the demise of Kenya's East African Publishing House in 1977 (Chakava 1993), and also killed off most of Kenya's scholarly journals. It took this embryonic research and publishing ecosystem a long time to recover.

Years of civil instability, IMF-led structural adjustment and funding austerity undermined these research cultures and made life ever harder in the African academy. The underfunding of university presses eroded their ability to publish new work. Growing numbers of students made teaching the main priority. Consultancy work replaced research and became an important way to supplement inadequate academic salaries. It was easy for outsiders to criticise. One Ghanaian academic based in Germany acknowledged these 'myriad' challenges, but still felt justified in criticising his University of Ghana colleagues for 'lagging behind their expatriate counterparts in research productivity'. For him, the answer was simple: 'pushing onto Publishville' (Bodomo 1999, 188), prioritising publications over teaching and administrative responsibilities.

Scholars of higher education began to focus on the gatekeeping exerted by 'foreign' journals, with Altbach and Rathgeber (1980, 31) highlighting the 'rising consciousness among Nigerian intellectuals of the ideological control exercised over their work by expatriate publishers', and the pressure to conform to 'viewpoints expressed by metropolitan scholars'. Cabral et al. (1998) wittily illustrate the many forms that these rejection letters took. Philip Altbach continued to use his knowledge of Indian publishing, applying them to African higher education and the core-periphery status hierarchies that structured the global university system (Teferra and Altbach 2003, Altbach 2004). Together with Damtew Teferra, he co-edited a series of volumes on the global publishing industry, publishing in African languages, knowledge dissemination (Altbach and Teferra 1998, 1999) and the challenges facing African journals and publishers from a range of perspectives:

practical, financial, technical, geopolitical and conceptual.

It was not just African universities that were under threat: African Studies in the UK was also hit by the funding cuts of the 1970s (McCracken 1993). With departments closing and fewer opportunities for dialogue, exchange and research, Crowder predicted an increasing 'mutual isolation' and the 'compartmentalisation of Africanists into two worlds – the rich Europeans and Americans on the one hand, and the poor African scholars on the other' (Crowder 1987, 109). Critical histories of the African Studies Association of the US (Allman 2019) reveal the consequences of a similar racial divide within the American academy.

The history of South African academic publishing offers another perspective on these broader trends. The country's institutions were segregated by race during apartheid, creating a systemic publishing barrier for black academics, even prior to the implicit bias that peer review can sustain (Le Roux 2015a). Presses like Unisa supported many journals, but radical academics were forced to publish internationally or with small independent presses, amidst a culture of self-censorship (Le Roux 2020). Tomaselli (2020) tells the story of one South African journal, *Critical Arts*, that started as a 'cottage industry' and survived for 25 years as an 'oppositional' journal before being given systematic institutional backing in the late 1990s. Co-publishing arrangements, such as that between Unisa and Taylor and Francis, have brought South African journals back into an international intellectual community, positioning local research in a global context (Le Roux 2015b).

The legacies of these divides are still visible in South Africa today, as scientometric scholars critique the low quality of publishing by scholars in the historically black institutions (Mouton and Valentine 2017). Others go beyond allegations of racism or editorial gatekeeping to call for more sustained attention to the 'managerial opacity of institutions' and the 'political–economic effects of measurement and reward systems' (Tomaselli 2019, 97).

As the next section shows, the global research economy continues to cast its shadow over African academic publishing. It starts with a short history of academic journal publishing and its commercial transformation in the 1950s and 1960s, led by publishers such as Pergamon Press. We describe how a few African presses and networks made valiant attempts to keep African academic publishing alive amidst the IMF austerity prescriptions and 'structural adjustment' policies of the 1980s. By the 1990s human capital theory was becoming increasingly influential. After neglecting universities for two decades, the World Bank began to fund African higher education once again (Lebeau and Mills 2008), and US philanthropy made major commitments to African university research 'capacity building' (Manuh et al. 2007; Jaumont 2016).

The chapter goes on to describe the emergence of a 21st century global science system, with journal articles (and their associated citations and impact) becoming the symbolic currency of a new research economy. In the early 2000s, responding to the emergence of global university rankings, there was ever more concern about African university research 'capacity' (Wendland 2016; Tousignant 2018). West Africa's research universities were beginning to stipulate that some publications should be in 'international' journals, a trend that began to undermine the reputation of long-established national journals (Adomi and Mordi 2003; Nwagwu 2005; Omobowale et al. 2014). Linking promotion decisions to research outputs created incentives to publish, a model akin to the rewards system that transformed Chinese humanities publishing (Xu 2019).

The arrival of the internet opened up new global networks for collaboration and research. Digital publishing software, such as OJS (Open Journals Software) offered the promise of democratising the publishing process, and became a realistic strategy for academic and several new independent journal presses launched in Nigeria and Ghana. For African academics frustrated by 'Northern' editorial gatekeeping and the languid editorial rhythms of 'local' scholarly journals, online open-access journals offered a quick, low-cost route to getting an academic publication (Smart et al. 2005).

Not everyone welcomed this diversity of publishing options, or the rapid adoption of an open-access business model funded by APCs. Article processing charges were first adopted in the sciences, responding to the serials crisis of the 1990s, where libraries were increasingly unable to afford the subscriptions to an ever larger number of journals. From the perspective of integrity 'watchdogs' such as Beall, this new business model had other problems. If publishing more articles ensured a greater revenue stream, what was to stop journal editors being encouraged to lower their editorial standards? Beall's list had profound consequences for academic publishers in Africa and across the global South, casting doubt on the reputation of older scholarly journals as well as on emergent publishing initiatives. African scholars readily took up Beall's language and normative discourse, researching the 'penetration' of Nigerian medical journals by so-called predatory publishers (Nwagwu and Ojemeni 2015), 'awareness' of the topic amongst Ghanaian researchers (Atiso et al. 2019) and the 'extent' of South African publications in such journals (Mouton and Valentine 2017).

Ghana's universities amplified this discourse, creating their own lists of 'approved' journals, or recommending their academics publish in journals included in the major citation indexes and databases, such as those owned by Elsevier (Scopus) or Clarivate (Web of Science). The dominance of a small group of international publishing conglomerates and their 'vertical integration' of the digital research infrastructure is key to understanding the challenges facing Ghana's scholars and publishers today (Atolani et al. 2019; Posada and Chen 2019).

The changing economics of academic publishing

Africa is both the cradle of human civilisation and the site of many of the first scientific developments, as evidenced in the early civilizations of the Nile Valley, Ethiopia and coastal eastern Africa. From the 7th century, centres of Islamic learning in Djenne and Timbuktu became important sites of scholarship and science, their mosques supporting libraries and large communities of scholars.

During the 17th century, European genres of scientific debate began to wield global power. The white 'gentleman scholars' benefitted from courtly patronage and independent wealth, sharing scientific discoveries across a self-proclaimed 'republic of letters'. Benefitting from the knowledge generated through travel, trade and imperial conquest, their scientific credibility was underpinned by authoritative institutions, such as the Royal Society, founded in 1662 (Shapin 1994).

Reflecting on this history, Shapin highlights the importance of scientific 'credibility': 'no credibility, no knowledge' (1995, 258). He explores the 'mundane processes' through which this new community of scholars acquired scientific credibility: personal networks, academic credentials, and authoritative institutions. These were networks of learning but also of exclusion: only privileged upper-class men were able to act as 'modest witnesses' (Haraway 1997). Scientific authority was located in particular places and with particular people.

Csiszar (2019) shows how during the 19th century journal publication became integral to European academic practice. The first journal of the Royal Society, *Philosophical Transactions*, launched in 1665, was initially an expensive collection of memoirs. By the early 19th century, a plethora of new specialist journals were being launched by scholarly societies. With a Victorian public culture eager for learning and reading, independent periodicals began to appear, published on a commercial basis. Perhaps the most famous example is *Nature*, launched in 1858 as a popular scientific weekly, and sold on newsstands (Baldwin 2015). Competing with the established learned society journals, *Nature* opened up science, becoming both financially profitable and academically respectable. Overcoming the suspicions of the scientific establishment towards their ephemeral status, periodicals acted to legitimate and certify new knowledge.

Despite its success, *Nature* remained an important exception to the primacy of non-commercial publishers. Fyfe et al. (2017) show how this dominant publishing ethos was sustained by learned societies and the university presses. They saw their mission as one of sharing scholarship and sharing knowledge. The Second World War proved a watershed for international scientific collaboration and academic publishing (Brown 1947; Hartcup and Lovell 2000). A new breed of commercial publishers capitalised on the inability of university presses and learned society publishers to keep up with the growth in global science. One of the first to do so was the Dutch publisher Elsevier.

The rapid rise of Pergamon Press exemplifies the commercial opportunities that emerged (Cox 2002). It was set up by Robert Maxwell, a Czech émigré who had worked in publishing for the Allied Command after the war. In 1951 he paid GBP 13,000 to buy UK distribution rights for Springer Verlag publications: six journals and two textbook series. By 1960 there were 59 journals, and circulation was growing at 5–10% each year. Pergamon continued to expand rapidly, launching new journals from the profits of existing serials, and developing a huge library of textbooks that sold throughout the world, as well as a highly profitable series of encyclopaedias. By the time Pergamon was sold to Elsevier in 1991 for GBP 440 million, it had published 7,000 monographs and launched 700 journals, of which more than 400 were still active. Cox demonstrates Maxwell's 'profound effect' on scientific publishing, which the debacle of his death, his debts and his misuse of the Mirror's pension funds has now 'eclipsed from history' (Cox 2002, 274).

The Cold War further drove superpower competition and new scientific collaborations. Governments promoted international scientific research initiatives, and the sense of a shared scientific community was fostered by the increasing use of English as the international language of science (Gordin 2015). In the late 1940s and 1950s, Dutch and British publishers pioneered the publication of English-language research journals targeted at international communities of contributors and readers (Meadows 1980). By the early 21st century, English-language journals were being published in countries all over the world (Fyfe et al. 2017, 8).

Some commentators classify publishers according to their institutional ethos and orientation. Thornton and Ocasio (1999) distinguish journals governed by an 'editorial logic' that treats the journal as a service to the disciplinary community, with the editor holding authority and prestige, compared to those with a more entrepreneurial 'market logic'. Under the latter logic, the ambition is 'resource competition and acquisition growth, and executive succession is determined by the product market and the market for corporate control' (Thornton and Ocasio 1999, 801)

The emergence of an international scientific, technical, and medical publishing industry was marked by the creation of its own trade association – called STM (Science, Technology and Medicine) in 1968. Whilst many journals are still owned by scholarly societies and universities, repeated take-overs and mergers have consolidated commercial influence over the sector. Scholarly publishing – and its accompanying set of research infrastructures – is now dominated by five major multinational companies: Springer Nature, Wiley, Elsevier, Informa, and Sage (Posada and Chen 2017).

Digital publishing and the dissemination possibilities opened up by the internet changed everything. There were suddenly many more opportunities to disseminate scholarly work, but journals reliant on income from print subscriptions suddenly found themselves threatened by new online-only open-access journals. New business models and community-led initiatives quickly emerged. The move towards an 'author pays' model created commercial incentives and opportunities for publishers, whilst the work of the Public Knowledge Project in developing the OJS (Open Journal Software) system provided a ready-made web platform for setting up new journals.

Shapin describes contemporary science as a 'credit economy', linking different groups of experts in modern differentiated societies. Lacking personal connections, they have to rely on 'shared institutional signifiers of academic credibility' rather than personal markers of trust (Shapin 1995, 270).

Measuring global science

By the 1960s, science was expanding rapidly. The challenge of keeping up with the endlessly growing flow of information inspired a young entrepreneurial US scientist called Eugene Garfield to publish a weekly pamphlet containing a copy of the lists of the contents pages of key journals (Grimwade 2018). *Current Contents*, as it was known, started in the life sciences. Its popularity led Garfield to develop a stream of other initiatives, including the first ever citation index (Garfield 1955). The ability to calculate an article's influence and 'impact' by the number of citations it received transformed the practice of science. Scientists could now measure the influence of their work, whilst universities were able to track productivity. This was at a time when pioneering thinkers like Robert K. Merton and Edward Shils were more focused on the power of disciplinary 'norms' and collective values in shaping scientific cultures (Merton 1973; Shils 1972). Accumulating enough data to rank journals by the frequency and impact of the citations their articles received (Garfield 1972), Garfield developed a highly effective way for academics and journals to compete.

By the early 1970s, historians of science could plot the exponential increase in the number of journals, increasing by a factor of 10 every 50 years (DeSolla Price 1961). Price forecast a situation where there would eventually be more than 100,000 journals. His modelling helped to launch the field of scientometrics, a discipline dedicated to measuring and tracking the circulation and citation of scholarly knowledge. Almost 50 years later, the global research system continues to expand. The number of papers indexed in Scopus jumped from 1 million in 2000 to 2.5 million in 2018, a 5% annual increase (Marginson 2021). Whilst many journals are still owned by scholarly societies and universities, there is increasing consolidation by commercial actors, and scholarly publishing is dominated by five major multinational companies (Posada and Chen 2017). These companies also own (or have bought) the bibliographic software for keeping track of references, the journal publishing software (if not the journals themselves), the indexes of approved and accredited journals, as well as the tools for measuring publishing 'outputs' and their 'impacts' – in short, the whole scholarly infrastructure (Posada and Chen 2019). At every stage of research, academics have become increasingly reliant on the tools of what Lariviere et al. (2015) call a 'publishing oligopoly'.

Despite – or perhaps because of – this complex new scholarly infrastructure, it is hard to know precisely how many academic journals currently exist. Responding to concerns about diversity and expansion, commercial publishers began to market their journal indexes as a tool to help scholars and policy-makers assess the credibility of new and emerging journals, and as a reassurance that editorial practices met minimum quality thresholds. Inclusion was key, and impact factor became a proxy for quality. Yet getting a journal into Scopus or Web of Science requires having an uninterrupted publication track record, a record of citation by existing Scopus/WoS journals, editorial and author diversity and meeting digital archiving requirements. Decisions are metrics-based, and applications from emerging journals and publishers are often rejected. As a result, journals based in Africa, South Asia and Latin America are effectively excluded from global circuits of knowledge production, citation, and recognition. Whilst some publishers offer subsidised or 'philanthropic' journal access to African universities, this access is often restricted or limited.

The largest commercial journal citation indexes are Web of Science, owned by Clarivate (Bell 2019), and Scopus, owned by Elsevier. They each have around 30,000–40,000 journals on their lists, though up to 20% of these are inactive. Around 90% of these are English-language journals. There are many other subject-specific and language-specific indexes, only some of which overlap with the coverage of the main citation indexes (Bell and Mills 2020). As new journals are launched to cater to new fields of knowledge, and as the demands placed on academics to publish their work, the economics and politics of publishing have become steadily more complex and fraught. The internet has added a further dimension, and further disruption.

Whilst science and politics have long been intertwined, a series of US scandals around scientific plagiarism and falsification has led to a new discourse around the importance of scientific integrity (Anderson et al. 2013; Price 2013). Since 2000, the rapid growth in research activity across the global science system, along with the rise of open-access publishing and digital technologies, has opened up new debates about the ethical values and publication practices of researchers. Existing cultures of disciplinary peer-review have been put into question. The ethos of a self-governing 'republic of science' is harder to defend in a research economy (Mills and Ratcliffe 2012) with fewer shared norms, more rewards for success, and a growing diversity of institutional drivers and commercial pressures. The geographical and status inequalities within and across this global system make measuring and assessing academic quality and reputation fraught and contested.

Africa's academic publishing renaissance

In 1984, a small community of independent African publishers gathered in Arusha, Tanzania for an event funded by the Dag Hammarskjold foundation. Despite its hopeful title – 'the development of autonomous capacity in publishing in Africa' – the focus was on the parlous state of indigenous publishing. It was the first of four 'Arusha conferences', as African publishers, editors and academics began to network. Led by pioneering publishers Henry Chakava and Victor Nkwanko, and helped by the assiduous record-keeper of African publishing Hans Zell, new initiatives began to emerge. The African Book Collective, an indigenous publisher's cooperative, was one of the first, alongside Northern NGOs such as INASP (International Network for Availability of Scientific Publications), based in Oxford, UK. APNET (African Publishers Network) was established in 1992, with funding from SIDA (Swedish International Development Cooperation Agency). Books began to appear on how to publish and run journals (Zell 1998), as well as regular updates on the state of academic publishing (Mlambo 2007). As part of the project of building technical capacity INASP helped to launch and fund the journal portal African Journals OnLine (AJOL), along with similar journal portals (called JOLs) in Bangladesh, Nepal and India.

In the 1970s and 1980s, journals run by pan-African scholarly networks (such as CODESRIA) survived, along with a few university presses. With donor support, CODESRIA sustained an impressive publishing profile of books, working papers and journals, many of which continue to this day. These included *Africa Development* (launched in 1976), and the *CODESRIA Bulletin* (from 1987), as well as co-sponsoring disciplinary journals in African universities.

Without international donor funding, many journals operated on a shoestring, and were run on a voluntary basis, with long backlogs of submissions, irregular publishing cycles and lengthy decision times. The gradual renaissance of African academic publishing in the 1990s was led by small book publishing cooperatives, and only later by the arrival of commercial publishing houses. A few not-for-profit initiatives and organisations such as INASP provided support for scholarly publishing, whilst Bioline International was the first journal platform. Today, CODESRIA launched several more journals during this period, including *African Sociological Review*, *African Development*, and the *Journal of Higher Education in Africa*.

AJOL began in 1998 as a donor-funded African journal database, and in 2005 became a not-for-profit company, based in South Africa. Starting by indexing 50 English-language African academic journals, by 2020 it was hosting 526 journals (of which around 300 were active). AJOL prioritises supporting editors and building the quality of the journals it hosts, ensuring in particular that journals cope with a transition of leadership. It regularly offers workshops and training for editors, and has developed a quality standards framework for journals, awarding them up to three stars. Yet its not-for-profit status makes it hard for AJOL to provide the levels of service and support that many journals need.

As Chapter 8 explores, a new generation of African academic publishers have been increasingly successful. Ahmed Hindawi and Nagwa Abdel-Mottaleb launched Hindawi in Cairo in 1997, under-cutting existing publishers and transforming the economics of publishing. Growing through acquisitions and journal launches, and quickly adopting an open-access publishing model (Peters 2007), Hindawi became a global 'top-ten' journal publisher before being acquired by Wiley in January 2021 for USD 300 million. No other Africa-based commercial publishers have emulated this trajectory, though many commercial publishers are also thriving. The *Journal of African Health Sciences* launched by Makerere academic James Tumwine in 2000, is now a highly successful journal, whilst the *PanAfrican Medical Journal* established in 2008, has become a research ecosystem in itself, offering grants, capacity-building, and conferences. In South Africa, with a generously funded research infrastructure supported by government subsidies, there are a growing number of commercial and non-profit publishers and journal platforms. For example, Unisa Press entered into a collaboration with Taylor and Francis in 2005, that led to 50 South African journals being co-published with the multinational. It helped reposition these local journals as 'international', with Taylor and Francis providing support and training for editors, and Unisa Press benefitting from its technical infrastructures and investment.

Beyond South Africa, the changing economics of digital publishing continue to tax many African universities. Faculty or institutional open-access journals are often set up and run on a shoestring or by academics with no publishing experience, and many struggle to sustain their presence. Increasingly university presses themselves lie dormant, or have become little more than textbook printers. A review of more than fifty African university presses finds that only half have websites, only a third had published monographs in the previous three years, and only four had experimented with open- access publishing (Van Schalkwyk and Luescher 2017). Highlighting the creativity of a few university-owned open access publishing initiatives Van Schalkwyk and Luescher imagine a future in which there is a shared commitment to the 'knowledge commons' (2017, 81).

The last two decades have seen a slew of 'capacity-building' reforms focused on increasing the quantity of research 'outputs' and publications with African universities (Mills 2020). Doctoral candidates are expected to publish before submitting their thesis, and promotion is dependent on publication outputs. Much less attention has been paid to knowledge infrastructures. The opportunities for African publishers today are very different from those in 1984. The challenge is to go beyond conferences and 'action plans' to focus on the everyday tasks of building publishing capacity across Africa (Zell 2019).

Meanwhile, journals and publishers in Nigeria and Ghana are publishing academic work that is focused on African scientific issues and national policy debates. This work is largely invisible to, and so ignored by, the international citation indexes (Harsh et al. 2021). Rather than see African-based journals as being undermined by the dominant commercial publishing platforms, can these regional knowledge circuits continue to survive alongside the dominant global research infrastructures? Their future depends on how much importance West Africa's universities place on 'international rankings' and publication metrics. Amidst global calls for more responsible use of research metrics (Wilsdon 2015) and less 'gaming and manipulation' (Biagioli and Lippman 2020), a change in university policy towards these global indexes could be key. A shift away from a focus on being 'world-class' might make research publishing a more sustainable aspect of African academic careers and regional research ecosystems. The alternative, as one South African scholar advocates, is learning to 'negotiate and navigate citation measurement systems' (Tomaselli 2020, 12).

Getting by

In the 1960s African science was optimistic and confident, reflecting the political opportunities offered by independent nation-building in a postcolonial world. New journals and conferences abounded, and Africa's scholars began to construct an Africa-centred research imaginary. Much has happened since. Repeated political and financial crises, from political coups to the crippling effects of structural adjustment policies, have undermined the fragile foundations of an African university research and publishing ecosystem. This chapter has sketched the demise and partial renaissance of African academic publishing cultures and infrastructures, together with the new challenges they now face.

Today, Ghana's academics have no choice but to negotiate Northern-dominated research cultures. The continent's academic publishers similarly labour in the shadow of a 'credibility economy' (Shapin 1995) and a digital infrastructure dominated by a few global companies. The major citation indexes, journal impact factors, and publishing metrics seem to define the rules of the game. The tactics deployed by Ghanaian researchers and the continent's publishers to simply 'get by' in this bibliometric economy are a recurrent theme in this book (Mills and Branford 2022). The next four chapters look at the experiences of Ghanaian researchers as they reconcile institutional demands, their own research ambitions, and the other demands on their time. The second half of the book offers case studies of Ghanaian journals and independent presses, as well as publishing houses from across the continent, analysing the changing political economy of academic publishing. The book ends by putting these different perspectives into dialogue, speculating on the future for Ghana's researchers and African universities.

Chapter 3

Why publish?
Surviving in the Ghanaian university system

At the end of the day some pride themselves that they have 101 publications, but the question is that what impact does those publications have on society? Some have just a few, and the few publications they have, have more impact in society than the battalion that someone else's have. I belong to the latter school of thought. (Issah, UDS lecturer)

Introduction

'Why publish?' might seem an odd question to ask academic scholars. Is it not obvious? How else does one share research, knowledge and insight? But there are many ways to communicate new ideas. Before the first scholarly journals were launched, 17th century scientists wrote letters to each other (Csiszar 2019). German research seminars began as shared conversations around domestic dining tables (Clark 2006). Generations of university students have learnt from textbooks and lectures rather than journal articles. Humanities scholars value monographs over journal articles. Yet, today, the centrality of journal publishing within academic work is undisputed. As Lillis (2012, 695) notes, 'whilst writing for publication is largely taken as a given, the specific workings, meanings and consequences of this activity at national and transnational levels tend to remain invisible'.

The rise of English, since the 1920s, as the dominant global academic medium of science (Montgomery 2013; Gordin 2015) has had a profound impact on many scholarly systems. More than 90% of articles are now published in English (Ammon 2012), whilst the proportion of non-English language articles in the Web of Science has declined from 15% in the 1970s to 5% today (Moskaleva and Akoev 2019). Whilst some point to the rich set of 'global Englishes' (Rose 2013) that now characterise academic dialogue, the dominance of English puts scholars from non-English speaking countries at a disadvantage, with English proficiency increasingly defined as a requirement for an 'international' profile (Curry and Lillis 2017).

Research on African academic publishing dates back to the 1970s (Altbach 1993; Zell 1977, 1984). African critics have long complained that 'scientific activity remains basically extraverted, alienated, dependent on an international division of labour that tends to make scientific invention a monopoly of the North' (Hountondji 1990, 9). The explicit emphasis on publishing outputs as a key to career progression with African academia is relatively recent. During the bleak years of World Bank policies of structural adjustment in the 1980s and 1990s, coupled with instability and a lack of government investment in science, many African universities had to go without basic research resources. Academics had to cope with bare libraries, no funding for research, and limited access to international journals (Lebeau and Mills 2008). Mouton (2008) described it as the 'de-institutionalisation' of science. Instead the focus was on surviving, and teaching ever larger numbers of students. Bodomo (1999) acknowledged the other challenges Ghanaian scholars faced, from caring responsibilities to poor ICT infrastructures, along with an emphasis on data collection over theoretical engagement.

Today there is much discussion about rethinking scholarly communication, and promoting other more accessible forms of writing, from blogs to tweets, as a way of maximising 'impact' and public engagement

(Weingart et al. 2021). There are many ways to develop one's scholarly credibility and influence. So why the continued emphasis on publishing in academic journals? This chapter explores the rationales and justifications offered by a community of almost 50 Ghanaian scholars. The question elicits blunt honesty and frank insights, illustrating broad patterns with anecdotes and reflections. The 'why' question is tough, almost existential, so the interviews started biographically. Our participants talked about their initial publishing experiences and how these early experiences shaped their subsequent publication strategies and practices, including the role of supervisors, mentors, and collaborative authorship. The conversation went on to explore where respondents chose to submit their work, and if 'chose' was indeed the right word. Did it connote more agency than many felt they had, struggling to keep afloat amidst myriad teaching and administrative responsibilities? Then the interview turned to the 'why' question.

Promotion and advancement

A key – if unsurprising – finding was how much emphasis respondents placed on promotion as motivating and driving their academic publishing strategies. Unprompted, more than half used the phrase 'publish or perish' during their interviews. The phrase captured how vital publishing had become not only for promotion but also for career survival. All knew how many articles they had already published, and could immediately cite this number. Promotion up the academic ranks required successively more papers in 'reputable peer-reviewed journals', including a specific proportion in which the candidate was lead author. Whilst promotion to professorship also meant meeting teaching and service requirements, publishing always dominated these conversations. Without this incentive, most felt academic publications would play a far smaller role in academic life. As Kosiwa, a senior lecturer and head of department at the University of Ghana put it:

> To be very frank, it is for promotion. We have publications tied to renewal of appointment; we have it tied to being promoted

to the next rank … Although we don't have much time to be sitting and writing these things, you have to write. They said 'if you don't publish, you perish'. So since you don't want to perish then you have to make the effort to publish. If they would look at our teaching, if they would use our teaching to assess us, then I am sure I wouldn't spend too much time thinking about publications. But because we are assessed based on publications then we have to make time to publish. I just want to be very frank. (Kosiwa, UG, senior lecturer)

Again and again, interviewees linked publishing to career advancement: 'If you don't publish you will perish. You cannot rise anywhere, so if you don't want to publish you don't come into academia' (Kofu, UG, senior lecturer). In response to the question 'what motivates you to publish?' a senior lecturer in social sciences replied simply: 'Promotion. And that is where our bread and butter comes from.' While UG academics were slightly more likely to emphasise publishing as a means to promotion, this view was common across both universities. One UDS health sciences HoD said 'the most important motivation to publish is promotion'. Similarly, Jonathan, a UDS lecturer, acknowledged that 'notwithstanding the effort that you put, you can be turning out students, you can be contributing to community work and whatever, the significant factor that drives people to do more publication is promotion. And as the saying goes, you either publish or you perish' (Jonathan, UDS lecturer, health sciences).

Career ambitions intersected with a general competitive ethos around publishing, especially amongst junior academic faculty. This echoes the broader global literature around the rise of academic hyper-competitiveness (Edwards and Roy 2017), and insights from research on audit culture, such as Goodhart's Law, where a measure becomes a target (Fire and Guestrin 2019). This sense of rivalry was summed up by a UG social science lecturer who said that 'because others are publishing, you also have to get it done'. This competition took different permutations, and not just for those at the start of their careers. Ibrahim, a head of a department of applied science at UDS described the competitive ethos of his faculty. 'It gives me sleepless nights and so I must work and catch up.' He felt that this sense of rivalry was 'a good motivating factor because if you don't sit up, they will go and leave you behind' and noted how 'the youth is in a hurry and so there is that level of competition'. Ibrahim noted approvingly that competition between lecturers within his department had led to many professorial appointments.

For others, the main source of rivalry was with contemporaries who had studied abroad, who had more opportunities to network and publish. Akuma, a UG social science lecturer, described how this played out in everyday rivalries, as her peers who were 'trained outside' tended to look down on 'those of us who were trained here'. It made her even more determined to develop her publishing profile and 'prove that I am better than them'. In particular, she wanted to show them that their profiles had depended on them being 'pampered' and supported 'out there', and to prove to them that 'they were publishing because they were out there, but since they joined us, they have not published'. 'Look,' she wanted to say, 'now you are here, on your own, you can't write'.

The perceived differences in the quality of academic training between Ghana and Europe or elsewhere 'outside' were a constant subtext in conversation. Kumi, a UG social sciences associate professor was candid about this constant sense of comparison. She emphasised that what really mattered to her was 'recognition' by her peers, both within her own university but also when traveling abroad. She didn't want to feel inferior 'when in Cape Town or Johannesburg or Basel' and wanted to have 'produced an output level that is commensurate with your rank'.

Kumi went on to insist that she 'wouldn't be enthused if I'm given a professorship by the University of Ghana, but have nothing to show for that', explaining that she would prefer to 'have a lot of papers that qualify me to be a professor while still only a senior lecturer ... it's more honourable than having people question how you got to your current rank'. Emphasising how 'recognition is extremely important in this industry' she felt that 'we are not only looking at it from within, comparing yourself with the lecturers here but with those in the other part of the world and you feel very competitive'.

Interviewees emphasised how published academic work had become the reputational yardstick with which to measure oneself against colleagues. When asked in the interview about their publications, people would sheepishly mention papers 'in progress', almost as a coda. The question possibly evoked a sense of embarrassment and fear that they are 'not measuring up' to expectations. This impression could be ameliorated by a sign that more publications were 'on their way'.

Ayi Kwei, a UG applied sciences lecturer, described how people used publishing metrics to judge each other. He explained that there was a 'tendency to look at the number of publications and use it to judge people: that absolute number, how many do you have?'. This was corroborated by how quick interviewees were to talk about their number of publications. Yet, as he acknowledged, this number 'never takes into consideration what you have that is either going out or yet to go out, the emphasis is on what is out there, not what you have that is yet to go'.

Ayi Kwei vividly depicted his sense of the publication 'pipeline'. He insisted there 'should always be a paper under consideration somewhere, and there should be a paper that you are publishing, and there should be a manuscript that you are writing'. He felt it was a 'continuous process', and that 'if you are not publishing then you are not doing the right thing'. His sense was that there were 'four stages that should be going concurrently and then you keep pushing them through from below'. He went further to suggest that 'the pipe should continuously be flowing until you hit retirement'.

The industrial pipeline metaphor captures Ayi Kwei's sense – and that of others – of the importance of constantly moving forward with one's career. He felt that 'if you don't publish then it is considered that you are not making progress and that isn't good'. This was shared by several other respondents. Yaa, a senior UG lecturer, admitted that 'it is difficult to see myself not making progress, I have to keep moving and that motivates me. I have to see that I am making progress in my career'.

Kwaku, a UDS social science lecturer, also warned against stagnating. He explained that the motivation to publish was both to 'fulfil the job description' but also because 'you don't want to stagnate or remain at the same role, or the same position that you were employed'. He went on to acknowledge that he had to 'serve his time' because he had been working outside of the university. 'I would have been a senior lecturer long ago but of course there are rules and when you return you have to serve before you can apply, so that is what is keeping me.'

Not making progress meant falling behind. Interviewees would tell cautionary tales of what had happened to those who lagged behind. Many emphasised the need to keep up with 'time', and the risk of being left 'out of the system'. Alongside self-imposed pressures, some described being admonished by university managers. Ibrahim, a social sciences lecturer at UG, knew of colleagues in another institution who had not met institutional publishing expectations, and were being taken to task by the administration. Using 'sitting' as a metaphor for responsiveness, he explained that 'when they were questioned, they sat up.' He noted how, after six years on a contract at a particular level of seniority, the university would 'come and ask questions, ask why the challenge?'.

Kwaku, a lecturer in the social science department at UDS insisted that 'your department can take you on and the university can take you on', leading to dismissal procedures. He elaborated that 'the university has written to people who did not meet the standards: that if they don't present certain publications at a certain point they may be asked to leave.' Akibu, a UG senior lecturer, suggested that the failure to move forward was a dismissible offence. 'If you are still not publishing, the university can take a decision to release you because it means that you are not really doing anything to improve on your academic career.' Whilst no interviews were conducted with anyone whose contract had been terminated on these grounds, several lecturers in their fifties suggested that they had not been promoted because of their limited publication records.

On the other hand, Jonathan, a UDS lecturer in health sciences, offered an optimistic biography of a colleague who had been 'struggling' with publishing, before finally achieving success. He noted how, despite joining the faculty in the 1980s 'he actually started publishing somewhere in the 2000s' and 'by the time that he came to speak at the workshop he was a professor'. Jonathan felt that 'sometimes you don't even know your way out, struggling to fix yourself into the system, and before you realise it, time is gone, and you have seen yourself lagging behind'. His challenge was 'how to pull yourself together to be able to publish'.

Asked explicitly about whether there was institutional 'pressure' to publish in 'reputable' journals, most agreed that 'pressure' was the right word. A few nuanced their responses. Kosiwa, head of a social science department at UG, insisted that 'I don't worry myself too much if the high impact ones are too difficult to get into, I would rather go for average'. Another senior lecturer insisted that 'I like to publish in international journals but am not pressurised', and a third did not see himself 'as under any pressure when I think of putting up my work in a journal'. Unsurprisingly, senior faculty seemed more detached from these pressures, having made it over the promotion hurdles set by their universities. The next chapter returns to the institutional rhetoric around 'international' journals and their reputation.

'Publish and perish'?

Talking to Ghanaian researchers about this research project, many immediately invoked the colourful adage 'publish or perish'. They knew their careers and promotion prospects depended on their research publications, especially those on which they were first author. Yet there was a fate worse than not publishing: that one might publish but still 'perish'. In an African academy at the periphery of global citation networks, choices about where to publish were freighted with risk.

Publish in the 'wrong' place and African scholars seeking to satisfy promotion expectations find themselves caught between 'sacrificing relevance for recognition, or recognition for relevance' (Nyamnjoh 2004, 333). Within the African academy, there are many consequences of what Nyamnjoh described as 'publish *and* perish'. Building on the critiques of Larson (2001) and Zeleza (1997), Nyamnjoh argues that being held to 'Western intellectual and literary standards' means 'cultivating insensitivity to issues, perspectives, and approaches of relevance to Africans, their realities, values and priorities' (Nyamnjoh 2004, 334). Taking up the anticolonial insights of African thinkers such as p'Bitek, Wa Thiong'o and Achebe, Nyamnjoh depicts the geopolitics of knowledge that weigh down African writers, arguing that the 'mediocrity of content, invisibility, remoteness, or the poor reputation of publisher, together with poor marketing and distribution (all) conspire to ensure that academics and writers perish, even when they have published.'

Nyamnjoh's critique resonates with many African scholars. Kamwendo (2014) calls for a rethinking of language policies within humanities journals, Vurayai and Ndofirepi (2020) point to the destructive implications of this 'neoliberal' ethos on junior African scholars, whilst Tarkang and Bain (2019) fear that repeated rejections from the most selective journals might push scholars towards lower quality and less reputable journals. The 'intellectual labour of engaging with different discourses and publishing paradigms is primarily borne by African scholars', points out Nolte (2019, 303). She identifies a growing division of labour between the empirical work expected of African scholars working in international collaborations (such as this one) and the theoretical contributions expected by funders and Northern journals.

Discussions of academic writing invoked metaphorical imagery. Talking about the pressure to be productive and publish, many respondents gave the image of 'sitting' a positive connotation. A person who is writing and publishing is 'sitting down' to the task, and not on their feet teaching. Issah, a UDS lecturer, invoked teaching in the negative sense of having no time for 'sitting down and writing'. Going on a writing retreat and being given the opportunity 'to sit down to begin to write and re-write, draft upon draft, initially it wasn't easy', he remembered. Similarly, Akuma, a UG lecturer, welcomed opportunities for dedicated writing retreats, where 'the department could always put aside some money and then take us out for a writing workshop, you sit down, there is a timetable, come and sit down and write', But one could also 'sit' in the wrong way. An academic who was not publishing was 'just sitting there', reflected Emmanuel, a UDS lecturer. Being serious about publishing meant 'sitting up': Kojo, a UG lecturer was not the only one to utter the phrase, 'we need to sit up'. For Ibrahim, a UDS senior lecturer, 'if you don't sit up, they'll leave you behind'. Akibu, a UG applied sciences senior lecturer, deployed the same image to describe the general state of alertness and hard work required of Africa's academics. 'The thing is,' he explained, 'that you need to sit up because it is not easy to combine your teaching, your marking, and research and all that.' Sitting 'up' was the best way of being agential and managing these different demands.

People offered a range of other institutional incentives to publish, beyond individual career progression. These included finding future collaborators, promoting the name of one's university, bringing revenue into one's research centre, or fulfilling the requirements of research funding. Nana, a UG agriculture academic explained, 'We are encouraged to publish because we are part of a World Bank Centre of Excellence. Our publications are money for us ... it is recognised by the World Bank as an indicator for a result and it is ticked against your name and it is converted to money for your institution'.

There are many consequences to the way that universities and research systems across the world now assess, measure and quantify academic work. The UK was one of the first to introduce a system of research assessment in 1986 as a means to channel limited research funding to the best performing universities, with other countries quickly following suit (Bence and Oppenheim 2005). The literature on the impact of an academic 'audit culture' is now more than 20 years old (Power 1997; Strathern 2000), but there is ever more evidence of the consequences of 'metricising' research and scholarly identities (Fire and Guestrin 2019). For Waters (2004: 41), the result is publications which few read, and scholarship with little innovation and insight: 'it's all form and no content'. There is also increasing attention on the gaming and manipulation (e.g. Biagioli and Lippman 2020; Moosa 2018) that results from the application of Goodhart's Law to academic publications – the measure becomes a target in a 'publish or perish' culture. The 'tyranny' of academic metrics (Muller 2019) is felt most acutely in higher education systems that have been reorientated to focus on publishing in English. Scholars in applied linguistics have highlighted the consequences of this global shift to English medium publishing (Canagarajah 2002; Curry and Lillis 2017), and the implications for non-English speaking authors (Hyland 2015).

In 2003, the world's universities were transformed by the publication of the first global rankings. Assembled by Shanghai Jiao Tong University, the measurements judged West Africa's universities harshly, with none listed in the world's top 500. The following year, the University of Ibadan began to require international publications for promotion (Omobowale et al. 2013), and many other Nigerian and Ghanaian universities quickly adopted similar approaches. With student applicants (and nervous governments) increasingly aware of the low rankings of African universities, many African universities introduced new publishing expectations on faculty seeking promotion. Over time, these have been gradually refined and tightened. One private university in Nigeria – Covenant University – is particularly ambitious, and in 2020 specified that candidates for full professorship should have a Scopus h-index of not less than three.

In recent years both the University of Ghana (UG) and University of Development Studies (UDS) have steadily revised their promotion requirements, setting out publication expectations ever more precisely. Both have broadly similar requirements, with UDS expecting at least 6 'refereed papers' for promotion from lecturer to senior lecturer, another 12 to associate professor, and a further 21 to full professor (UDS 2018). UG also requires 6 publications for promotion to senior lecturer, 12 to associate professor, and then at least another 14 to full professor, depending on teaching and service commitments. UG has recently adopted an elaborate evaluation and assessment scheme for teaching, research and service, and requires at least 50% of submitted 'exhibits' to be first-authored publications in 'peer-reviewed, reputable' journals (UG 2019). UG also sets limits on the number of articles submitted to the same journal. There is also a limit on the duration one can hold a certain seniority of contract. In both universities, journal publishing has become a career survival strategy. As one social sciences senior lecturer at the University of Ghana concluded, if you are not publishing 'you become so frustrated, and eventually leave the system completely dissatisfied'.

Within this pervasive culture of metrics, the pressure to publish weighs heavily. Having a long list of academic publications is no longer a guarantee of promotion. The new danger is 'publish *and* perish'. If these articles and outputs are not in 'reputable' journals they might not be deemed eligible by appointment and promotion boards. But who defines 'reputable'? Ghana is on the margins of global disciplinary communities, and reputational hierarchies are largely dominated by 'Northern' scholarly journals. Publishing six peer-reviewed articles becomes less important than ensuring that they are in internationally 'respected' journals. This is easier in some fields than others. In the health sciences many scholars are involved in international research and writing collaborations, providing access and funding for open-access payments. Others, particularly scholars in the humanities and social sciences, find it more difficult to get published in the 'elite' journals and, amid a dizzying range of outlets, are often unsure of which journals to aim for.

Contributing to knowledge

The second major response to the 'why publish' question was the one most expected. Half the interviewees emphasised their responsibility to contribute to knowledge through publishing. The idea of contributing to knowledge was expressed in various ways. People talked of 'filling gaps', 'extending knowledge', 'taking an idea further', 'expanding the frontiers of knowledge', 'building on what others had done', 'improve what we know', 'disseminating knowledge' and 'getting the information out there'.

Some acknowledged a sense of pride that came from contributing. As Kumi, a UG senior lecturer in the social sciences, put it, 'you feel somehow important and you are recognised as having contributed to the global discourse in the area of scholarly publication'. Kosiwa, a UG applied sciences senior lecturer, explained that 'you spend so much time carrying out your research ... the fact that once you publish the findings out there, people can also learn from it, that also motivates me'. She went on to describe the 'satisfaction' of 'my work going somewhere' as a key reason to publish.

Richmond, a UDS senior lecturer, admitted that 'you are supposed to publish to get promoted ... but it is not just because I want to be promoted that I would publish anything; I publish to help mankind'. Some sought to have it both ways. For Issah, a UDS applied sciences lecturer, 'promotion is part of it but not the main thing'. He felt that when his colleagues sought rapid promotion the quality of their work suffered. 'Unfortunately too many in our climate say to themselves that the end justifies the means. They tend to be more focused on quantity at the expense of quality. So, people are more or less selfish. People like us who tend to be so strict about quality may not get ourselves promoted as early or as fast, but not because we can't do it'. A few interviewees offered more normative accounts of where people should publish, rather than reflect on their own experiences.

Compared to UG, many UDS academics espoused a strong commitment to sharing knowledge for the benefit of the local region and its people. Their university's community-orientated ethos (the UDS motto is 'Knowledge for Service') still involves students spending the third trimester of each year on practical fieldwork in local communities. This ethos is reflected in the applied research interests of its faculty and the expectation that student learning happens in community settings. For Lahiri, a UDS applied sciences senior lecturer, 'whatever I do, I need to share the information for people to know'. She went on to say that 'the fact that my information is out there and others are reading and citing me, it gets me motivated that I want to publish more'. Others expressed a similar sense of duty to get academic knowledge 'out'. Emmanuel, a UDS applied sciences lecturer, articulated this as his scientific vocation. 'You know when you have done something yourself, and you have information, you have to share it, for the world to know that there is something like this'.

A common theme across the interviews was the sense that, without a publication, it was as though the work had not been done at all. Many called the result 'a waste'. As Kofi, a UG health sciences senior lecturer put it, 'as a researcher if I work on something and people do not see what I have done it is not worth it'. He went on to explain that 'if I investigate any issue and I don't put it out there for people to review and know what I have done, and critique what I have done, then that is not work'. Without getting the information 'out there,' it is as though the work does not exist.

Contributing to knowledge by publishing was seen as a way of helping others. Joseph, a UDS lecturer in applied science, emphasised the importance of 'exposing others to look at what I have done'. He was unusual in emphasising the importance of using ResearchGate and similar platforms (such as Academia.edu) for ensuring 'people benefit from my publications', but also for monitoring how many people were reading his work.

Disseminating information to benefit society and 'humankind' was a motivation for several interviewees. Ayi Kwei invoked Pasteur's legacy, saying that 'you may be dead and gone. But whatever work you did and whatever information you gave out, if it was very useful it stands the test of time.' He went on: 'If Pasteur hadn't made his work available today, we wouldn't have pasteurisation and there are other many things that people have done that based upon their work it has influenced food processing, food packaging, the way we consume food and so on.'

The importance of making health-related discoveries was a recurring theme in interviews. Academics pointed to examples of 'cures' for hypothetical disease (including, in one case, Covid-19) to show how academic publications can have a profound impact on people's lives. A few identified journals and publications that were likely to have the most influence or impact.

As in health sciences, utility was also emphasised by UDS researchers in the applied sciences. Faculty spoke about research on water purification, drug delivery and food preservation, explaining how they were motivated to see their findings being used in practice. Participants differed only on the degree to which publishing was seen to be the best means to ensure this wider utility. To Richmond, a UDS head of department and senior lecturer, getting information 'out' benefitted both society and contributed to knowledge production. He felt that 'data cannot be kept on the shelves otherwise why do you do the research?' For him, 'you publish for people, also for scientists or researchers to get an idea, and also maybe something that would help mankind that you couldn't do.' Richmond's hope was that others would 'carry on from where I ended because my lab may not be able to come to a real conclusion of the research, but somebody else could continue and finish that work'.

Issah, another UDS applied sciences lecturer, felt that research and publishing was often selfish, and not necessarily the most useful way to help develop Ghana. His dream was not 'to earn more status for myself' but rather to 'change peoples' lives'. He wanted his research 'to be commercialised and developed into [a] small- or medium-scale industry, especially in rural and urban communities, to generate employment, to create jobs and to create wealth'. He wanted to give 'people in the village a better quality of life, even if nobody gives me gold or silver for it'.

The importance of university research making a 'useful' contribution to society traces back to Bentham's 'utilitarian' vision and the founding of University College London. In a Ghanaian context, UDS was the product of Nkrumah's call for universities grounded in, and responsive to, the needs of society. Its original mandate was to 'blend the academic world with that of the community in order to provide constructive interaction between the two for the total development of Northern Ghana' (Kaburise 2003). Whilst this mandate, and the radical community-based learning models that came with it, was increasingly placed under threat by the demands of academic research, many UDS scholars still shared this vision.

A few questioned whether journal publications had a direct impact on society. Donkor, a UG senior lecturer in health sciences, insisted that his motivation was the bigger goal of 'benefitting humanity'. 'The more we share, the more we learn, the more humanity benefits.' He felt it was important to 'diversify the premium that we put on academic output', and not emphasise 'journals, book chapters and books'. He admitted that 'we publish for academics to consume, but after consumption it has to have a bearing on humanity'.

On not teaching 'outdated knowledge'

Ever since Wilhelm von Humboldt set out a vision in 1810 for a new university in Berlin that would unify teaching and research (Von Humboldt 1970), academic commentators have reflected on how best to strengthen the research and teaching nexus. Contemporary debates, initiated by Ernst Boyer (1990), see a divide between idealists who emphasise the value of the connection (Clark 1994) and realists who recognise how difficult this is to sustain in practice, especially as universities get 'unbundled' (McCowan 2017) and pulled in different directions (McKinley et al. 2020). Amongst our Ghanaian respondents, few advocated separation. Instead several talked to the importance of carrying out research to inform one's teaching. Farhanah, a UDS health sciences lecturer, felt strongly that 'I have to be up to date on whatever I am teaching … I shouldn't go to the classroom and be using outdated knowledge.'

Others felt strongly that their students should be able to read their work, or that in order to mentor postgraduates through the publishing process they too should be publishing. Kofi, a UG senior lecturer in health sciences, made a compelling case for the positive impact of his own research on his students, insisting that he was motivated by being able to point my students to 'work in the setting that they are familiar with, they can look at work from different places by different people but they can also see work that I have done and then they can relate it with what I am teaching them'.

Maana, another UG senior lecturer, noted how research provided lecturers with a wealth of examples to illustrate their points while teaching. She felt that as well as the students finding this 'exciting', it helps you to find 'overlaps between teaching and research so that our students know how theory and practice come together'. For Farhanah, being able to talk about her recently published work boosted her teaching confidence. She described telling her students about papers she had recently published, and one had said 'yes, doc I saw your paper, and I read it'. This gave her a feeling that she was 'on top' of her job, and a sense of satisfaction that 'what you are telling them, it is out there'.

Teaching and research were often experienced as rivals. Many mentioned the tension between the emphasis on publications, and their own wish that teaching and community engagement played a bigger role in promotion requirements. Abenayo, a senior lecturer at UG, voiced her frustration at the way that 'if you don't publish you don't get promoted, then it is like you are not doing anything, even though my department is a teaching department'. She felt that teaching 'didn't carry a lot of weight' and that 'whether you like it or not you have to publish if you want to be promoted'.

Abenayo's striking description of how teaching was now seen as 'not doing anything' was echoed by many interviewees. Francis, a UDS applied sciences HoD commented that, 'if you don't publish you will not be promoted, no matter how hardworking the fellow is'. Others, like Gabriel, emphasised the UDS 'triple-criteria' system for assessing one's work. He explained that it 'is not just teaching, it is teaching, research and extension, and that if you just do one aspect of your role, you are not doing much'. He insisted that at UDS 'your job description is teaching, research and community extension'. He aimed to ensure his research and teaching benefitted the community and welcomed being assessed for promotion on all three areas

UDS faculty voiced the most disquiet about the way their university was prioritising research and publishing over teaching. They sensed a growing divide between the public mandate of UDS as a community-focused university and these publication requirements. UDS faculty emphasised the importance of community engagement in their work, while UG faculty focused more on the need for international recognition.

Again, there were dissenting voices. Patrick, a UDS head of department in the health sciences, disagreed that faculty were overburdened by teaching. He questioned the claim that promotion should be based primarily on an assessment of teaching. He felt it was his 'primary responsibility to create and share knowledge', and asked 'if you say you don't have time to research and publish, what are you going to be using to teach your students'. His concern was that without that, 'you are going to be using what others have created all the time and there wouldn't be any innovation from your side'. Worse still, 'you do not know how the person went about that work, but if it is yours you know what you did, you know what went in there, and then you know the quality of it'.

These tensions are a consequence of the idealisation of the teaching-research nexus (McKinley et al. 2020). This unity of academic purpose may be an important principle, but it is hard enough to sustain in rich UK universities (Shields and Watermeyer 2020), let alone in resource-constrained Ghanaian universities where new faculty are given extensive teaching responsibilities with limited support (Alabi and Abdulai 2016). A significant proportion of junior faculty have yet to finish their PhDs, making this yet another pressure to juggle (Alabi and Abdulai 2016).

'Honour' and 'inner joy': the affective rewards of publishing

As in most university systems, publication is partly driven by a sense of competition, and a determination to make a contribution. Yet many interviewees also felt that scholarly recognition had its affective rewards, including pride, satisfaction and honour. This sense of pleasure comes through in Kosiwa's anecdote about a paper she wrote whilst a lecturer at UG:

> I had this experience where an authority in one of the areas in which I publish – somebody I quoted very well in my works, he is an authority, a big man in the area – sent me an email and I felt so honoured. [Burst into laughter] Imagine that even this small paper that I had written was recognised by such a well renowned person. That alone gave me satisfaction. I felt really honoured that at least my work is going somewhere. So that is also one of the reasons why I want to publish.

The joy of recognition helps academics to continue. As one UG health sciences lecturer put it, 'You meet organisations that are quoting work that you have done – I think it motivates me to continue.' Recognition, building a name for oneself, and contributing to knowledge intermingle. Kojo, a UG social sciences lecturer, describes 'the joy of seeing yourself contributing to knowledge':

> That inner joy alone is enough so that at a point when everything is successful, you are able to refer your colleagues to it and say that I have also contributed to this issue so they can read it. Or apart from being a requirement for promotion on the academic ladder and so on, the inner joy of having been able to contribute your quota to an issue, maybe it could be a national or global issue, it cannot be mentioned without your name there.

Similarly for Kumi, a senior lecturer in social sciences at UG, the 'innate satisfaction' that comes from 'having a number of publications and being cited' made him 'feel somehow important'. Receiving 'emails from people all over the world, you are recognised as having contributed to the global discourse in the area of scholarly publication'.

Many spoke of the satisfaction of being recognised as an author, of having one's work read, cited, and known about. This was not just about status. It was about being recognised for one's scholarly contribution to a scientific field. Whilst Akibu, a UG applied sciences senior lecturer, admitted that 'you have to sell yourself', he felt that 'you want people to get to know what you are doing'. Kumi saw publishing as a means 'to advertise yourself', and 'make yourself known and visible because when you are a researcher and you don't make yourself known, how would people get to know you?' Akuma, a UG social sciences lecturer, explained that you want to 'get to a level where people are looking for you, because you are an authority in that area'. Her hope was to be known 'out there', and for other researchers to 'come to me anytime they want to do something in Ghana in reproductive health'.

Recognition led to appreciation and even admiration. For Fredua, a UDS applied sciences lecturer, 'when you do the research, you have to publish it so that people can appreciate the work you are doing'. Online platforms make this 'appreciation' more palpable and several mentioned their sense of pride at reading readers' comments on platforms like ResearchGate or receiving notification of people downloading their work. Shaibu, a UDS health sciences lecturer said, 'for people to get to know the kind of work you are doing, you have to publish ... the few papers that I have published, when people read your work they give you a notification that, "oh somebody has read your work".'

Not everyone identified writing as a source of innate pride and satisfaction. For some it just came with the day job. Akosua was unromantic about the academic vocation: 'I guess for me you are in the academic enterprise, this is what you are supposed to do, so you do it.' Similarly, Adjoa, a UG senior lecturer in social sciences, described publishing as 'just a routine thing that you do as an academic. I think it is an expectation that once you are in that field, you really want to be sharing your work ... I knew I was already in the system; I knew I had to be doing that'. Another UG lecturer in social sciences said, 'what motivates me? I am in academia. This is the field I find myself and as part of the job you have to publish.'

Revisiting the 'why publish' question

The answer to the 'why publish' question for Ghanaian academics highlights a complex weave of personal motivations and institutional rationales. Four broad explanations emerged from the interviews, often at the same time and even in the same breath.

For most, the first reason for publishing is the immediate goal of career survival and advancement. Publication was not an option, but a requirement. Both universities set explicit numerical publication targets as part of their promotion criteria. This led one respondent to compare research to a production process, a factory churning out papers, echoing broader critiques of 'audit culture' and its impact on British universities. Many were honest about the institutional pressures on them to publish, even if uncomplaining about the focus on numbers of outputs.

The second most common explanation invoked the complementarity of research and teaching: that an active research and publishing record was the key to being a good academic teacher. A third was more outward-looking: the ambition to share knowledge and make a difference to policy and practice beyond academia. The fourth theme to emerge was the intrinsic motivation to carry out curiosity-driven research, and the affective rewards that this brought. None of these motivations were unique to Ghana, but the prioritisation of career survival reflects the material realities of making a living that sustains family members and dependents.

Rationales varied by age and seniority. More senior faculty were the most likely to invoke their own research vocation (Weber 1948) and the intrinsic rewards that come from making a scientific contribution. A few spoke less of their own motivations than of what good science 'should' involve, using phrases such as 'that is why most people are publishing'. One or two insisted, perhaps disingenuously, that promotion was not important to them. And, very occasionally, people admitted that they had not initially realised the pivotal role that publishing played in academic career progression.

Any attempts to categorise researchers by purported publishing rationale overlook how most respondents were keen to apply for pro-motion, to teach well *and* to share their scientific insights and knowledge. As well as shared rationales, differences in perspective depend on age, seniority, disciplinary culture, training, and research biography.

Individual staff experiences of, and views on, publishing are best read in the context of the growing importance accorded to research by these universities. UG's aspiration to be a 'world-class' research-intensive university increases the focus on publication 'outputs'. Whilst UDS academics highlighted their university's unique mandate to work with local communities, they too now find themselves under pressure to publish in 'reputable' journals. It is no wonder that some feel the goalposts have changed.

These rationales and explanations are commonplace amongst researchers, but the stakes for those working at the peripheries of a global science system are higher. They find themselves forced to choose between global reputation and local relevance (Nyamnjoh 2004), between English and their native languages (Casanave 1998), and between different reputational economies (Hyland 2015). These are not easy choices, especially as the reputations of long-established national scholarly journals are increasingly put into question.

Chapter 4

In search of the 'international' journal

I submitted a paper to an international journal that receives papers from anywhere, only for the editor to write to me asking me to submit the paper to a Ghanaian journal because he knew this was a paper coming from Ghana. (Awudu, UDS lecturer, social science)

What I have seen is that most data from Africa is said not to be credible, and so when you send it to European journals, usually they don't publish them. They may just reject it. Sometimes they wouldn't give you any concrete tangible reason. They may just say, "not suitable for the journal," or "send it to this or that," because sometimes they will say that this is an international journal. So, if data is collected from Ghana is it not international? (Kwaku, UDS lecturer, social science)

Introduction

With an ever-growing number of scholarly journals and publishing platforms, deciding where to submit one's research for peer review can be a high-stakes decision. In Ghana this 'choice' has additional complexity. As shown in Chapter 2, researchers' decisions about where to submit their work are guided by what 'counts' for promotion at both universities. UDS promotion guidelines require 'books and articles published in refereed journals', whilst UG similarly expects publications in 'reputable, peer-reviewed journals' (UDS 2018; UG 2019). Terms such as 'reputable' and 'refereed' are left undefined in these institutional policies, leaving scope for uncertainty, interpretation and contestation. For researchers keen to progress their careers, every article needs to count. Whilst the official university guidelines make no mention of 'local' or 'national' journals as opposed to 'international' journals, the terms are used constantly by academic faculty themselves.

Postcolonial critics of the African academy have long highlighted the damaging consequences of academic 'extraversion' (Bayart 2000), with the continent's research priorities structured by its colonial histories and its orientation to the agenda of the 'Global North' (Hountondji 2009). This external intellectual orientation is manifest in Ghana's university strategies (Gyamera 2019), in data on international publishing collaborations (Mêgnigbêto 2013) and even in the way Ghana's researchers joke about 'African science' as they bemoan the poor quality of their laboratory facilities in relation to those in Europe (Droney 2014). Gyamera (2019) highlights how the University of Mawuta – a pseudonym for the 'oldest and biggest universities in Ghana' (Gyamera 2019, 927) – adopts a 'do or die' approach to internationalisation, quoting one senior administrator as chastising departments that were not publishing sufficiently, saying 'if you want to die, we will help you to die'. Mêgnigbêto (2013) shows how 70% of the 3,300 articles published by Ghanaian researchers from 2001 to 2010 were part of international research collaborations, primarily with colleagues in the US and UK, and only a small proportion were with other African countries (around 3% with South Africa, and only 1% with Kenya and Tanzania). Droney (2014) argues that the Ghanaian scientists he worked with are still committed to national development, but mock the notion of African science. They want to present themselves as 'global scientists not contained by the word African', and 'want the best careers they can achieve – in Ghana or elsewhere' (Droney 2014, 381).

Across Africa and beyond, the rise of the globalised publishing industry has reshaped the priorities and values of researchers (Carré 2016; Curry and Lillis 2017). Ghanaian researchers feel the pressure to publish 'internationally', but are also aware of the risks of publishing in the 'wrong' journals (Atiso et al. 2019). Like most of the world's researchers, they are aware of the power of new publishing metrics, and the importance of publication in 'top' peer-reviewed and indexed journals (Nicholas et al. 2017).

There is a growing literature on the contested nature of the 'international' within African universities. Adomi and Mordi (2003) were the first to note the trend of Nigerian promotion boards expecting a proportion of articles published in what they called 'foreign' journals. Ten years later, Omobowale et al. (2013, 2014) made the case that this was leading to a trend towards publishing in 'foreign paid-for' journals, with 'peripheral' Nigerian scholars choosing journals that were domiciled in developed countries in order to meet the 'international' threshold, even though these were sometimes of low quality and sometimes conducted minimal peer review. Omobowale et al. (2014) argued that these were sub-standard, if not 'predatory', journals that benefitted from 'desperate customers', and that the work so published was ignored by the scholarly mainstream. Tarkang and Bain (2019) take up this argument to suggest that African researchers should publish in peer-reviewed 'local' journals, and call for an accredited list of African journals.

This chapter develops this work by demonstrating the difficulties of delineating a strict set of journal quality markers. It explores how interviewees interpreted the meanings of terms such as 'significance' and 'quality' in university guidelines, how they judged the reputations of journals, along with how they felt peers judged their work. There are many different factors that people used to assess potential journals, including the disciplinary scope, readership, reputation, publishing 'brand', frequency of publication, speed of review, and perceived impact. Many also pointed to the influence of personal scholarly networks – including whether a peer or senior colleague had recommended the journal, and who else had published in the journal.

For some, this more nuanced and field-specific process of assessment was reduced to a focus on symbolic geography, and whether the chosen outlet was an 'international' journal, especially an 'indexed' journal that had an impact factor, rather than 'local' journals. The chapter describes how respondents emphasised journal indexes and rankings as the most reliable guide to publishing. It goes on to discuss the specific influence of, and views on, Scopus. The next section is on the challenges of getting an article accepted, including the perceived affordability of some journals, as many charged prohibitive APCs (article processing charges), and these journals' relevance to Ghanaian research and policy debates. Publishing 'locally' was often seen as a second-best option, given the negative associations that 'local' journals invoked. The final section discusses how people perceived the consequences of what they saw as the 'wrong' decision, namely publishing in a low-quality, or even worse, what they perceived to be a 'predatory' journal.

Choosing a 'top-tier' journal

In 2014, UG published a ten-year strategic plan that set out its ambition to become a 'world class research-intensive university' (UG 2014). The plan was many months in the making. It set out several KPIs (key performance indicators), including the university's aim to rank in the top 20 African universities, and for faculty publications in 'high-impact' journals to increase by 200%. The vision is reiterated on the university's website, in its brochures and in a decade of efforts to meet the research targets of a pan-African university benchmarking exercise (Cloete et al. 2018).

It is this that informed the University of Ghana's lengthy process of consultation and revision of its guidelines on promotion (UG 2019), with a stronger emphasis on teaching and service as well as detailed guidance for faculty on publications. Schedule F of the university statutes sets out that 'the key ingredient should be significance not volume', and that evaluators 'can judge the significance of a publication by examining the quality of the journals in which it appears, the use to which other researchers have made of it or by requesting testimony from distinguished scholars or authors in the candidate's field of research'. The promotion guidelines insist that the 'emphasis should be on the quality which encompasses originality, significance, rigor and impact in the discipline' (UG 2019, 5).

How then do faculty make sense of this guidance? Interviewees talked through their strategies for choosing a journal. Several used websites or journal indexes to check whether a journal was 'recognised', and so not 'predatory'. Some did this in a very thorough way. Yaa, a senior lecturer in the social sciences at UG, scoured a database of economics journals, assessing whether their profile matched her research area. Her research paid off. 'Thank God that was the journal I selected as they seemed to like the work and so they accepted it'.

Whilst there are many sources of online advice, few mentioned using such guidance. Instead, many recalled looking over their colleagues' publication profiles to find suitable journals, decided as a research group, or relied on the advice of co-authors. Akosua described how her co-author's ambitions had led to them publishing together in a 'top-ranked' journal, and that, on her own, she would not have made a list of such journals'. Mavis, a UDS lecturer in applied sciences, carefully negotiated her choice of journal with her research team leader, describing how it took time to 'eventually agree', ensuring it best 'suited the results I have'.

Established UG staff were most likely to be familiar with the best university presses and commercial publishers, and their respective status. Kumi, a senior UG lecturer, described his 'minimum criterion' for choosing a journal. It had to be a 'recognised publisher', which he then explained meant 'Taylor and Francis, I'm talking about Springer, I'm talking about Oxford University Press, I'm talking about Chicago, Emerald, and Sage and all the major recognised and a few institutional journals'. He admitted that some strong journals were not published by these 'major' presses, but they were 'institutionalised' because they were hosted by a university.

Another researcher described how she went through all the journals looking to see how they were ranked by indexes within her field, using the Australian business school ranking of journals (ABDC), to guide her judgement as to the 'good journals'.

Not everyone was conversant with this global publishing landscape. Researchers at UDS were less likely to be familiar with the major citation indexes and their role in adjudicating impact and quality. Some referred to Springer, PubMed and Scopus as libraries. A few even pointed to ISSN and ISBN numbers (easily purchased for registration of any publications) as signals of journal authenticity. For every researcher who could immediately name the most influential journals in their field, there were others with much less knowledge of these status hierarchies.

In search of the 'international'

> My preference is for international journals and not because I think they are better but that is my inclination. You want to be good where you are, but you want to be internationally competitive as well … It is not that I don't like local journals … but then you have to take into account other considerations. (Yaa, UG senior lecturer, social sciences)

When our interviewees described their journal choices, they would often juxtapose 'international' and 'local' journals. The contrast was used as a proxy for journal quality, even if both terms themselves were left vague and undefined (Omobowale et al. 2014). Their use in everyday conversations created a powerful spatial and symbolic opposition. This reinforced and stabilised the sense that Ghana's journals (and by extension, its researchers) existed at the periphery of a global academic publishing landscape. Neither university used these terms in their own promotion guidance or official discourse. Work by Thomas (2018) highlights how a similar imagined geography drives the publishing strategies of Tanzanian scholars.

Abenayo, a UG senior lecturer, pointed to the artificiality of this geographical divide, and its implications for Ghana's own journals. She described how in university meetings about promotion requirements, 'we are told to publish in "internationally recognised" journals'. She insisted that 'if we don't publish in our own journals, then who would publish there?' Despite saying this 'out loud wherever I go', she felt that there was no choice 'but to publish in international journals'.

She went on to talk about the pressure she feels from her peers and 'from above' when they see that she has three 'local' publications. They look at her CV and say 'you are doing well but you have to be mindful of where you are publishing' because it 'looks like you are publishing in local journals'. Despite only having '3 out of 16 publications in local journals I am still told not to publish there'.

Staff in sociology tended to be more critical of this imagined global/local hierarchy, whilst researchers in the health and applied sciences were keener to be globally visible. Adjoa, a UG senior lecturer, framed 'international' as a way of gaining research visibility, whereas with 'local journals, you would make noise within your [country] and so you are a local champion, and it does not go anywhere.' She went on to discuss a paper critiquing the low coverage of 'African' journals within systematic reviews. She felt that such reviews only cover 'high impact' journals, such that 'if you really want the true picture of what you are trying to do your systematic review on and you look at these low impact journals then you will not get anything'.

Publishing internationally presented many challenges. Several pointed to the exorbitant APCs charged by some open-access journals. Others highlighted delays, editorial gatekeeping, and the risks of being discriminated against as a Ghanaian scholar. Awudu, a UG lecturer, recalled submitting a paper to an 'international journal', only to be shocked when the editor wrote 'asking me to submit the paper to a Ghanaian journal because he knew this was a paper coming from Ghana'. This was doubly frustrating as Awudu felt that 'our local journals do not look professional'.

Several people pointed out that whilst the 'official' university guidance was to publish in both local and international journals, they knew which was most likely to 'count'. Attah, a UG applied sciences lecturer, insisted that promotion assessors felt it was more 'authentic' to publish in international journals. She felt that the 'local' journals were looked down upon 'because you can easily publish there', and that it was the 'international journals that they want now'. Asked if she had published in any of the 'local' journals, she said that she 'had not even tried'. However, because 'she was not hearing anything' from the international journals about the papers she had sent, she was considering submitting them to local journals, even if there was a perception that if 'you go local, you are not recognised'.

A few explained their choices as being less about differences in quality than about gaining respect. Yaa, a UG senior lecturer, described how in searching for a journal, 'when I come across a respectable person, somebody I have a lot of respect for, and they publish somewhere and they do the same type of work that I do, I will look at where they published and I would want to get there as well because they have published there'. She went on to describe how 'the professor in our department has published in a journal on gender and economics, and so, if I happen to get a paper focused on gender issues, I feel that because she has published there I can also get it there'.

The Scopus factor

The two universities had a great deal of influence over individual publishing strategies. The library and research office of the University of Ghana emphasised choosing journals within indexes such as Scopus, though this is not a requirement in the promotion guidance or statutes. Scopus is prominently listed on the University of Ghana library homepage, as if it is a comprehensive journal database. As Akibu, an applied sciences senior lecturer said, 'we have been given a list of journals where we can publish or where you know your work can be recognised by the University of Ghana'. 'For now,' she continued, 'I know that I don't want to publish in any journal that would not benefit me. It means that I wouldn't want to publish in a journal that is not identified or recognised by the institution in which I work.' UDS occasionally circulated a list of approved or recommended journals to its faculty.

Scopus is the brand name of Elsevier's abstract and citation database. It was launched in 2004 and allows researchers to search for articles and citations from a database of more than 24,000 active journal titles, from almost 12,000 publishers. Along with its rival Web of Science (WoS) – the first ever citation index – Scopus is heavily marketed as a research tool, and many training webinars are offered via Elsevier's Africa YouTube channel.

UG interviewees talked about the expectation on them to choose Scopus-indexed journals. Ten interviewees explicitly mentioned the index, and others valued the training sessions and webinars offered by Elsevier. Kosiwa, a UG senior lecturer in applied sciences explained that 'every lecturer on campus knows that it is Scopus, so nobody even bothers to go out of Scopus anymore … they have already looked for the possible journals that you can publish in'. She went on to say that 'you just look in that list and then you pick one, so I think they have made life easier for us in a way by limiting us to Scopus: we don't really worry about whether this is a predatory journal or not'. She praised its convenience, noting that finding journals would take 'a lot of time when we didn't have this Scopus to guide us'. 'We go online on Scopus,' she reiterated, 'and I look out for keywords in my topic and then that is what helps me select a journal.'

Gabriel, a UDS social science lecturer, added that 'for promotion they now look to see if your papers are published in Scopus'. Kumi, a UG social sciences associate professor, put it more strongly, explaining that publishing in a journal not indexed in Scopus was 'like an exercise in futility'. He qualified this by saying, 'You may want to put some papers in local journals to disseminate the findings because the consumers are typically from within.' He felt that there would be a 'better readership' in a 'Western journal', but, sadly, 'they wouldn't be able to make much of it'.

The key to the success of indexes like Scopus and WoS is the data it generates about a journal's impact factor, a measure of the average number of citations a journal article receives. Twenty-eight of our respondents mentioned that they look at impact factors when deciding which journals to publish in. Many, like Nana, a UG applied sciences lecturer, were enthusiastic about the impact factor 'metric'. The last thing she wanted to do was to 'publish your high quality work in a journal that is not widely recognised' as 'it is a lot of work to just throw away like that'. For her 'the impact factor more or less encompasses everything because you know that once it has a high impact factor, more people are reading it, and when more people are reading it, it reaches a wider audience and it would have that impact that you seek'.

UG faculty were particularly attentive to journal impact factors, and several highlighted that this was the first metric they considered. Their university's focus on becoming a 'world-class' university translated into a greater awareness of such measures as a proxy for journal reputation. Many UG faculty include their personal 'h-index' in their promotion portfolios, as well as the impact factor of each journal they had published in.

Was everyone invested in this metricisation of quality? Only four respondents were critical of the impact factors, suggested that this was not the only priority, or that it was 'overhyped'. Mohammed, a UDS lecturer, was ambivalent about Scopus, questioning the validity of its metrics. 'I don't consider the impact factor of a journal,' he explained, saying 'people just want to put their journals on a certain level'. Provided it wasn't 'predatory', he felt that the impact factor shouldn't determine where to publish. 'If you put your work there it will be read by people.' Akuma, a UG lecturer, was also unenthusiastic, explaining 'that this has never motivated me'. She was only interested in whether it was a 'recognised journal'. That said, Akuma also admitted that she was not immune to its appeal: 'later on if I check and if it is high I am okay'.

A few were hazy on journal details. One person wrongly insisted that no African journals ('apart from a few hosted by South African Universities') had an impact factor, and incorrectly claimed that the *Ghana Medical Journal* was excluded from the Scopus citation index.

With a bewildering array of journal 'choices', recognised publishing 'brands' were a way of narrowing one's search, an approach encouraged by librarians. Commercial signifiers were seen as reputational markers and sources of security. UG faculty seemed most aware of these signals. Akuma described how her seniors ask her where she is publishing, knowing that she needs to name 'well-known' journals. 'When you mention "oh Taylor and Francis", it is good and "Springer", it is good'. She went on to say that 'these are the places I look at; I don't look elsewhere'.

Taiye, a UG health sciences lecturer, felt that she needed to be publishing in journals that are 'prominent to the research world', and as a result chose 'journals that were recommended to us such as *PloSOne*, Springer journals and the rest'. Maana, also at UG, felt reassured that 'I know that when I am picking *BMC* or *BMJ*, I am comfortable right, and so anything that is under *BMC*, I am comfortable'. She went on to explain that 'the reason is that you know *BMC* has credibility and publishing in that mother of journals, I'm covered'.

Some felt that the most prestigious high-impact journals were out of reach for early career researchers. Whilst they aspired to them, there was always the risk of being discouraged by rejection. A few respondents described how they aimed to 'graduate' from lower to higher tier journals as they gained expertise. These different 'tiers' are conceptualised in relation to journal impact factor. Moving 'up' the tiers required developing one's academic self-esteem, reputation, and understanding of the types of work published by journals, rather than just the development of technical research skills.

Kwami, a UG social sciences lecturer, was one of several who talked about initially 'targeting' low-rank journals, and that 'only when you are able to build that reputation you can now try a high ranked journal'. A similar sense of tactical progression was evinced by Gabriel, a UDS social science lecturer. He pointed to the emotional consequences of rejection, and how they were told 'as beginner researchers it is important not to look at very high impact factors because that is going to discourage you'. He described the fragility of academic confidence, such that 'you might not be able to succeed and that can discourage you so you must gain some level of competency and self-esteem before you can go to these high impact factors'.

Emmanuel, a lecturer in applied sciences, was even more precise about how he used journal impact factors to measure his own level of expertise and professional competence. 'You begin to realise that you have achieved certain things and you realise that you have graduated from that level, and you are in a different level.' He vividly described the journey in terms of 'somebody who will start with a journal that has impact level of maybe 0.5, then along the line he now starts eyeing a journal of 1.5, maybe later he goes to look for 3'. Emmanuel felt that 'as you read more papers you are being pushed left and right to understand certain things, you then know the type of research you could send to bigger journals that are out there'.

The expectation on researchers to choose a journal indexed in Scopus or WoS consolidated the power of these indexes and their quality infrastructures, reinforcing existing journal hierarchies and weakening the reputation of the many African journals who had not been indexed. A few worried about the consequences of this. Kwaku, a UDS lecturer in the social sciences, explained how his peers would 'talk of the fact that it [the journal] should be in the SSCI – the Social Science Citation Index' or Scopus, because these were seen to be highly reputable. 'But,' he went on, 'there are certain journals that are very good, but the classification does not allow them to be included there because those journals for example do not publish online.'

He was well placed to comment on the gaps in the coverage of theses indexes, as he had studied for a PhD in China. Here, he had become aware of the indexes' minimal coverage of non-English language journals. 'The rankings are not so objective,' he insisted. 'The Chinese publish a lot, but they publish in the Chinese language in Chinese journals'. As a result he felt 'they can't come to the top because those that are going to review, review only the English aspect'. He went on to insist that 'science has no language whether it is Chinese, French, English or whatever, it is scientific'. Whilst his claim that 'they don't know Chinese' was not strictly accurate, as there are 316 Chinese language journals in Scopus (though only 22 in Web of Science), there was truth in his critique.

Did people know the impact factor of Ghanaian journals? Adjoa, a UG health sciences lecturer, was unsure, and admitted that he did not know the impact of the *Ghana Medical Journal*. But, in any case, he admitted, 'it would not be as high as these other ones, and because of that you go to the international one'.

71

The risks of 'thinking local'

For all the emphasis people placed on choosing 'international' journals, others highlighted the importance of supporting what they called 'local' journals. 'Local' was understood flexibly. It could mean Ghanaian, regional, or even African. The term was deployed relationally, and juxtaposed, sometimes negatively, to European- or American-run journals. Research on the tension between 'international' and 'local' in the publishing expectations placed on West African academics goes back more than 20 years (Bodomo 1999). Adomi and Mordi (2003) tracked the trend towards what Nigerian universities called 'foreign' journals, whilst Omobowale et al. (2013, 2014) use the language of 'foreign paid' publication. More recently Atolani et al. (2019) documented the damaging consequence of journal impact factors on local journal cultures.

A few, like Ibrahim, a UDS senior lecturer, were very positive about the experience of publishing with Ghanaian journals. He rightly pointed out that his university 'wants you to publish in both local and international journals', and went on to say that the 'few local journals that I published about three or four articles in so far have been good'. He felt that they take 'their time to do a good scrutiny and they give much attention to little details', they 'don't want to dent their image' and so 'they take their time to do a good job'. Their big challenge was attracting reviewers. 'If they are able to get good reviewers for the local journal, they will do good work,' he concluded.

Others spoke positively about their experience of editing and reviewing for Ghanaian journals, and how they had improved in quality. Gabriel, a UDS senior lecturer, described how he reviewed for a UDS journal that 'when they started it was not anything to write home about'. Over time the quality had improved, and submissions are received from 'outside', including from Nigeria and across the continent.

Such voices were in the minority. Many more were ambivalent about publishing locally. Nana, a UG applied sciences lecturer, admitted that he had been encouraged to publish locally, recalling his professor's views that 'we should not always be looking at the journals outside'.

In his mind, the local journals did not 'look strong, and probably don't even have impact factors'. He went on: 'I don't know if there are any that are indexed, or whether they would even count towards your promotions or not.'

Others complained about 'local' journals having low impact. One researcher's solution was not necessarily to choose an 'outside' journal, but rather one recognised for its quality and its standards. Awudu, a UG social science lecturer, focused less on the credibility that inclusion in the global journal indexes provided, and instead on the visibility that resulted. 'You realise,' he explained, 'that many of the local journals are not indexing to several sources where the paper can reach people, so it is just their website that they have and that is where it is and unless you go to that website, nobody will see that paper and that is one of the reasons'. Awudu went on to talk about the aesthetics of publishing, comparing international journals where 'you will see the layout, and everything looks very nice' with 'these other local journals of ours' that 'just do not look professional at all'.

Donkor, a UG senior health sciences lecturer, noted that online open-access journals were more accessible because they were not behind what he called a 'financial firewall,' where 'you must pay before you access'. But this was not enough if they were to 'catch up' with the international journals from Europe 'that are of higher credibility and everyone wants to publish there'. As a result, 'if I am pushed to make a choice as to whether I am publishing in a low tier journal or local or high obviously I would want to publish in a journal that is recognised by my peers either locally or internationally'.

He also worried about academic credibility. 'If it is not indexed, people will not see it as credible and it is also not going to be visible'. Donkor also emphasised impact, 'and not just impact, academic impact with factors, we are talking of direct impact with ordinary human beings'. He admitted that 'if you are a professor and you truly are interested in making impact locally, of course I would continue to have a mix, a few in international, some in local, and even beyond journals'. By this he meant that he was also keen to 'publish in non-academic portals, the dailies, newspapers, all those places, but it depends on the stage of the academic'.

Despite being positive about his experiences of peer review, Gabriel, a UDS social science lecturer, complained about the perceived lack of professionalism of 'local' journals and their slowness in editorial decision-making. He bemoaned the feeling that 'locally we have no sense of time and people are not paid for reviewing journals like the editors'. As a result, 'most local journals publish once or twice in a year'. He went on to disparage his colleagues. 'You submit your paper and you want it to be published early for your promotion and what have you, it has to go through a lengthy process. Some of the foreign international journals attach seriousness to it. Our own people, it may not be like that'.

Gabriel pointed to a number of 'dormant' local journals, including one published by his university's medical school, as evidence as to the frailty of the local publishing economy. He had once been an editor of that journal, and admitted that as editor he used to receive papers from Nigeria, South Africa and Kenya but could not remember the last time the journal had been published. 'It is about reviewers, he complained, 'we don't have reviewers'.

Many commented about the tough peer review assessments they receive from local journals, with Kosiwa, a UG lecturer, reflecting that 'we are too critical of our own'. He reflected on his 'disheartening' experience of a paper being rejected by a 'local' journal. Kosiwa blamed this on the reviewers' lack of expertise with social science research. He described how he then sent the paper to an 'international journal – a renowned one in the social sciences – and you wouldn't believe it, but the same paper was accepted'. 'So,' he explained, 'based on that experience we would rather try the international ones first before coming down to the local ones, because we feel that the local ones are too critical when they are assessing.'

Poor-quality reviewing was a common complaint. Gabriel admitted 'I have never sent any article to some reviewers because the review is not of quality. So, when they review your paper, at the end of the day when they publish it, you yourself, you read the thing and you can see that'. Akuma, a social sciences lecturer at UG, admitted that she chose not to publish in 'these journals we have on campus' because 'when you publish here it is just on the shelf'. She went on to acknowledge that it is partly about impressing 'your seniors' by mentioning 'Taylor and Francis' and 'Springer', and that 'these are the places I look out for, I don't look elsewhere'.

Questioning the 'international/local' divide

Can one judge the quality of a journal by its geographical provenance and its publisher? The Ghanaian social scientists interviewed were quick to question this problematic 'geography of credibility' (Powell 2007) and its use to judge journal reputation, and to deconstruct an imagined hierarchy between 'local' and 'international' journals. Abenayo noted that 'the content should be looked at and not the journal'. Noting that the issues are 'complicated', she pointed to the contorted geographical imaginaries that surrounded authenticity. She felt that some of her colleagues saw 'everything from Europe, North America as international, so if you are published in Nigerian journals, that is not international'. As a result, 'people are more likely to say that this is a local journal, this is an African journal'.

Mensah, another UG social sciences lecturer, put it more starkly, complaining about his colleagues' 'terrible misconception' that publishing in journals that are 'supposedly based in the UK' was a marker of reputational quality. 'Some of the local journals,' he pointed out, 'even the editors are more experienced, more proficient than some of these so-called "international" journals that we use.' He developed his critique, saying 'they think that the local journals are actually more frustrating than the international journals'.

He went on to bemoan the 'vicious cycle of the way we do our things' and the way that 'if you get a local reviewer who already doesn't value the work he is doing, his attitude towards that work is zero but he thinks that the journal from America or Europe is an important journal'. This led to a distorted sense of priorities: 'He pays much more attention to that journal and so he would quickly respond to those ones than the other ones'. For Mensah, this was 'where some of the difficulties also come from', and he felt that 'until we stop and begin to value our own these are some of the things that will happen'.

Talking about his single experience of publishing in a local journal, Mensah admitted that one of the reviewers had never responded. However, he pointed out that 'it is a bit frustrating for editors of local journals as well because people don't treat them with the same respect that they do for other international reviewers'.

Mensah felt that his social science faculty had 'a very good journal'. He asserted that the 'university wants us to publish in journals of high repute and it doesn't really matter whether it is a local or international journal'. Insisting that it was more about reputation than geography he went on to say 'we do have the idea that it has to be an international journal, but I have always had the opinion that we can also make our local journals international ones'. He used the example of Nigeria, where 'Nigerians have also made their local journals of international quality'. 'I know,' he went on, 'because they prefer those journals and so we can also make our local journals international ones, where people from outside will also come and publish in our journals because the so-called international journals are local journals in their respective countries'.

Kofi, a UG senior lecturer in health sciences, reiterated this sense that it was about choosing the right journal for the right audience. 'When I think of putting up my work in a journal', he elaborated, 'I don't first of all consider whether it is a local or international journal.' Instead, 'I consider whether that journal is reputable enough to carry across my message.' Noting that 'that journal may be a local journal but may have the audience that I want to reach'. On the other hand, he went on, 'that journal may be an international journal but may actually have a lot more local audience than the local journals'.

Kofi pointed out that as a health economist he would never publish in the *Legon Journal of International Affairs* but would certainly prioritise the *Ghana Medical Journal* over an international medical journal if it had 'the audience I want to reach with my particular message'. Akibu, a UG applied sciences lecturer gave a similar example of having 'developed an appropriate technology that may be specific towards the local people', and that you 'may want to publish it locally to benefit Ghana'. He acknowledged that somebody might say, 'this journal is not recognised' but 'they should consider the content of the paper'.

Some UDS academics described how looking at international journals undermined their confidence, making them realise that their 'own' journals and methods were now out of date. For Mavis, a lecturer in applied sciences, it was 'a little intimidating when you go into the journal and you realise the kind of research that is there'. She realised that 'what you are bringing on board are just these old methods, you see people are using very new methods'. This led her to realise that 'if I send my paper here it will be rejected, so you just know that well you have done something, but where to put it to be accepted makes you develop cold feet.'

The political economy of article processing charges

The high article processing charges (APCs) charged by many open-access journals were a frequent cause of complaint for interviewees, especially for faculty at UDS who admitted to sometimes paying these fees from their own salaries. For Ntim, an applied sciences lecturer at UDS, 'a lot of times you can get a good article to a journal and when it comes to the cost of publishing, you don't even want to think about that journal'. He went on, 'these journals with good impact factors, you have to understand that you have to pay, and me seated here, where would I get the money?'.

Interviewees felt trapped by a publication economy that depended on universities covering these costs, when their own institutions weren't able to do so. Emmanuel, a UDS applied sciences lecturer, pointed out that scholars like him in 'low-income countries', are 'removing USD 1,500 or even USD 1,800 to pay for a journal, from your pocket.'

Fredua, also in the applied sciences at UDS, emphasised the additive costs that came from publishing several articles, 'if you have five papers to publish and each one costs about 500 dollars', their annual research allowance 'would not reach anything'. One consequence of this for her, is that it affects 'the number of papers you can publish within a year'. Some admitted that open access was an important principle, but associated it with prohibitive costs. 'I would rather opt for other options than to go for open access because of the charges,' declared Mavis, a UDS lecturer in applied sciences.

Respondents highlighted their reliance on the APC fee waivers that many journals offered to researchers in low-income countries. Francis, a UDS applied sciences senior lecturer, pointed out that 'the issue is we are not a rich university so everything you publish is coming from your salary'. However, access to these waivers has declined as Ghana has now been classified as a middle-income country, making previously accessible journals no longer affordable. Without a fee waiver, a journal is effectively out of reach for many Ghanaian academics. Awudu pointed out that 'if you are supposed to pay and you don't have the funds, you don't consider that one'. Others, like Yaa, a UG social sciences senior lecturer, gambled that she might get an unofficial waiver down the line. 'There have been two journals so far that have asked for publication fees,' Yaa explained, 'and I would simply write back and ask for it to be waived, and I believe that if the work is good they will give it a waiver and God has been good, they waived it for me'.

There was always the risk that waiver requests could be turned down. 'I wanted to publish in *PloSOne*' (one of the first mega-journals that adopted an APC business model), explained Richmond, and they 'wanted to charge us a huge sum of money ... I think it was about GBP 2,000 plus'. If all the authors were in developing countries, they would have been awarded a waiver, but two of them had US affiliations. 'I pleaded,' he recalled, but 'they said no, so then I had to withdraw it and publish it in another journal'.

One UDS respondent described a disagreement in their research team over whether to 'send an article out' or to publish in their own *UDS Journal of Development Studies*. The disagreement revolved around the relative status of the two journals, and who would cover the cost of the APCs required by the international publication. Ntim was registered for a PhD at a Dutch University at the time, and so he was able to publish work from his doctoral research for free because of the 'read and publish' contract that the university had with a major publisher. Others were not so lucky. Likewise, Lahiri, a UDS applied sciences senior lecturer, explained that 'when I was working with

Danida [Danish International Development Agency], they were paying and making sure that I published in international journals. But now I am alone, it is very challenging to publish in such places.' Her framing of being a senior lecturer but also being 'alone' underscores this sense of not being supported by their university, a particular concern for UDS interviewees.

Where institutional research allowances were available, they were not always easy to access and often took a long time to process. Paul, a UDS applied sciences lecturer, noted that, 'if you submit your paper and it is confirmed that the paper would be published then the university can support you if you wait for it, but I have been working on my own. Last Friday I had to go and pay 300 cedis (USD 50) for one of my papers to be published.' Asked how his university could better support faculty, Ntim suggested that they provide a larger research allowance with more funds for publishing, commenting that 'if I were the only one who had to pay the 900 cedis almost all my research allowance is gone, and if you add the cost of data collection you will be going negative'.

The cost of doing research inevitably left little for paying APCs. This is compounded by having to pay APCs in foreign currencies at expensive exchange rates and through cumbersome transfer procedures. These challenges are distilled in two UDS social science lecturers' remarks. Haruna felt that 'I think cost is a big issue in Africa in terms of publication'. For Kwaku 'sometimes the money [for APCs] is so huge and in the African context we can't raise such money'. Participants were frustrated about both the inadequacy of university support and the wider structural forces limiting their involvement in global scientific debate. Staff at UDS were most likely to raise the topic of APCs, reflecting a discourse that emphasised publishing in such journals, but also the lack of institutional funding available to them.

Revisiting Jeffrey Beall

In 2012 a new concept entered the scholarly discourse: 'predatory publishing' (Beall 2012). The term was the invention of University of Colorado librarian Jeffrey Beall. He had already been blogging about the challenges of open-access publishing, and in 2009 published a review of Bentham Open, a publishing house that he described as 'flooding scholarly communication with a flurry of low quality and questionable research' (2009). He began to assemble an ever-lengthening list of other such publishers. In 2010, he labelled such publishers as 'predatory' because 'their mission is not to promote, preserve, and make available scholarship; instead, their mission is to exploit the author-pays, open-access model for their own profit' (2010, 15). He went on to say, more acerbically, that 'the gold open-access industry is being tainted by a perfidious group of fast and loose upstart publishers who exploit these funding agencies for their own profit, agencies that are all too willing to pay author fees'. The article describes some of the nine publishers as 'dumping grounds' (2010, 15). A 2011 version of this list named 23 publishers and using racialised stereotypes, described a West African publisher as a 'Nigerian scam' and a South Asian publisher as a Pakistani 'storefront' operation. Beall's 2012 op-ed column in *Nature* has been cited more than 700 times. The discourse of 'predatory publishing' entered the academic lexicon, conjuring up images of aggression and animal-like behaviour.

Beall continued to add to his list. He also declared that four further publishers (including Hindawi) were on his 'watch list' as they showed 'some characteristics of predatory open-access publishing.' In early 2012 Beall launched a new blog, *Scholarly Open Access*, dedicated to 'critical analysis of scholarly open-access publishing'. Each edition had a prominent link to a 'List of publishers'. By January 2013, this list had extended to 269 names (Beall 2013). By 2016 the list included 1,028 publishers (Beall 2016). The blog was suddenly taken down, with no explanation, the following year.

Beall's lists of supposedly 'predatory' publishers bluntly divided academic knowledge and dissemination outlets into good and bad, legitimate and illegitimate, true and 'fake'. Promoted and circulated by journals, librarians and universities alike, its Manichean worldview generated anxiety in many emerging academic systems. The discourse – and the practices of list making and accreditation that it has generated – has far-reaching implications for the African academy. Long-established

African journals suddenly became less reputable and legitimate because they were not included in these 'recognised' global citation indexes. This effacement of knowledge production and scholarly expertise undermined a long history of efforts to build 'research capacity' within Africa's universities (Atuahene 2011; Mills 2020).

South Africa's Department for Higher Education and Training (DHET) was the first in Africa to publish an annual list of 'accredited journals' in 2006 (Mouton and Valentine 2017). A development of an existing publication subsidy model, it incentivised individual academics and institutions to publish as much possible within these accredited lists. Almost 15 years later its distortions continue (Muller 2017; Tomaselli 2018). Questioning the inclusion of some social science research indexed in IBSS (International Biography of the Social Sciences), Mouton and Valentine (2017) developed a detailed analysis of more than 4,000 papers published by South African scholars in journals they judged to be 'probably or possibly predatory'. As a result, DHET removed accreditation from most of these journals, leading to further tensions and recriminations (Le Grange 2019; Maistry 2019).

Scholars of publishing have highlighted the damaging consequences of labelling some forms of academic practice as 'illegitimate' (Bell 2017; Eriksson and Gert 2018). The conflation of 'predation' with questions about quality leads to a narrow, normative defence of supposedly 'proper' scholarship. The discourse generates anxiety, suspicion and prejudice whilst reinforcing existing reputational hierarchies. There is growing evidence from numerous African countries of the creative ways in which academics 'game' the lists of accredited journals created by government ministries and university promotion boards, leading to yet more distrust (Mouton and Valentine 2017; Nwagwu and Ojemeni 2015; Teferra 2019).

Beall's list provoked a crisis for several African commercial publishing houses. Chapter 8 discusses the impact of being listed on the Nigerian publisher Academic Journals. Set up by a biotechnology researcher, its first journal promised to 'provide the most rapid turn-around time possible for reviewing and publishing, and to disseminate the articles freely for teaching and reference purposes' (Tonukari 2004, 124). The formula appealed to researchers and proved commercially successful. Making the most of the digital publishing platform, the founder launched a series of other journals, and by 2011 its stable included more than 100 open-access journals. In that year, the publisher was one of two Nigerian presses to be named and shamed by Beall as 'probably predatory'. Despite strongly appealing the ruling, Beall refused to reverse his decision, and the negative publicity forced Academic Journals to sack employees and cut back its operations (Mills et al. 2021).

Not all the work published in these journals was of questionable quality, in the same way that not all articles in Scopus-accredited journals are rigorous, cited or even worth reading. The 'predatory' label was a blunt but effective weapon that cast doubt on many new and emerging open-access journals, but also ignored the challenges of developing research capacity within a resource-scarce environment (Memon 2019; Nwagwu and Makhubela 2017). Beall's list reinforced existing academic norms, knowledge hierarchies and centre-periphery relationships (Bell 2017). The list is maintained on mirror sites, and new alternatives have emerged, such as the commercial service offered by Cabells.

Lists of accredited journals have particular implications for African universities seeking to increase the quantity of their research 'outputs' and publications. Increasingly doctoral candidates are expected to publish as a requirement for graduation, and universities incentivise staff to publish in 'accredited' journals (Tomaselli 2018). This places pressure on researchers to find the right places to publish, often with little prior knowledge of how to assess journal quality. Some of the most relevant and important African journals may not be in Scopus or Web of Science. This can mean that useful policy findings aren't disseminated effectively, and publications that aim to support regional development priorities and societal needs are overlooked (Chan et al. 2011). Amidst the many research 'capacity-building' initiatives in African universities (Adriansen and Møller 2019; Akuffo 2014; Analoui and Danquah 2017), there has been insufficient attention accorded to the challenges of publication and dissemination. The next section explores how these debates about publishing in the 'wrong' journals played out in Ghana's universities.

Making the 'wrong' choices?

Many respondents expressed anxiety about having published in journals that they described as 'not good' or with publishers that had been classified by their university as 'predatory', echoing the emotive language of Jeffrey Beall (2012). It was difficult to ask this question directly, but the term 'predatory' quickly came up when people were asked whether they were aware of journals in the field that were not seen as 'legitimate' or 'valued'. The question was designed to prompt reflections on how academic legitimacy is acquired and bestowed, and to acknowledge the 'credibility economies' that structure academic fields (Mills and Robinson 2021; Shapin 1995). Of the 43 researchers interviewed, around a quarter admitted to having made the 'wrong' publishing choices at some point in their career. But who was judging these as right or wrong, and had this normative judgment been made? The shame of being associated with what many were quick to call 'predatory' journals deserves more thought and analysis.

Maistry is one of the few authors to publicly confess to 'naivety and ignorance' (Maistry 2019) after having published a piece in a journal that the South African Department for Higher Education and Training subsequently identified as 'predatory'. At the same time he points to a 'punitive' system of 'accountability and surveillance', and the pressure on him to publish, that had led to this sequence of events. Responding, Le Grange (2019) questions the moralisation of this debate, and calls for the democratisation of access to publishing opportunities.

Many Ghanaian interviewees dwelt on the difficulties of identifying and weeding out poor quality journals, or of just feeling that something was not quite right. One described having to do all the editorial work himself on a paper and so 'felt within me that this was a predatory journal'. Several talked about the training webinars regularly promoted by both universities (Mills et al. 2021). Shaibu, a UDS lecturer in health sciences, recounted an orientation where 'we were taken through how to publish, where and where not to publish'. He explained that this 'was where the predatory journal issue came, and we were told not to submit our work to predatory journals because they will not be recognised and they will not consider them for promotion because they are not of quality'.

People were quick to list the techniques they used for filtering out journals, including 'being pestered for manuscripts'; spotting what appeared to be an unrealistically fast turnaround time for review and publication; checking whether the editorial board were real people (or actually attached to the journal); whether the quality of the articles aroused suspicion; whether the scope of the journal seemed unworkably broad; whether the journal appeared on Beall's or other blacklists; or whether the journal simply lacked the imprimatur provided by indexing, impact factor or publishing brand.

As Kofi, a UG health sciences lecturer, explained, personal connections were often the best way of verifying credibility. 'I remember getting a call', he recounted, 'to review a paper from a journal I have never heard of'. Because he 'suspected it was a predatory journal' he contacted one Ghanaian editor, asking 'do you know this journal and who are they?'. He described how she replied saying 'yes, it is a new journal but they are trying to do something'. This felt to him to be a useful way of 'checking predatory journals'.

Some suggested that grammatical errors were a sign of a so-called 'predatory' journal, and others asserted that journals from certain regions were inherently suspicious. Nigeria and India were repeatedly singled out, reflecting both cultural rivalry of an African neighbour and a level of xenophobia (Shipley 2017). Another sign was the speed of editorial decision-making. Ibrahim, a UG senior lecturer in health sciences, described wanting to publish a paper 'quite fast'. Three days after submitting to a journal that only charged USD 50, they accepted it for publication. He began to doubt if it could have been peer reviewed by two different people, knowing that the normal review time is two weeks. He felt that the 'paper was not in good hands', a feeling made worse by seeing that the journal claimed to have an impact factor of 2. Having previously published in journals with impact factors of 'like 0.5, 0.6' he got suspicious and tried (unsuccessfully) to withdraw the paper.

Most felt that publishing in a so-called 'predatory' journal would blot their reputation. The fear of making a mistake evoked strong emotions, and the 'shame' of being 'found in lists of predatory journals'. Such articles would not meet the criteria for promotion, and that this meant 'losing' or 'wasting' a paper. Akibu, a UG applied sciences senior lecturer acknowledged that to go through all the hassle of doing the research, 'only for you to throw your work into a journal that is not recognised is not something that anybody would want to go through'. Lahiri, a UDS applied sciences senior lecturer, laughed, going on to say that 'academia are not accepting such journals, so if you have a hundred papers in those predatory journals it wouldn't score you anything!' Others adopted a more pragmatic approach, such as submitting many more articles than required in case some were rejected. As Francis, a senior applied sciences professor at UDS, put it: 'So when you submit these articles and there are those ones there, they will say "no, these ones don't meet our standards", but they wouldn't tell you that.' The response when they 'hit back' was to say 'okay, I have agreed, I will take them out', as 'you still have others'.

Mavis, a UDS applied sciences lecturer, discovered that her first paper as lead author was published in a journal subsequently grey-listed by her university in a list sent out by email. She was devastated. 'That particular paper – it was the major findings from my master's programme – had a lot of information, and so when I realised the journal was predatory, I was very devastated because that is just information gone and I can't republish it anywhere.' The sense Mavis felt of having 'lost' this knowledge is striking. The experience had stalled her publishing record. Despite having been a lecturer for nearly a decade, she had not published again since her master's. 'I have a lot of data which I haven't published ... I have a lot of work done and the data are sitting.' She felt that she was developing 'cold feet' as a result of her experience with the journal, so 'now it's like you are scared to put an article in a journal, and then you realise that it is a predatory one'. She mused on her experience as 'a hard lesson' to learn. Others were less anxious or intimidated. Maana, a head of department at UG with a long publication record, brushed off her experiences with a laugh, saying, 'If I have one or two [publications in those journals] and at that time I really did not know, it is fine, but like I should have about

30 publications and if half of these papers are coming from predatory journals then I would get scared.'

A few respondents questioned the validity of 'predatory journals' as a category, pointing out that many valuable articles are published in journals considered to be 'predatory', and that all journals have better and worse periods. One UDS senior lecturer – Gabriel – suggested that some of these journals were 'gradually evolving' and suggesting that they had 'moved away from predatory' and were being 'accepted in most of the Scopus' and even had 'impact factors and all that'. Others, in his view, did not want to pay the costs of getting accredited and just wanted to maximise their profit.

Emmanuel, a UDS chemistry lecturer, queried what could be done when a journal declined in quality. 'In 2010 or 2011 a journal was of good standard. Now maybe in 2016, 2017 or 2018 you see it falling on the list of predatory journals. What do you do with the paper that you published in there?' If this happens, he asks, 'will you go back and withdraw that paper to send to another journal?'. He pointed to situations where a journal becomes 'corrupted, polluted and all that'. Donkor brought up the way the 'ethical transgressions' of a publisher might 'overshadow the quality of the paper you have published'.

Beyond local versus global

This chapter has explored the implications of Ghana's universities' expectations that faculty publish with 'recognised' academic publishers and in 'reputable peer-reviewed' journals. It has shown how journal credibility is imagined and constructed in geographical and relational terms, leading people to judge West Africa's journals and research ecosystems negatively. Given that promotion is a key motivator for publishing, the views of one's peers about journal 'choices' were critical. Most researchers interviewed were acutely attuned to journal metrics, impact factors and citation indexes. At the same time, the charges and the selectivity of 'top' journals within each field meant that these 'international' journals were felt to be out of reach, especially for those at the start of their careers or who had not yet reached the 'right' level of expertise.

Despite Ghanaian universities emphasising quality and significance, most faculty erected a strong spatial and status dichotomy between 'local' and 'international' journals, differentiating them by perceived quality and professionalism. This academic discourse and distinction is long-standing (Adomi and Mordi 2003; Archibong et al. 2010; Nyamnjoh 2004) across West Africa. Many interviewees seemed to internalise the imagined geographies and status hierarchies that have resulted, echoing evidence from Nigeria and beyond (Lillis and Curry 2010; Omobowale et al. 2013). A few social science faculty, especially those at the University of Ghana, questioned and critiqued these distinctions, pointing to their damaging consequences for 'local' journal cultures and endogenous research capacity (Hountondji 1997). Very few doubted the existence of so-called 'predatory' publishers and journals, but instead insisted that these presented an existential threat to academic integrity and their own academic careers. This led many to 'play it safe', choosing journals indexed in Scopus rather than risk publishing with the 'wrong' journal. These choices ensure that metrics are increasingly used as a proxy for credibility, but in doing so, also risk undermining long-established Ghanaian journals.

Chapter 5

Learning how to publish:
Mentorship, supervision and co-authorship

I published that with my supervisor and so he served as a mentor. He guided me through, and he suggested journals to me as well, and so that made it relatively easier. (Awudu, UG lecturer, social sciences)

If anything like mentoring exists it's more or less … a form of 'godfatherism'. (Issah, UDS lecturer, applied sciences)

It is like everybody for himself and God for us all. (Shaibu, UDS lecturer, health sciences)

Introduction

A first academic publication is a key rite of passage for many researchers. The initiation takes many forms. Historically, many social science researchers waited to complete their PhD projects before submitting papers. As academic CVs become ever more competitive, institutional expectations and research cultures are changing. Increasingly even undergraduate students are encouraged to think about publishing their work. Samuel, co-author and key member of the research team, had been a member of several international research collaborations for years, publishing extensively before submitting his doctorate.

One hypothesis guiding this research was that getting into the 'right' publishing 'habit' early was key, and that this depended on having engaged research supervisors. Asking participants to reflect on key research relationships, interviews explored how publishing practices and strategies evolved and developed.

Amongst those who study research creativity, scholars are divided as to whether new researchers are likely to be more productive. Some point to Kuhn's (1962) argument that young researchers bring new perspectives on scientific problems, and are less likely to have been socialised into dominant scientific paradigms. However, most scientometric studies suggest that academic fields operate according to Mertonian principles, with progression up the scientific hierarchy meaning more publications and more impact. This leads to the 'Matthew effect', where those with the most academic prestige accumulate still more. Only a few academics can become 'top performers'. In his analysis of Polish researchers, Kwiek (2018) argues that these tend to be men, with a mean age of 50, who work long hours and are internationally orientated. African research suggests a similar pattern of publishing output increasing with age, albeit mediated by institution, gender, and disciplinary field (Mouton and Prozesky 2018).

With the growth in collaborative research (Marginson 2018), there are more opportunities for African doctoral candidates, postgraduates, and even undergraduates to publish. Yet being a junior member of a research team is no guarantee of future productivity, especially if the relationship is extractive and hierarchical. As this chapter shows, more important are the personal networks that many academics rely on, helping them to keep the publishing 'pipeline' flowing. Whilst formal mentoring programmes are rarely successful, these informal support networks are key to guiding new researchers through a complex research publishing landscape. This chapter describes the reflections of Ghanaian early career researchers on these informal networks of mentorship, guidance and support, and what their insights add to existing research.

Starting out

> I looked for the journal, but he did everything ... so I don't know
> how he did it. (Gabriel, UDS senior lecturer, social sciences)

There is growing policy attention to doctoral education as nation states compete in a global competition for research talent (Mills 2020), such as South Africa's ambition to become a doctoral hub for the region (Mouton and Cloete 2015). Some call for reform to doctoral education (Cardoso et al. 2020; De Wit and Altbach 2019; Nerad and Evans 2014; Yudkevich et al. 2019), advocating less focus on the thesis as 'product' than on doctoral research as a 'process' and pedagogy (Bao et al. 2018). Reviews of doctoral training across the continent highlight low completion rates and poor supervision quality in many countries, again compared to South Africa (British Council 2018). Alabi and Mohammed (2018) focus on the challenges of doctoral capacity building in Ghana, whilst Molla and Cuthbert (2016) worry that ambitious policy rhetoric is not matched by an attention to implementation, fearing that the 'pursuit of the PhD' becomes a 'numbers game', about volume rather than quality.

Studies of doctoral education have focused on how early career researchers are socialised and mentored, and their subsequent 'identity trajectory' (McAlpine and Amundsen 2017). Others have focused on the struggles that many doctoral students face (Acker and Haque 2015). Their work complements the many tomes of practical advice on doctoral writing and publishing (Kamler 2008; Kamler and Thomson 2014). As Kamler notes, 'doctoral publication is not a given ... it flourishes when it receives serious institutional attention' (Kamler 2008, 284).

Understanding doctoral identity in relation to academic writing and publishing (Xu and Grant 2020) is an important focus for policy and practice. Li (2016) explores the emotional consequences of publication pressures on Chinese doctoral students, whilst Hill and Thabet (2021) describe how doctoral publishing is being prioritised in an emerging UAE research culture.

There is relatively little research on how institutional publishing expectations are reshaping Ghanaian doctoral training and supervisory practices. There is more focus on the teaching and administration challenges that new academics face, given their lack of preparation or training (Alabi and Abdulai 2016). Others have offered advice on the value of writing courses and communication training (Afful 2017; White and King 2020).

Analysing survey data on more than 7,500 African academics, Mouton and Prozesky (2018) find that a third had only published their first article at age 40 and above. They found that research productivity was mediated by age, gender and scientific field. In the same vein, interviewees with the most publications were older male public health scholars, but even here, publication rates varied widely.

In East Africa's research universities – including Makerere and Nairobi – two academic publications are required for a PhD, and one for a master's degree. Whilst this is not yet a requirement in Ghana, a third of Ghanaian respondents published from their undergraduate or master's dissertations. Many were encouraged to do so by supervisors, or had been part of a larger team. For more than half, their first publications emerged from dissertations (Table 4), demonstrating the importance of supportive supervision.

Table 4: First publications of Ghanaian academic interviewees

Source and stage of first publication	Undergraduate dissertation	Master's dissertation	PhD dissertation	Total
	4	12	8	24 (out of 43)

Being quick off the mark with a first paper was not necessarily a predictor of future publication output. One person who published an article from their undergraduate dissertation published only five articles in ten years, while others had published 30 or 40. Neither did disciplinary field determine one's publishing trajectory. Some were energised by their experience, others lost confidence. It all depended on institutional context, competing responsibilities and, crucially, guidance and support.

Nelly, a UDS applied sciences lecturer, published her first article with her undergraduate supervisor. Her next publication, from her master's dissertation, turned out to be in a so-called 'predatory journal' and this knocked her back. Gabriel was another early starter, publishing an article from his master's dissertation with his supervisor, before being consumed by teaching responsibilities. 'Honestly,' he admitted, 'if some of us had known about all these things from the beginning' things would have been different, but 'for the first five years of my life here, I wasn't motivated to publish not because of anything, but by then we were young, all we did was teaching'. Neither had been involved in choosing the journal or in responding to reviews and revisions, and so had learnt little about the process, or the dangers to look out for.

Many other UDS respondents described being immersed in teaching at the start of their academic careers, and not being encouraged to publish. As Issah, an applied sciences lecturer, reminisced, 'the first few years we were just busy teaching and teaching not knowing that it is not all about teaching ... at a point you get to realise that publication is very important'. He admitted that 'if I look at my first publication now, I am not so happy. Anytime I look at it now, I say I could have done it better.' Then he laughed, and added, 'but sometimes I confirm to myself that if I didn't start that way maybe I couldn't have started ... or my status would have been further delayed'.

Kwaku, a senior lecturer at UDS who had done a second PhD in China, felt that the prioritisation of teaching at UDS was a particular challenge for new faculty. He admitted that 'for the first two years I didn't publish because we didn't know the significance of publications until other senior members encouraged us that it was important to publish'. He described how 'no one really teaches you the dynamics of publishing' and contrasted this with his experience in China, where it 'was part of the requirement you have to publish before you graduate ... students are encouraged from the word "go", so you know that if you even finish your thesis and you don't publish you can't graduate'. He felt that this was important, as it 'forced the student to learn the art of publishing before graduating because when you graduate no one is there to guide you'. Yaa, a social sciences UG lecturer, went further, admitting that publishing felt like a guessing game. 'I did not know as much as I know now', she reflected, and so it was just a matter of 'pick a good journal, do good work and then pray to God'. 'Now,' she said, 'I know a little bit more.'

Others, at both UDS and UG, were intensely aware of institutional expectations. Attah, a UG lecturer in applied sciences, explained that 'when I was appointed, I was told my promotion would be based on my publications'. For Mensah, a UG social sciences lecturer, 'when you decide to be in the academia you are made to know right from the onset that publication is one of your expectations, one of your "deliverables" and you are told that your ability to be promoted is related to how active you are in churning out a new set of work'.

Some explained how their rationale for publishing had changed over time. Akuma, a UG social sciences lecturer in her thirties, suggested that she now only wants to make 'ground-breaking' interventions that 'everybody would cite'. She compared this to her earlier attitude, where once 'you have found something, now you publish'. Now, she went on, 'I am trying to read more, understand the area that I research and identify something that is pressing and needed but yet has not been researched.'

The role of the doctoral supervisor

If most first publications emerge from dissertations, then supervisors play a key role in kickstarting the publication journeys. Kojo, a UG social sciences lecturer, explained this vividly:

> If you want to take the journey of an academic career, what will make you is publications. We need to start with how it dawns on you that there is something called publication. I started searching around because at the time, all that we knew about an academic career was knowing your stuff and teaching others. Yeah, it's about the teaching; how good you are at helping with presentations, solving questions for students and the rest, but little on the area of research. But

after my supervisor drew my attention to it and the first publication went through and then getting the sense that eventually I might find myself in academia, then it dawns on me that we need to sit up and then get more serious with it.

Interviewees were appreciative of the support and guidance they had received from their supervisors. Shaibu, a UDS health sciences lecturer, recalled how his supervisor had made publishing a goal from the outset. 'The person who supervised my work told me that he wants me to do quality work and to be able to publish something out of it. So, when I graduated he was always calling me to get a paper out of the work, and he really had time to guide me in how to go about it.'

People described a range of ways their supervisors had focused attention on publishing. One raised the question of publication midway through their supervisee's research degree, another after thesis submission. Some supervisors had recommended conferences, encouraged students to keep trying when rejected, acted as first author on a joint publication with their students, helped field reviewer comments, helped select journals, and pushed supervisees to submit funding proposals.

Nearly everyone starts out with the support of others. Nine respondents described co-authoring their first paper with their supervisor. Seven others mentioned other forms of supervisory guidance with their first paper, while a further ten mentioned the involvement of mentors who were not explicitly named as supervisors but were often referred to as 'mentors' or 'senior colleagues'. Only two said their supervisors had not been involved in their papers. As many of those studying for doctoral degrees in Ghana's universities are also employed as lecturers, there is the additional challenge of being supervised by one's colleagues and academic peers. It is no surprise that friendship, guidance and support comes from a range of sources, and not just one's 'official' supervisor.

Supervisors often benefitted from being co-authors on their supervisees' publications. Some felt that involving one's supervisor was inevitable. Farhanah, a UDS health sciences lecturer noted, 'there is a lot of work the students are doing and I am supervising so we can easily use what they are doing, the raw data and analyse it well and then do some publications after it'. Supervisors felt that this work was for the benefit of the students. Kosiwa, a UG applied sciences head of department, admitted that 'just to push them [students] up, we rather write it and then we ask them to maybe edit it, add a bit of input, and then we add them as co-authors'.

Akuma, a UG social sciences lecturer, described how one of her early publications was 'from my PhD … I did basically everything, but I still included my supervisors' name by way of thank you'. She recounted how her supervisor had assumed he would be lead author on a publication from her master's degree. Gabriel, a UDS lecturer, felt he had no say in the matter. 'In fact,' he reflected, 'at that time your supervisor will put his name on it and there is nothing you could do about it'. Indeed, he felt that it would give the paper more credibility if he was the lead author 'even though I did a lot of writing on that paper but eventually he finalised it'. As Gabriel's supervisor was also the corresponding author, 'until the thing was finally published I didn't know what was going on'.

Mavis, another UDS lecturer, had a similar experience with publishing 'an extract from my undergraduate work with my supervisor. She explained that it was 'his baby idea', and that he 'needed the data', so whilst she did the data collection, 'he was impressed with the way we worked so he needed to publish the paper', leading him to do 'the final writing of the manuscript'.

Even where supervisors left supervisees to do most of the work, mentees still valued their guidance. Adjoa, UG senior lecturer, recalls how she published a piece of work with support from her mentor. She 'conceptualised the project, collected the data myself, did the analysis myself, and obviously wrote the first draft'. She felt it had been an 'exciting experience' to be 'guided … through the process of what I needed to do in terms of structuring the paper'.

Making a supervisor a co-author provided support, but also put pressure on the relationship. Lahiri, a UDS applied sciences senior lecturer, recalls how 'before we could even publish, my supervisor would guide me to put the paper in good shape because her reputation was at stake'. She described how it 'went back and forth' between them for some time before being published. But then it was rejected by their first choice of journal. Lahiri felt 'very bad for the fact that my supervisor was very much in love with that journal, she actually wanted it to be published in that journal because of the impact factor'. She described how rejection 'was a big blow to me and to her … it wasn't pleasant'.

Not every supervisor sought authorship rights. Donkor, a UG senior lecturer, recalled how his undergraduate supervisor had encouraged him to apply for funding to the Ghana National Aids Control Programme. He had then presented his research first to his department and then the Ghana Science Association conference. He got further support to help prepare an article for submission to the *Journal of the Ghana Science Association*. This gave Donkor invaluable research and publishing experience for his subsequent career.

Mentoring

In one revealing interview, Kumi, a senior faculty member at UG, offered a frank appraisal of his own publishing profile. He admitted that 'I think I have about three or four [articles] in most of these unrecognised journals,' a fact he blamed on not having had a mentor. He now devotes his efforts to mentoring his colleagues and spreading awareness of so-called 'predatory publishing'. 'This is one of the academic injustices we find in the system and so I am talking from experience,' he explained. 'As a young scholar you just want to publish so you could have a good paper that may end up in a poor journal because of lack of mentorship or knowledge.'

Studying for a PhD in Germany, Kumi fashioned his own alternatives: 'I did not have the opportunity to be mentored so sometimes I just look at people who are doing well and get inspired by their exploits. I watch what they are doing and their publication history, I get motivated that I can get to that level.' Kumi also remembered the editors of one of his first papers:

It was published in a Francis and Taylor [sic] journal, which I'm still excited about, although it went through about three rounds of revisions. The editor was very generous. He realised that he was dealing with … an amateur in the publication process, so I was mentored until the paper came out.

Whilst not helped to publish in the early stages of his career, Kumi recognises the academic landscape has changed, and he pushes his students to publish early. He noted with pride his 70 publications. Emphasising the importance of grit and commitment, Kumi explained that 'to be a very good publisher' meant working into the early hours and making sacrifices.

Some sustained close working relationships with former supervisors long after finishing their PhD, sharing work for comments and guidance. Encouragement can also come from one's colleagues, as Abenayo, a UG social sciences senior lecturer explained. 'My first publication was from my MA thesis, which was on the experiences of women with HIV/Aids. When I was appointed, my new head of department said I could write a paper out of my MA thesis, which I did.'

Mentors helped new faculty adjust to academic life. Akuma, a UG social sciences lecturer, explained how she had struggled to get work published. 'I am sending papers, and it is becoming difficult.' Her mentor pointed out that her PhD supervisor had 'corrected it several times before you got it published'. She recognised that publishing 'was a process' and that she should take her time.

Few departments had formal mentoring procedures, and most relied on personal networks. As Mensah, a UG social sciences lecturer, explained, 'informally, you can get that kind of support, and you need to nurture it' because 'it becomes critical in your field'.

Mentors provided both academic but also emotional support, as Kwami, a UG social sciences lecturer, explained. 'You need a mentor,' he insisted, 'to guide you through the process'. Pointing to his own PhD experience, he felt it is 'so disheartening if you spend time writing a paper and it gets rejected, you feel so bad'. He felt that those without a mentor go 'completely off' as a result.

Most felt that the onus was on early career academics to approach potential mentors. Maana, a UG social science senior lecturer, advised that, 'if there are not mentors, you can find one yourself and so I identified some'. He went on to explain how, 'when I drafted the paper, I gave it to them to review and I made sure I took every comment very seriously.' For Ibrahim, a UDS applied sciences head of department, 'you ask a senior colleague who is already in the system and who knows about these things ... I think they are prepared to assist you.' Similarly, Kofi insisted that you shouldn't 'expect a senior person to come to you', but that instead 'the onus is on you to approach someone and say I want to put out this paper and can you help me look at it?'

Several senior respondents portrayed a supportive department culture, and a commitment to reviewing junior colleagues' work. Francis, the head of a UDS applied science department, described his department as being 'like a family, so anyone's problem is everyone's problem'. He felt that at an 'informal level we try to encourage each other' and 'we want to see your contribution, even though you are not yet a senior lecturer, you are as important as anybody else'. If his colleagues had a draft paper, he was always happy to 'look at it and forward it'.

On the other hand, Kosiwa, a UG applied sciences head of department, suggested that junior colleagues were too short of time to seek out the help of senior faculty. 'We encourage them, saying "write it, bring it",' he exclaimed, and then 'we edit it and they send it out for publication'. Yet this rarely happened. He felt that 'the truth is, the younger ones are even busier than we are, so they end up not bringing anything.' He explained that he regularly 'was pushing them' and 'encouraging them' to seek support, but 'getting them to do it is the problem'.

Attah, an early career researcher in the same department, was more critical, suggesting that informal support from senior colleagues was limited and depended on individual personalities. He felt that if 'there were systems then the senior ones will be ready to take the younger ones through, and of course that would motivate us to do more'. Bemoaning the lack of a formal mentoring programme, he admitted 'you have to choose who to go to and sometimes you go, and the person is very busy you know'.

A similar comment about the need for a better organised mentoring arrangement was made by Shaibu, a UDS health sciences lecturer, who wanted to send a paper to a senior colleague for review, but was aware that 'that person is also busy doing something and he may not even have time to look at it for you'.

Finding a mentor depended on who was prepared to help. For example, Margaret, a UG applied sciences lecturer, explained that she had given her work 'to another lecturer to review it for me and give me his/her comments on, we have that peer review within our department, and I will say it is helpful'. Those who had never been mentored were very aware of what they had missed out on. Paul complained that he had 'not had people that we could look up to for inspiration and all of that', so that instead 'I had to find my own way out'.

Several UDS faculty were frustrated at the lack of formal mentorship programmes in their university. Issah, a UDS applied sciences lecturer, explained that 'on paper we have the mentoring documents, but in practice, it is almost non-existent'. He went on to bemoan the lack of 'proper orientation or guidance, learning from those who have gone this way before'. He wished that 'the seniors among us' could offer more 'seminars, workshops, and so on and so forth'. A UDS health sciences head of department had a similar opinion, explaining 'that there is no structure in this institution that supports mentoring'. He felt the blame needed to be shared between senior faculty 'because we don't know where to start from' and junior faculty 'who are not willing to come and ask'. Personally, he felt that this had held him back in his own career.

Compared to universities in the 'developed countries' where new faculty had mentors, it had initially been challenging not to have a guide and that this 'contributed to the late start of the process'. Shaibu put it even more bluntly. 'It is like everybody for himself and God for us all.' These tensions reflect the demands of working within an institution seeking to raise its research profile but having few senior colleagues on whom to call.

Sometimes personal collaboration links led to joint publications, as Kwaku, a UDS social sciences lecturer, describes. He had tried to publish as a single author with a South African journal, but 'they punched a lot of holes into this thing' and 'sometimes where to publish also matters'. Talking to a senior academic , 'he told me to withdraw it'. Instead they worked together, and Kwaku benefited from 'somebody who is experienced' who helped him with comments and suggestions: 'let's do this, let's do that'. This person added his name 'and we sent it somewhere and then it was published'.

Informal peer-review arrangements were often gendered, explained Akosua. She felt that 'the senior male colleagues have a more informal networking where they look at each other's papers and have those kinds of conversations'. In contrast she adopted a 'very systematic manner' to support a younger woman researcher, helping her to 'review her papers and show her how to strengthen the arguments in ways that are more likely to get it published'.

A few interviewees disagreed with the emphasis placed on mentoring, highlighting the risks of some being excluded or marginalised. Issah, a UDS lecturer in his fifties scoffed at its value, seeing it as a source of ego gratification and patron–client relations. 'If anything like that exists it is more or less I will say a form of "godfatherism" sort of thing.' His distaste for patronage was captured in a visceral metaphor. 'I don't know how to lick bowls.'

Many felt that their university cultures compared poorly to those they had encountered while studying or working abroad. A UDS health sciences head of department who had studied in Belgium felt that mentoring was 'lacking particularly in this institution, and we were fortunate because we went outside'. Kwaku pointedly highlighted the encouragement he received 'from the word go' during his training in China.

A mentor's comments can also create tensions and frustrations. As Maana, a UG senior lecturer in the social sciences, recalled: 'When the comments come it is like you would say, what is this person saying? It means I have to revise the whole paper or what?' But then, 'when you are done working on the comments, you would realise that you have added more value to the work.'

Publishing as part of a research team

Over the last 20 years, the proportion of papers co-authored with international collaborators has grown from 13% to almost 23% (Marginson 2018). This is reflected in the experience of many Ghanaian interviewees, even if disciplinary cultures of collaborative authorship differ markedly. One noted that multi-authored papers are the norm in health sciences and in applied research units. Meanwhile, a UG social sciences lecturer had sole-authored all nine of his articles.

Participants emphasised the benefits of collaboration, from the combining of different disciplinary perspectives, to collective decision-making about publication strategies. Francis, a UDS applied sciences head of department, described this as involving 'everybody' in helping to 'read through and make his comments'. He said 'you put something down – "that is the way I see it" – and somebody else says, "this is the way I see it: and sometimes you argue among yourselves as academics and you arrive at a conclusion'. He insisted that this 'was the support we get from each other', but it also could produce 'new combinations of ideas'. As Yahuza, a UDS social science lecturer put it: 'We are talking of the same phenomenon in different perspectives, so when we come together with those things, we will be able to add up ideas and move forward.'

Co-authorship also has the benefit of increasing one's overall publication tally. Some admitted they had informal 'quid pro quo' arrangements to include each other's names on publications. Farhanah, a UDS health sciences lecturer, described how it was difficult for new faculty to break into such arrangements. 'If you want support, it is like you have to go collaborating with people.' She went on to admit how, for 'those who are new, we just came, so it is like people already have their groups – you add my name when I am publishing, and I also add your name … and then sometimes I would be there and then someone will come and say, "when you are publishing, try and add my name".'

Such admissions about 'gaming' the numbers reflect the pressures many felt. Fredua, a UDS applied sciences lecturer, insisted that her fellow early career researchers should band together to increase their outputs. She felt that if they all 'formed a group where you all take one topic each to develop, within a year you could get like five or six papers and that is another technique you can use to have more papers within a shorter time'.

Another advocate of collaboration to boost one's 'output' was a UG health sciences senior lecturer. Kofi's approach captures the problems of measuring academic publications (Biagioli and Lippman 2020). 'My philosophy', he began, 'is one of the things I learnt early on and I think it really helped me, was collaboration'. Kofi went on to say that 'I think that was the single most important thing for me: working with people'. He questioned the strategy of 'young people who feel they can make it on their own'. For him, the benefits of strategic co-authorship were indisputable:

> If in a year you can work on three papers for publication and you are doing that alone, you are the only one doing that. If you do that every year, at the end of five years how many do you have? Fifteen. That is if you get to publish them. If in a year you can work on three, I can work on three, and another person can work on three, and there are four of us. So, I work on three, I am the lead person, but then you contribute to a certain part of it, you contribute to a certain part for all of us. At the end of year, if all of us get to publish, you have three times four which is twelve in one year ... So, I think that is one thing that early career people would need to learn. That it is collaboration and the collaboration is not being a free-rider, it is not just putting your name there and not doing anything. Making time to put a certain contribution, contribute something to that paper and getting your name there, and I think that is one of the key things.

Collaborative authorship comes with complications: negotiating author order and ensuring everyone does their fair share. The consensus was that lead authors would conceptualise and draft the paper, respond to reviewer comments and take care of the corrections. For

Ibrahim, lead authorship reflected that this paper 'is your baby', whilst for Yaa, it was about being 'in the driving seat'.

A major task for the lead author was making sure that co-authors met their responsibilities on the project. This meant the administrative burden of scheduling tasks and circulating updates, and the diplomacy that required. As Kofi noted, 'you have to coordinate all of them, get comments – sometimes conflicting comments – and you have to find a way to sort all that out'.

Lead authors hold both power and responsibility. Kwaku, a UDS social science lecturer described how he would be asked by senior colleagues to collaborate as a co-author, noting that 'as time went on and I gained more experience, I also initiated the research process, with others as assisting authors'. A few people mentioned the risk of co-authors doing the work while senior lead authors coasted, contributing very little. International collaboration presented further risks, and cases where African researchers have been treated as little more than data collectors have led to important critiques of the coloniality of much research on Africa (Nolte 2019; Kingori and Gerrets 2019).

Exploitation can happen in different ways. Kofi warned that 'it depends on who you are working with ... there are some publications that I virtually played the role of the lead, the one who does all that, but because of the other people you are publishing with, you then find yourself not being the named lead'. Kumi, a UG social sciences associate professor, was more blunt, saying 'we [the juniors] did the greater part of the report writing and yet 'as usual when you have bosses, you put their names there'. Senior faculty stood accused of exploiting junior contributors, as Yahuza, a UDS social sciences lecturer, recounted. 'My head of department was using me,' he complained, 'and I was writing proposals for him and other kinds of things, but I didn't know it was meant for him'. Yahuza admitted that 'he used it for publication without putting my name on it, and it was later I got to know, it actually pained me'. Some collaborations fail, as Farhanah, a UDS health sciences lecturer, frankly admitted. 'Sometimes there is politics all over,' she pointed out, 'people don't want you to progress, they want you to stay where you are so whatever that will make you progress, they don't really like it'. She rightly pointed out that the university is 'a human institution, so I am not surprised'.

Participants had different views on the co-author role. Kosiwa, a UG applied sciences head of department commented that, 'if you are co-author, it is a bit more relaxing because you don't go through all the stress that the lead person has to go through'. Ayi Kwei, an applied sciences lecturer, found himself having to chip in to pay for expensive corrections when the lead author had failed to spot errors in the galley proofs. He felt that 'as an author whether you are a lead or co-author, you should probably behave as if you are the lead on every paper that has your name on it because once your name is on it your reputation is on the line'.

Lahiri, a UDS lecturer, saw co-authorship as a partnership of equal investment and effort. 'You are working together and whatever you have to publish, you are all inputting ideas, so the person being the lead author is sort of like just the name'. She insisted that 'the contribution to the paper, it is for all of you ... the experience of being the lead author is the same as being a co-author'.

Attitudes to co-authorship varied by discipline and expertise, but also brought up questions of ethics and responsibility. Yaa described how she felt 'particularly invested in my papers, and I don't often depend on the co-authors because it is my idea and I want to make sure I see it through to the end. Even if they have contributions, I tend to oversee'.

Donkor pointed to conventions around authorship credit, but admitted that some of his colleagues 'may not truly be ethical authors' given their lack of contribution. 'Either you contribute intellectually to the design of the study,' he explained, or 'to the data collection, to the drafting and proofreading', but in our setting 'you don't have a lot of people fulfilling their obligations'.

Co-publishing as part of an international research team can make heavy demands on junior members of the team, especially if they are tasked to write up the different contributions. One UG health sciences senior lecturer, described his first collaboration being part of his master's thesis with 'four of us working on the same topic but from different continents'.

Equitable authorship?

Academic research, writing and publishing has long been team-based in the sciences, but it is increasingly a collective project across the whole academy, with all the possibilities and risks that this creates. From first publication to senior researcher, respondents benefitted from support, but also were vulnerable to manipulation.

This chapter has highlighted the role that supportive writing relationships can play within Ghana's universities, as well as the challenges of collaborative authorship. At best, these relationships help orient researchers to the structures and hierarchies of a global publishing landscape, helping them understand what to aim for and what to avoid (Xu and Grant 2020). At worst, junior faculty are exploited, with senior colleagues using co-authorship as a means to boost publication outputs.

Researchers at both Ghanaian universities made very clear how much they valued supportive mentors. Yet institutional mentorship programmes were rarely implemented, especially at UDS, leaving people reliant on personal networks or individual patrons. Whilst some senior colleagues have experience of co-authoring and collaborations, there seemed to be little systematic guidance and support for handling the complicated interpersonal dynamics and power relations that result.

Given the structural, epistemological and economic inequalities that bedevil international research collaborations (Halvorsen and Nossum 2016; Parker and Kingori 2016), it would seem unfair to expect individual researchers to manage these relationships alone. Making international research and writing collaborations more equitable has to be the ultimate aim, drawing on decolonial critiques of 'academic extractivism' (Cruz and Luke 2020), and finding the right ways to incentivise genuine co-authorship rather than a culture of 'glorified data collectors' (Odjidja 2021).

Chapter 6

Scarcity and Ghanaian research culture

Even if you have a paper, there is no time to work on it. Holidays, you are marking ... and you don't even have time for yourself, let alone to have time to write papers and publish. (Attah, UG lecturer, social sciences)

Introduction

This book has explored the lived experiences of academic publishing amongst Ghana's researchers, and the demands of working in universities being redefined by a global research economy. The first chapters described why researchers feel under pressure to publish, the challenge of knowing where to publish, and who one publishes with. The analysis now turns to the affective dimensions of academic research when time and money are in short supply. How are academics managing with limited research resources, unreliable internet connection and patchy journal provision? How does it feel to never have enough time to write? Such pressures are differentiated by institution, age, gender and discipline. Some try to speed up the publishing process, but then risk the disapproval and disdain of their seniors. The peer-review process makes further demands. Women in academia have to balance family and professional responsibilities.

There is an extensive literature by African scholars on the impact of neoliberal financial reforms (including the World Bank's structural adjustment programmes) on Africa's public universities and their research infrastructures (Lebeau and Mills 2008; Mamdani 2007; Mazrui 1997). After the optimism of the 1960s, exemplified by Nkrumah's vision of an African scientific modernity, came three decades of financial austerity. It had a profound impact on academic working conditions and research cultures across the continent.

Ghana is now classified as a lower middle-income country, and is relatively prosperous in comparison to neighbouring Francophone West African states. However it spends less than 0.2% of GDP on research and development, and there is no national research policy or national research fund (Fosci et al. 2019), leaving university researchers with little institutional support. All faculty get a small annual book and research allowance, regardless of outputs, projects or research activity, and attempts at reform are highly controversial.

None of this is unique to Ghana, or indeed to Africa. There is a growing corpus of critical higher education scholarship on the changing nature of the academy across the globe, as commercial logics and a reliance on private funding reshape 'public' universities. Critiques of academic capitalism (Slaughter and Rhoades 2004) and the university 'in ruins' abound (Readings 1996), but nearly all are written from the perspective of the Global North. Fewer offer detailed accounts of how African universities are being transformed by the rush to market (Mamdani 2007).

Ghanaian researchers have documented the impact of these reforms on the research careers of a whole generation of African academics, and on women in particular. Prah (2002) draws together a range of data sources to highlight the statistical and political invisibility of women academics and administrators in Ghanaian universities. Tsikata (2007) offers a vivid case study of one woman scientist in her fifties who felt that she 'would have been a professor but for the proper equipment' (2007, 32, 37). Tsikata goes on to argue that 'gender inequality is a foundational characteristic of the university', shaped by exclusionary 'informal networks' and the expectations placed on women to 'fulfil their roles as wives and mothers, and then still to take on mothering roles at work' (Tsikata 2007, 40). The literature on the highly gendered nature of Ghana's academic workplaces (Prah 2002; Mabokela and Mlambo 2015; Tsikata 2007) highlights how women struggle to develop academic careers with relatively little workplace support, and face a culture of deference to senior male professors. These insights are developed in the work of Mabokela and Mlambo (2015, 2017), who focus on the cultural factors and expectations that constrain women's academic careers in Ghana. One list of Ghana's top 50 scientists has only eight female academics, including five from UG.

Across many global higher education systems, the continued decline in public funding, coupled with the growth in student numbers, are changing employment and working conditions for academic faculty. Bringing together insights from sociology and political economy, the field of critical higher education studies has foregrounded the consequences of institutional and career precarity for academics (Ivancheva et al. 2019). An important stream of work has reflected on the changing temporality of academic work, and the way that competition and rivalry has led to an urge 'to accelerate' (Vostal 2016), with speed emerging as a response to the demands of academic knowledge production. Again, this work needs an African lens. Debates about the precarity of academic work attend to time scarcity, but less to the challenge of juggling different temporalities. The voices of Ghanaian researchers offer insights into the struggle to get by in a research economy over which they have little power.

Science amidst scarcity

In the UK, science policy-makers used to talk of the 'well-found laboratory', a concept initially used to justify high levels of British government funding for science in the aftermath of the First World War. It was defined as the minimum level of laboratory equipment, facilities, and funding needed to conduct basic research and train postgraduates. Many of Ghana's university laboratories are often far from 'well-found'. Both UDS and UG scientists spoke of their struggles to access basic chemicals, equipment, and supplies. The additional costs of paying APCs to publish in open-access journals is a further burden.

Wherever it is conducted, most academic research is resource and time intensive. Without basic equipment and laboratory facilities, basic science becomes impossible, a situation made worse by the prohibitive costs of much scientific equipment. This sense of lack was felt especially strongly by science researchers in UDS. Many were frustrated by the lack of equipment. One UDS science lecturer, Issah, felt that 'we have the ideas, but the infrastructure and the facilities to make them a reality is greatly non-existent'. This was not just a concern for junior faculty. The head of a health sciences department complained that essential medical instruments could only be accessed in Tamale, many miles away. For Richmond, a UDS head of an applied science department, 'the problem we encounter in Ghana and in Africa, how our research is done, because of the lack of some equipment, some things that we were supposed to do – we couldn't do it'.

Material constraints shaped research practice and specialisms in both universities. This was a particular challenge for researchers at UDS. A senior UDS social science lecturer suggested that a lack of laboratory facilities had driven academics to focus on 'nutrition, anthropology and social sciences, because that is where you can now deal with the human without needing laboratories'. This is evident in the applied science profiles of most UDS departments, as well as the work done by the UDS social sciences (e.g. work on social media) that does not require extensive fieldwork. Certain fields were easier to practice when 'equipment and laboratory facilities were insufficient for the serious pursuit of science' (Tsikata 2007, 29). This has implications for the types of research that could be pursued. Joseph, a UDS applied sciences lecturer, dwelt at length on the tensions generated by a system where a standard number of publications are required for promotion:

> Those of us in the sciences, I think we are being cheated some-how … we are spending much more in research, more than other colleagues in mathematics. For example, if you want

to do research in our laboratory, we need some chemical reagents. If you want to look at the cost implications it is too much and that might even delay our work ... Those people at the mathematical faculty, they are being promoted more than those people in applied sciences because they are getting more papers. Why? Most of their work does not require laboratory work. You just go get something and then they start writing something and they are promoted. Maybe by the time they have written five you may still be here struggling because of the cost implications. We want them [the university] to know that it's not that we people we are lacking, but these are problems we are facing for us to be able to publish. We are ready to do a lot of work if all those things are available before us to do.

The government also came under fire for its lack of financial support from Issah, a UDS lecturer, who felt he had to say it 'raw': 'If there is any quality research that is going to be done in Ghana or Nigeria or many countries in the West African sub-region, you can be sure that the money is from abroad.' He admitted that 'there is a lot of noise about science and technology, but our government are not welcoming it at all'. It was 'much more challenging in places like UDS', as the 'little money – less than one hundred dollars – that the government gives may not be enough for me to buy a bottle of some important chemical to carry out my research'.

Issah's views are backed up by the conclusions of a 2019 assessment that Ghana's 'research system appears underdeveloped and under-performing relative to the country's wider economic trajectory' (Fosci et al. 2019, iv). Fosci et al. point to the political sensitivity of reforming the annual research and book allowance currently paid to all academic faculty, regardless of research activity. Government attempts to reform the subsidy have led Ghanaian academic unions to stage a series of strikes.

As well as despondency about the research facilities, there was a sense of envy about facilities in European and American universities. As Akibu put it, 'where I did my PhD, it is easier because you have everything you need to do the work: that is not the same here'. Emmanuel, an applied sciences lecturer, described how he looked to the 'top journals' from America and wished he could do research in those types of labs. He felt that a prestigious publication record might be as much about access to well-resourced labs as about academic brilliance. 'I once had experience in a lab in Kenya, where I realised that most of these people who are making names in these big journals, it is not that they are very intelligent.'

Scientists at UDS bemoaned their limited laboratory facilities, comparing them to those that are 'far better for those that are down in the south who have been here for long'. For Kwaku, a UDS social sciences lecturer, 'some universities have more resources than others – University of Ghana of course is outstanding. If you compare it with newer universities that are less than a number of years old, you are making a mistake.'

As a social science senior lecturer in his mid-fifties, Kwaku felt that the key point of comparison was his institution's own past. In his twenty years of being at UDS he had watched as the university's infrastructure had grown and eased things for younger academics. He painted a picture where at first there had been no laboratories for research, nor administrative support for teaching. 'For years there was nothing to write, there was not a laboratory.' He laughed and continued. 'Even when teaching you were suffering, so we who were pioneers here, we suffered so people have come here, and they are enjoying'. He pointed out that for the first ten years of his role he didn't have an office, and now 'they came here and everything is here'. Belatedly applying for promotion, he faced the risk that these difficult years would be largely unrecognised in an increasingly research-driven promotional system.

Staff and students regularly admitted to self-funding their publications. Emmanuel explained that the 'consumables in the laboratories, they are not there'. Instead, 'out of yourself, you have to sacrifice'. This meant bringing 'money from your pocket and see how you can put it together with that of the students, to work together and come out with something'.

111

This frustration about the university's research facilities is echoed by Issah, a UDS lecturer in the applied sciences. 'I don't know whether you can even call it a laboratory,' he joked, 'and yet the conditions of service, what I must accomplish to get me promoted to move forward, is the same as someone who is from the University of Ghana, Cape Coast, or KNUST where they have better facilities, and the working environment is much more conducive.' He went on to question whether his university had 'misplaced priorities' given the constant focus on 'predatory' publishing and their 'injunction' to publish only in high quality journals. 'Every now and then,' he explained, 'they come out with some list [of journals to avoid] here and there, but I doubt if the authorities have local standing because they don't create a conducive environment for me to do a quality job'. Did they have the right, he asked, to 'demand this level of quality … if the environment and the facilities are not of high quality'? He drove home his point, rhetorically asking: 'Do they support me to move forward in my career and create enabling environment for me to work?' The answer was 'a big no'.

Others, such as Kojo, a UG lecturer, acknowledged the 'temptation' to publish in so-called 'predatory journals', especially 'if you are looking for promotion' and 'those standard journals are going to take forever to publish your work'. 'So why don't I just put one here', he asked, 'and see what would happen.' He felt that these 'might be the thoughts that would be running in the minds of young researchers'. That said, 'after a year you know that once you are in this career your reputation is very, very important', and that 'throwing your papers there, you are more or less killing your own career and affecting your own reputation'. As he points out, such decisions were a way to save time when other resources are scarce. Time becomes a precious currency, and an awareness of this value structures every decision and emotion.

Time and the gendering of scarcity

Time, and the sense of its scarcity, was a second key dimension of the Ghanaian research economy. There is a growing sociological and educational literature on academic temporality within the Euro-

American academy. Work has focused on universities' constant orientation towards the future (Clegg 2010), the demands that temporal 'flexibility' makes on learners (Raddon 2007; Sheail 2018) and the consequences of the 'acceleration' of academic work (Vostal 2016, 2021). Writing about a Chilean higher education system transformed by neoliberal policy reforms, Guzman-Valenzuela and Barnett (2013) perceptively describe how Chilean academics are involved in 'time-bargaining', trading their own commitments to teaching and university to make time for themselves, seeing time as something that can be bought in exchange for services rendered. Attending to temporal agency, Vostal argues for the importance of the skill of 'agentic synchronisation' (2019), whereby researchers carefully synchronise the different temporalities of academic work. These different temporalities, of research, writing, publishing and promotion, were visible in interviews.

In both Ghanaian universities most interviewees felt that there was no substitute for time, no matter how well managed or budgeted. Akosua summed it up perfectly. 'I know what I need: time, and I can't invent it.' One-third of respondents pointed to the particular challenge of balancing teaching and research. Asked about the challenges of publishing, Yaa, a UG social sciences senior lecturer, emphasised how 'extremely time-consuming' the process of 'rigorous' research was, starting with 'collecting your own data', because 'you have got to have good data' to do 'good analysis'. She went on to talk about the time needed to write an introduction and full literature review, and to 'set it out properly'.

'Putting in' enough time was not optional. As Yaa pointed out, work that is not methodologically rigorous risks being rejected by a journal. Even after the hard work of data collection has been done, carving out time for writing presented its own challenge. This was parsed as the difficulty of being able to just 'sit down' and write. Kosiwa, a UG applied sciences head of department, explained that 'combining writing with our job as lecturers is a bit challenging. You start, get halfway, just leave it somewhere there, pick it up later. The main challenge was in writing.' This sense of frustration with staccato writing rhythms, intermittently picking papers up and putting them down again, was echoed by other respondents. 'I have like three or four papers at various stages and I don't know the last time I looked at them,' admitted Adjoa, a UG health sciences senior lecturer, while Mensah – a UG social sciences lecturer – admits that, as a result, 'you might have forgotten your train of thought'.

Making time for writing also raised the question of finding a conducive space for writing. Perhaps paradoxically, the university was not that space. 'When you are here students will come and knock on your door looking for you and you have to attend to them. So, for me the first thing is the time,' said Akuma, a UG applied sciences lecturer. Some of the UG faculty mentioned 'write shops', writing retreats such as those funded by international donors, as well as seed grants which funded 'time away to write-up research findings for publication'. Mensah, a UG social sciences lecturer, praised this 'innovation' and described how they would go to a hotel in Koforidua for a week, and that it would 'take you out from your familiar zone, they go there, a hotel room reserved, and then you are there, write'.

Akuma, a UG social sciences lecturer, agreed that dedicated time and space for writing provided a valuable reprieve from the relentless demands of family management. Her thoughts are worth stating at length:

> But for some of us who are women, it is difficult for us to make time to write. Going away for a week just to go and write, not cooking for somebody and thinking about what to eat, and all being catered for, I think it helps. The department could always put aside some money and then take us out for a write shop. You sit down, there is a timetable, come and sit down and write, no interference. Because some of us are women – I don't want to make it a woman issue or a gender thing – but as women, in the morning you take care of your children, take them to school and come here. If you start work, by 7:30 I am here, 3:30 I have to be out of here. When I get home what can I do? I can't do anything – all I do is I take care of my children

and sleep. So, I only have a few hours to publish. If they want to get more publications from us, they can at least take us away for one week. If your husband knows that you are not around for the next one week, he would manage it.

Not everyone agreed. Kosiwa, a UG applied science head of department, felt that out-of-town workshops were not necessarily the answer for the women in her department. She pointed out that 'family issues make it difficult to attend such workshops'. Only women respondents foregrounded the challenges of combining academic and family life in interviews. The gendered disparities in reproductive and caring labour continue to affect female Ghanaian academics (Tsikata 2007) and women in many academic systems. The different perspectives of these two UG lecturers on writing workshops reveal how writing practices are mediated by age, caring responsibilities, marital status, and attitudes of husbands to spouses being away from home.

The academic time economy is gendered in both its daily patterns – such as the demands of the school run – as well as in the shape of the overall career trajectory in relation to motherhood (Tsikata 2007). There are also seasonal rhythms, as school holidays or family occasions mean more caring responsibilities rather than a chance to write or relax.

Akosua, a UG social sciences associate professor, recalled receiving comments back on one of her papers just before Christmas: 'The deadline for revisions was 30 December, and I just thought, "I can't do this over Christmas".' Her children help anchor her sense of time in her recollections of publishing, as she says, 'I actually have a paper, whose galley proofs were done in 2006, and I remember very clearly being heavily pregnant, and I remember that when it was published my son was five.'

Akosua went on to declare a 'time crisis'. She felt that the 'problem in this department is not about knowing where to publish'. Instead, she declaimed that 'the crisis is that you come in, and you have to develop courses and you have your course material to teach, and then you also have to publish your own work. You have young children, and you have to balance all of that'. She was adamant that this was the issue that was 'inhibiting' her colleagues, not a sense of not knowing how to publish.

The competing demands of publishing and teaching were mentioned by almost one-third of respondents, including faculty of both genders from both universities. Arguing that publication was being over-emphasised in promotional requirements, Kosiwa, a UG applied science head of department complained that the demands of research could mean teaching was not kept up to date. 'When you are teaching,' she said, 'you need to read, update your knowledge and all that, prepare your notes, slides'. Yet 'if you have to use that time in writing papers or articles then there is the likelihood that you keep repeating all your old slides without inculcating current things into it'.

Shaibu, a UDS health sciences lecturer, made similar points about promotional criteria. 'Though publications will enhance our teaching, and so everybody would want to do publication, but the teaching takes a lot of time actually and yet you still have to work on papers.'

Teaching responsibilities varied widely, depending on faculty to student ratios. Yahuza, a UDS social science lecturer, spelt out the pressures on him. These included being 'exam officer of my department', requiring him to spend weekends conducting exams for part-timers, as well as the demands of teaching and the deadlines of marking: 'immediately after the examination they give you two weeks to upload your results, so you have to mark'. He went on to list all the courses he was teaching, before explaining that 'they have pinned me down to an extent that if I were to be given enough time, I could have done a lot of publications, but the teaching and marking of other things have taken a chunk of my time'.

When asked what the university could do about the lack of time faculty have to write and publish, Yahuza said, 'we need more hands on deck so that the work is reduced. If they recruit more faculty and the work is reduced one can have enough time to do the publications.' Gabriel, another UDS senior lecturer in the same department, pointed out that 'there is a load of teaching here ... and we are just about five or six lecturers.' Akuma, UG applied sciences lecturer, criticised the promotion criteria in light of staffing levels and teaching loads. 'It is not good,' she complained, 'to just copy another university system and use it for promotion'. She felt that 'you must look at your local settings and the realities of your situation' pointing out that, given the large number of students she had to look after 'where is the time?'.

Both universities placed similar publishing expectations on their faculty. Like her UDS peers, Attah a UG applied sciences lecturer, worried about peoples' 'development and welfare'. Sometimes, she reflected, the 'workload is so much that you don't even have the time, even if you have a paper, there is no time to work on it'. 'Holidays you are marking,' she said, and 'in our department we are few and the students are many. Even if you are teaching two courses,' she went on, 'you are busy marking and you don't even have time for yourself, let alone to have time to write papers and publish.'

Many interviewees spoke about how academic work spilled into weekends. Akosua, a UG associate professor, described how she 'writes all the time', and that 'I don't actually have the kind of time I need to be able to do the amount of writing I would like to do, so I spend a lot of my weekends at home working'. She was very clear about what was missing: time.

Others did try and 'invent' time by foregoing or altering their sleep patterns. Yahuza, a UDS lecturer explained how he copes: 'It is of late that I developed a strategy that I don't sleep throughout the night. I go home, eat and sleep early, and wake up around two and start marking these things.' Shaibu, a UDS health sciences lecturer, worried that 'a lot of people don't sleep because you want to do teaching and publication at the same time [so] you may not be able to sleep as a normal person'. Collegial life too might become 'deprived'. He felt that his colleagues lacked time to read each other's work, attend professional development workshops offered by the university, or even just socialise with colleagues.

Going too fast? Academics in a hurry

Staff at all levels spoke of the time pressures their work placed upon them, but junior faculty found themselves particularly burdened, with heavier teaching loads and larger classes. Kosiwa, a UG head of department, sympathised with them, noting how they have 'to struggle with this [heavy workload], preparing slides to teach, marking, and then to worsen matters, because they are master's students, they have to start a PhD'. He went on to acknowledge that the 'young ones virtually don't have time for publications or anything like that'.

This was also the case at UDS. Kwaku, a social sciences lecturer, pointed out that for most early career researchers in his department, the process is 'something they cannot manage with their teaching load'. In explaining why he had not published much at first, he recalled that 'when I joined the university, the first two years I was loaded with a lot of work, courses to teach'.

Some more senior academics seemed to disparage 'youth in a hurry', over-eager to publish and secure promotion. For Akosua, this desire for speed and sense of inviolability reminded her of dangerous driving, and she described being pressured to write a reference for a colleague who she felt was going too fast:

> I was actually upset with a junior colleague who applied for a fellowship. I was writing the recommendation letter, so I asked him to send me his CV so that I could use that to help him, and I noticed an error in his CV. It was such a glaring error that if he had shown it to anybody, they would have seen it. So, I said to him: 'I hope you showed your proposal to somebody else.' He said 'yes' but from the way he said it, I knew he hadn't and I was just a bit surprised, because even those of us who are associate professors, when we write, we show it to other people. I actually don't think we need a seminar to be told that. It is a real kind of hubris to think that I am good enough! It is the kind of self-confidence teenagers have; you know, when teenagers fly off or they drive their parent's car at certain speeds, they think they are invincible, right? Nothing will happen to them. But you get older and you realise that if you drive foolishly, you will have a foolish death.

Donkor, a UG applied sciences lecturer, also worried about the risks of his young colleagues 'sacrificing quality for quantity'. He felt that there were 'more important challenges' than waiting for journals to respond. Given that 'rewards are associated with a certain quantity of papers produced', his fear was that people who wanted 100 papers 'would end up submitting to where they are not supposed to be submitting'.

Several pointed to intergenerational frictions created by junior faculty who were 'jumping the queue'. Arguing that teaching service and publishing should have equal weight in promotions, Gabriel, a UDS social science senior lecturer in his mid-fifties, felt frustrated that younger faculty were 'forcing the balance'. He complained that some of the 'young' seemed to 'come in from nowhere, before you say "Jack" they are just there getting to professor, and you are here trying your best'.

Gabriel went on to point out that faculty promoted too quickly were lacking in experience and expertise. Using the metaphor that 'the sweetness of the pudding lies in the eating', he insisted that 'those things that are sweet you have to eat to know that they are really sweet'. He went on to say that 'people are professors but they don't know why they are professors, they are just there', and that 'even if you engage them in their own field you would see that they don't have any idea … some of them are always running away from engagements'. He felt that it was 'not about how quickly you got your professorship', but about 'being in a field for a long time, so there is no area that we cannot engage'.

While many senior faculty spoke about the need to mentor early career academics through their first publications, others conveyed a breakdown of unspoken academic norms by 'youngsters' who hadn't 'waited their turn' but instead published their way to seniority. A more traditional academic culture of 'waiting' (with promotion partly based on length of service) sits incongruously with this new culture of measurement and maximisation. Whilst UG regulations require at least three years in each grade before applying for promotion, many senior faculty would have taken much longer to be promoted. 'We are living in a very competitive environment,' insisted Mensah, a UG social sciences lecturer in his late thirties. While some young academics were accused of 'being in a hurry', there was a shared sense of trying to do a lot, trying to get ahead, and trying to do so in a time-scarce environment.

Waithood: the slow rhythms of journal publishing

In the context of internalised pressure to work fast and multi-task, the slow publishing time-frames of journals, especially in the social sciences and humanities, was a source of considerable frustration. Most galling for many was the long wait for an initial response after submission. Jonathan, a UDS health sciences lecturer, pointed to 'instances where people submit, and it would take a year or even more before you get a response. When it happens that way, it demoralises.' He went on to say that this waiting gets in the way of a planned 'line of action'. Abenayo, a UG social sciences lecturer, also complained. 'Some of them, they wouldn't even get back to you. There was a paper that I sent, and the journal had it for more than six months before they got back to me, only to tell me that we are sorry we cannot publish it. And I said, "What were you doing all these months?".' Akuma, a UG social sciences lecturer, described waiting two years for a response from an African health journal, while a UDS applied sciences lecturer said he had been tempted to withdraw papers from 'silent' journals. This waiting could 'fill the author with regret' for sending it to an 'unresponsive' journal according to a UDS health sciences lecturer.

Most felt that the whole review process was too drawn out. Taiye, a UG social science lecturer, bemoaned the whole 'back-and-forth kind of thing ... the first coming back to you takes forever to happen, and then you work on the comments and sending it back also takes a longer time, and that is the process that I don't like'. Similarly, Yahuza, a UDS social science lecturer, complained how 'when they respond to you the questions and other things are so much, and you have to do it again, send it, it would take another three months or whatever before finally the paper is published'. He felt that 'there should be a quicker way of assessing the papers through the reputable journals in order to enable it to come quickly'. Waiting made Yahuza anxious. 'Sometimes ou submit it and are waiting, three, four months, with no response and, in the course of that the anxiety is there.' He pointed out that this 'affects the pace at which you sometimes want to go, because when you submit it [to one journal], you cannot submit to another. You have to wait until whatever response that you have.'

Anxiety was a recurring theme, and even senior faculty had vivid memories of their early experiences. Lecturers in health sciences at both UG and UDS described waiting for decisions from the BioMed Central suite of medical journals as particularly difficult. For Kofi, 'I still remember the sleepless nights that came before the decision of the editor to publish it.' 'When I submitted,' explained Patrick, 'the anxiety of waiting for the reviewers' comments was unbearable.' He waited almost a year, and that 'waiting wasn't a pleasant experience at all' because 'my PhD – my graduation – was linked to the number of publications that I had.'

Paul, a UDS applied sciences lecturer, controversially suggested that things could move faster if authors could instead submit to multiple journals at once, where 'the first to send you a reply is the one you should work with'. Taiye, a social science lecturer at UG, explained the problem these delays caused for career progression within the Ghanaian system. 'You have to get a certain number of papers published before your next step, and so if you want to progress your time will be limited to the amount of time used by the journals.' In one case he had a paper 'that took almost two years, and that is two years of waiting'. He was 'counting how many papers before I can get to lecturer, to senior lecturer, to associate professor', and felt that waiting for such a long time 'impedes you, delays your progress'.

This timescape of frustration with slow peer review and editorial delays partly stemmed from a fear of being left behind by one's academic rivals. Nana, a UG applied sciences lecturer, described being 'afraid of the delay', but also 'afraid that your results would be redundant'. He recounted an experience of being 'in the final stages of being accepted, a paper came out; the same area, the same molecules I had worked on, the same group of things that I have worked on, from China'.

A few insisted that the careful and time-consuming process of peer review was necessary for high quality work. When asked about delays in getting feedback from journals, Lahiri, a UDS applied sciences senior lecturer, said: 'The time varies but it is fine for me because I know at the end of the day, they are going to do good work for me. So, I do not have a problem with the time.' She compared this good work to journals which publish papers within a week or two of submission, noting that 'I review papers and I don't think it can take me one week to review.' Kojo described how she frowned on this 'almost instantaneous response and acceptance of the paper'. Instead she felt that 'on average I think a fairly good paper should travel the length of maybe nine months to a year'.

Longer waiting times were associated with more prestigious journals, even if this was frustrating. Adjoa, a UG health science senior lecturer, felt the review process was inefficient and added that 'these so-called high impact journals, they take forever and frustrate people'. Nana agreed that selective journals were likely to take their time making a decision, but still felt this was unnecessary. 'I will tell you something,' she began, 'in academia, it is seen as a good journal if it delays quite a bit.' From her point of view 'if you put in a paper today and it comes out tomorrow people feel that good work wasn't done'. This mean that it was 'usually, some three to six months, then they feel that that is good work, but this is a lot of delay for you'.

Shaibu, a health sciences lecturer at UDS, was resigned to such delays, putting them down to the journal's popularity, and that it 'takes a longer time to hear from them because they have a lot of reviews to do'. She commented that it 'would take a long time before they will even acknowledge receipt of the paper, and it takes some time again before they will give you feedback'.

For Kosiwa, these delays all added up to a disincentive to submit papers to 'good' journals. 'They tell you they have received it,' he explained, but the 'review could be three, four months, and if you are unlucky even a year.' And then 'it takes forever for them to even publish it, so those are the things that deter us from sending it to the good journals'. If you can 'get one that will do it in a month or two for promotion,' she asked, 'why wouldn't you rather use them instead of these ones that would delay you?'.

Rejection, shame and stigma

If waiting was difficult, getting a rejection or 'revise and resubmit' notice brought its own demands, especially when accompanied by critical peer-review comments. Emmanuel, a UDS applied sciences lecturer, compared it to being hit. 'At times, when you are a beginner, it is as if someone is punching you inside. You don't know that he is propelling you to be what you are supposed to be.'

A few felt that it was better to not receive many comments. Major revisions were seen as 'very annoying' by one lecturer, as rewriting was time consuming. Nelly, an applied sciences lecturer, wondered 'how to write a paper such that you get minimal comments from reviewers ... at least that will encourage people to write [rather] than if you write and get comments that are not palatable from reviewers'. Repeated rounds of reviewing and rewriting made more demands on her time.

In addition to conflicting reviewers' comments, some were annoyed when reviewers did not seem to have requisite expertise. Emmanuel felt that 'there are situations where some of the reviewers are not specialists in the area ... You may be a physicist, but you may not be a specialist in theoretical physics. Then you talk on something that you don't know the details of.'

Extensive review comments were described as 'disheartening' or worse. 'They will toss you, tell you this, tear the whole paper apart,' felt Gabriel, a UDS senior lecturer. For some, the relationship between the Ghanaian academics and 'international' reviewers was particularly raw. Patrick, a UDS health sciences head of department, was blunt about their impact on his faculty: 'It demoralises and it demotivates researchers, particularly from developing countries.'

Rejection generated sadness, distress, and confusion. Four respondents phrased this as 'feeling bad'. For example, Shaibu said that after his paper was rejected by a journal, 'I felt bad, very bad, because that was the first time and I did not understand what it meant to get such comments, and I really felt bad. Now I understand how these things happen.' Many other respondents also spoke of a sense of confusion about why their paper had been rejected. Kwami, at UG, recounted that 'the editor came back after a very long time, after I had sent a mail to the editor about the paper, then he came back and said that they are rejecting the paper with some reasons that it was difficult for me to understand'. Akuma, also at UG, recalled sending a paper to the *Journal of Child Health*, but then they 'would come back and tell you it is not suitable for their journal'. 'At times you are confused,' she admitted, 'I am working on children, and I have a paper on children, and I send it to them, and they tell me it is not suitable for their journal.'

Talking about rejection sometimes led to animosity towards editors and reviewers. 'If you are not lucky, they will reject it with some flimsy excuse,' said Gabriel, a UDS social sciences senior lecturer. Some felt that this reflected Ghana's marginality within the global science system. Awudu, a UG social sciences lecturer, was very critical of journals that 'reject with the reason that it does not fit into the journal, meanwhile it does'.

Nana, also a lecturer at UG, admitted feeling similarly angry on receiving a rejection. 'Waao! Usually, you come up with all sorts of things to help your mind calm down ... you are panicking: "these people are not serious", "you don't think good research can come out from an African lab", and things like that.' She described how she gradually calmed down, questioning her initial assumption that they had been rejected because of their African university affiliation, admitting that 'professionally, it is just divergent opinions; somebody does not agree with you on what you have done and what you have submitted'. On reflection, 'you move from one place to another'.

Kwami felt it was less deliberate prejudice against African researchers than journals having different specialisms, saying 'some journals don't publish stuff from Africa, they don't publish stuff from Ghana, and you have to look at all these things before you submit your paper to the journal, and that is how to do it'. On the other hand, Kwaku pointed out the double standards that seemed to be at work:

Or I go to a journal and I see that all the work there is done in the UK, US, France or sometimes collaboration between China, Japan, and what have you. They have not even seen any data collected from an African country. Then you submit your paper, everything about it is okay. But they are just telling you not suitable. Not suitable probably because it is from an African country and they say it is an international journal, so is the African country not part of the international? But the readership of the journal most of the time may be limited to certain countries, so they are familiar with the ideas in those countries. But when you say 'Ghana' maybe not many people know much about Ghana, so the data looks isolated. And so, it is not about your methodology, it is not about your introduction or your objectives, but the data you collected seems not to fit into what they want.

He wondered if Euro-American editors felt that they lacked the 'ability to test the data and to objectively assess it', but also pointed out how South Africa was an exception to this exclusion, arguing that 'where the data is collected matters'. From his perspective, 'South Africa is more or less like a "European country" so most journals ... have accepted publications from South Africa'. He went on to use the example of someone wanting to 'validate' a research instrument from the West in Africa, so 'they do it in South Africa, and it is accepted, but in most other places the paper ends up not getting accepted, getting declined, and so on'.

Several authors talked about how journal rejections often used Ghanaian academic English as an excuse for rejection. Abenayo described how 'we teach and do everything in English, but normally because of where we hope to publish, when it goes, they always have issues with our language' (Abenayo, UG social sciences lecturer). She described how 'disheartening' it was to have a journal reject you saying 'your English is not good'. Abenayo recounted how this happened to a paper she wrote with colleagues from the university's English department. They found themselves bewildered, and wondering 'what type of English they were looking for' because 'you have done whatever it is that you are supposed to do'. The legitimacy of new genres of global academic English (Galloway and Rose 2015, Canagarajah 2012) has been recognised by scholars in applied linguistics, but not by every journal editor.

Rejection increased other anxieties. For Kojo, there was an ever-present fear that personal interests and rivalries played a role in editorial decisions. 'Initially,' he said, 'you think somebody has a personal grudge with you and … wants to kill your career or something, but I have seen that it is part of the game.' He felt that this had become a 'norm, so we no longer think about it.' Patrick, a UDS health sciences senior lecturer, also wondered about personal rivalries and competition, explaining that 'sometimes you read the reviewers' comment and look at it, you will shake your head because you don't know where those comments are coming from'. He even wondered if 'they have a similar thing that they want to bring out and they don't want yours to get out first or whatever, I cannot tell'.

Knowing that senior colleagues have work rejected can be comforting. Kwaku, a UDS social sciences lecturer explained why. 'People who are even more experienced, sometimes they send their papers to a certain place and the comments they make for them is discouraging. Meanwhile this is also a senior, even a professor.' On the other hand, several acknowledged that the relationship with editors and reviewers could be positive and productive, with review comments designed to help authors develop their work. Others, like Awudu, a UG social sciences lecturer, prepares his mentees accordingly, making it clear to them that 'you will get all kinds of comments and all sorts of things would come but you just have to have a very thick skin to absorb that and push it through'.

Instead of searching for international journals to publish African research Kwaku called for more Ghanaian journal publishing. Echoing calls to build continental research infrastructures (Okune 2021), he felt the answer was to encourage 'African universities to develop local journals and try to accept publications from local people because we are familiar with our own issues, we need to indigenise knowledge'. He pointed to the problem of collecting 'some data from Ghana and sending it to a European journal to review' as 'they may not appreciate what you are talking about, they may not understand it'. Instead, he felt it was better to use peer reviewers 'who understand the concepts and what the local people are talking about', rather than take it 'outside'.

The virtues of persistence: theorising academic agency and vocation

Given the emotional demands of research and publishing in a time-poor and resource-constrained academy, what motivates people to continue? The virtue of 'persistence' emerged as a strong theme in interviews. Issah, a UDS lecturer in applied sciences, spoke of sitting down to 'write and rewrite, draft upon draft'. 'Initially it wasn't easy,' he admitted, 'when you are trying to move to the higher quality journal, there were frustrations but yet we persisted.'

Persistence and determination was a constant refrain, and a repeated coda to stories of difficulty. When asked whether a rejection discouraged him from publishing, Taiye, a UG social science lecturer, explained that 'the first experience was good and so when I got the rejection, you know it did not disturb me. I was still encouraged that this is something you can do, and so with the rejection though I felt bad I moved on quickly to submit other papers even after that one, which were accepted.' Similarly, Adjoa, a UG social science senior lecturer, said, 'so for me the paper that was rejected, I actually felt challenged to do it better.'

A Weberian ethos of scientific commitment had become part of many professional identities, seen as a mark of the 'real' academic. Three different UG social science lecturers underscored their resilience. Akuma insisted that 'I haven't given up, as I am someone who does not give up … It is not easy writing, is not an easy task. Anybody who says it is easy, it is never easy. But once you start and you tell yourself you will finish you will go through and finish it … You just have to continue working hard.' Talking about the delays caused by peer review, Mensah, a UG social sciences lecturer, admitted that while 'it has the potential to affect the passion and enthusiasm that you require as an academic … you can't give up, it is frustrating but you can't give up'. He was emphatic, insisting that 'the majority of my people will tell you that they have not given up'. When asked if rejection deterred him from publishing, Adjoa replied 'No, no, no why would I say that? He instead insisted that he hadn't got to the point of 'not knowing why you are in that field … those who do not know why they are doing certain things, they would probably be thinking of something like that.'

Others espoused a similar level of determination. Asked the same question, Haruna, a lecturer at UDS agreed, explaining that it was 'probably because I am in academia – I am sure if it were other people who are not in the academia, they would have given up because it was quite cumbersome'. Donkor, a UG lecturer, admitted that aspiring academics should be 'ready to really work hard because it takes a lot of time, a lot of energy'. He went on to describe one particularly arduous experience of getting a paper published which included writing a fourteen-page rebuttal letter. He ended the interview with a rhetorical question. 'Who would be interested to do this if you are not motivated?'

The Cameroonian philosopher Mbembe (2001, 1) vividly describes the destructive power of 'negative interpretations' where the African human experience is never presented as 'possessing things and attributes that are properly part of "human nature"'. Africa is seen to be of 'lesser value, little importance, and poor quality'. This discourse continues to get reproduced across the continent. Talking to Ghanaian scientists, Droney (2014) encounters a similar sense of Ghana's 'lack' in relation to global science, albeit expressed through irony and dark humour. It is hard to escape this rhetoric of lack, as interviewees described the unfairness of their working conditions, and the inequalities that emerge within and between Ghanaian universities and disciplines. UDS faculty feel their laboratory resources are inadequate; chemists feel the promotion system discriminates against their field; and women academics feel the pressures of time scarcity more than men.

Again and again, respondents focused on the particular challenge of making time to carry out and publish their research. Their pursuit of the scientific vocation, despite the gendered economies of scarcity, defines an African academic ethos and professional identity (Tousignant 2018; Wendland 2016). Pragmatism determines the types of research pursued and papers published. People are determined to keep going, and many saw persistence as a key scientific virtue. Writing and publishing is emotionally demanding, with joy at success mixed with inadequacy and the frustration of rejection. Time to research and write is a precious resource, unequally distributed by gender and seniority.

An awareness of academic temporalities and under-resourced research infrastructures is integral to understanding academic agency in research and publishing across Africa. Concerns about time and money shape choices about which research to pursue and methods to use. They can deter researchers from publishing in local 'scholar-led' journals, if peer review is seen as slow and cumbersome. When time is limited, choosing a more commercially-orientated journal and rapid review process makes sense. On the other hand, publishing in 'elite' academic journals is no easier, given editorial gatekeeping, demanding peer-review protocols and high APCs.

Acceleration is an option for those without competing responsibilities and commitments. Others urged patience, given the need for peer review. Then there is the rivalry and silent resentment felt towards younger scholars who seem to be publishing too quickly. Vostal (2019) offers a nuanced analysis of the different temporalities of academic work, and questions simplistic accounts of science speeding up. He sees 'agentic synchronisation' at work, where researchers skilfully align different experimental, cognitive and institutional temporalities. This focus on agency captures the capacity of some to combine both speed and patience. Researchers are constantly aware of the need to meet targets set by institutional promotion boards. Women faculty face additional challenges of combining caring responsibilities and professional roles. This is the context in which Ghana's journals have to compete and survive.

In the African publishing landscape, academic journals hosted by universities compete with independent publishers that offer professionalised web hosting, responsive 'customer' service and efficient decision-making. The next two chapters explore the diversity of their publishing models, offering case studies of Ghanaian institutional journals and independent publishers from across anglophone Africa.

Chapter 7

What does the editor think?
Perspectives from Ghanaian academic journals

The publishing landscape today is much more fraught ... where you publish has become more contentious ... We now assume that the top journals are the most important. (Editor, *Contemporary Journal of African Studies*)

Introduction

This book has documented the academic publishing strategies and experiences of researchers at two Ghanaian universities. With research 'outputs' a key metric determining career advancement at both institutions, it has explored researchers' publishing rationales, choices, and calculations, as well as analysing the guidance they have received from supervisors, mentors and collaborators. This picture would be incomplete without the perspectives of journal editors and publishers themselves. Given the disciplinary diversity across the Ghanaian scholarly research ecosystem, it consists of detailed case studies of different journals, including those hosted by universities and professional associations. Despite their different histories and institutional settings, all face the same pressure of university expectations on staff to publish 'internationally' as much as in Ghana's own journals.

The Ghanaian academy has a long and rich tradition of scholarly publishing. Complementing colonial-era journals, the *Transactions of the Historical Society of Ghana* (founded in 1953) was followed by others in the early sixties, as the University College of the Gold Coast became the new University of Ghana in 1961, four years after Ghana's independence.

The journals and publishers profiled here play an important role in building Ghana's national and regional research ecosystem. One is supported by a professional association, two by universities, and one by Ghana's national science council. They publish work in science, african studies, development studies, horticulture, and education. The oldest was founded in 1962, the youngest in 2009. All publish at least one issue a year, and all are now published online and open access. Only one charges APCs.

These case studies aim to understand how the changing publishing landscape – including digitisation, open access and commercialisation – is reshaping the role of Ghana's scholarly journals in a regional research ecosystem. Informal and wide-ranging interviews with journal editors allowed them to reflect on their histories, reputation, and business models. Many talked of the challenges of meeting publication deadlines, garnering sufficient submissions, ensuring timely peer review, and sustaining scholarly standards. Nearly all the editors worked on a largely voluntary basis, and funding is an issue for all the journals profiled. Being a journal editor can be a thankless task. As Professor Atia Apusigah, a founding editor of the *Ghanaian Journal of Development Studies* noted, 'no one appreciates the time you put into it'.

Most of these journals have benefitted from the support and training offered by the South African non-profit foundation African Journals Online (AJOL), an NGO dedicated to building journal capacity and quality. The last part of this chapter draws on an interview with its current director, Susan Murray, to discuss AJOL's support for this fragile African publishing ecosystem. It ends with a reflection on the future of professional association academic publishing, and the challenges of sustaining the socio-technical infrastructures that are now needed.

Ghana Journal of Science (GJS)

The *Ghana Journal of Science* (GJS) is published by the Council for Scientific and Industrial Research (CSIR). The Council is Ghana's national research agency, funding and carrying out research. The journal publishes two issues a year on the AJOL portal, with papers from a whole range of fields of applied science and technology, drawn from Ghana and across the region.[1]

The journal's origins date back to the founding of the Ghana Science Association in 1959. It held its first conference in 1961, and the second, held after a major international peace forum entitled 'The World without the Bomb' (Allman 2008), attracted eminent scientists such as JD Bernal. The association launched its journal in 1962 (Yanney-Wilson 1961, 1962), holding biennial conferences throughout the 1970s and 1980s. CSIR was established in 1968 as a Government agency to support and fund research, and now includes ten applied science research institutes, and the Council began to fund and support the journal. The *Ghana Journal of Agricultural Science* is also funded by the Council. In 1999, the Ghana Science Association launched its own journal, and is no longer involved in publishing the *Ghana Journal of Science*.

The journal has an editorial team of 11, based either at the University of Ghana or CSIR. Its current editor-in-chief – Professor George Odamtten – is a mycologist at the University of Ghana. He makes final editorial decisions based on reviewers' reports. The CSIR technical editor, Akilakpa Sawyerr, oversees all aspects of the publication workflow, from the receipt of a manuscript to its publication, including initial manuscript checking, database entry, invitation of referees, summarising referee reports, copy-editing, proofreading, and uploading onto the indexing sites. He is employed by CSIR, as are others involved in technical production.

The journal aims to provide an avenue for Ghana's scientists to share their knowledge with the general scientific community. Its emphasis

---

1   https://www.ajol.info/index.php/gjs

is on helping African academics to promote their research and 'make their work more visible to society'. According to Sawyerr, supporting authors to improve their work, as well as publishing an open-access journal, are important to GJS. 'Africans should support their own and help lift the credibility of their journals, not only concentrating on impact factors of foreign journals'. He expressed his frustrations that Ghana's academic promotion procedures required publications in Scopus-indexed journals – remember that very few Ghanaian journals are indexed in Scopus – and asked why local journals are not also valued.

The journal's history reveals the ebb and flow of its fortunes. Until 2010 only one issue was published a year, each with between five and ten articles. There was a brief period in the 1980s and 1990s where more than 20 articles were published each year. The move to electronic publishing made the production of the journal much easier and more consistent. The technical editor described how the previous editors had been struggling to keep up with manuscript submissions. He vividly described arriving to a huge pile of paper manuscripts in his office, and the manual process of reviewing creating a backlog that made it difficult to follow up with authors and reviewers. This corroborates with the experience of Francis, the UDS lecturer who sent his submission to GJS and then waited patiently for a year, before hearing that two of the three reviewers had not returned their reviews. He was asked to wait a further six months before finally receiving three positive reviews.

A key challenge for GJS is recruiting enough reviewers to ensure all submissions go through a double-blind peer review process. As is normal practice, the journal does not pay reviewers. The assumption is that established scholars should do this work 'gladly', because 'it was done for you to get to the position you are'. The ideal is one of collaborative reciprocity, but reviewers are often overladen with other duties and so the journal often relies on junior faculty who use their reviewing experience to boost their CV; all reviewers are offered a certificate of honour after reviewing a manuscript.

The journal continues to receive regular submissions across the whole range of the applied sciences. The most recent 2020 issue includes an article on the economic returns of education for twins, another on the road use of Accra's primary-school children, and a third on the highway code. In 2020, issue 61.1 published 12 papers, and rejected a further 4 for not meeting requirements. One reason for its continued presence, according to its managing editor, is its age. 'The journal has been around for some time, therefore [it] has a lot of clout, so submissions come in numbers without soliciting, especially from researchers in scientific institutions in Africa.'

GJS does not charge APCs, and all costs are borne by CSIR. In the long term, however, the journal aims to develop its reputation to the extent that it can begin introducing APCs, allowing the journal to become financially self-sufficient. AJOL (African Journals Online) has provided significant support for GJS, helping the journal obtain DOIs, sorting out copyright, and providing training. The journal was indexed with EBSCO in 2019 and is working towards a JPPS star, AJOL's quality assurance kitemark. A journal that has been in existence for almost 60 years and launched at a time of global prominence for Ghanaian science remains insecure and financially vulnerable. It is not listed in any of the international indexes, and depends on the subsidy of the CSIR.

The fortunes of the Ghana Science Association have also been mixed. Donkor, a senior lecturer at UG, described the value of attending the biennial conference of the association as a student, and of being encouraged to submit his paper to the journal. Francis, another senior lecturer at UDS, had a less positive experience. He described his experiences of submitting an article to the *Journal of the Ghana Science Association*, and how it was rejected after a very long delay. He recalled being 'a bit frustrated', asking why he had not been told earlier, despite reminding them several times. 'I kept on reminding them because I had confidence in that paper, so I didn't want to send it out to some of the journals we know are predatory'. He later found out that one of the reviewers had been travelling, but that when it takes more than 'one year six months, you are not too happy because you lose your faith'. He was unusual in stating that he preferred sending articles to 'our local journals' and had sent papers to other science journals hosted at KNUST.

Contemporary Journal of African Studies (CJAS)

The *Contemporary Journal of African Studies* (CJAS) is an open-access African Studies journal hosted by the Institute of African Studies at the University of Ghana and published on the AJOL platform.[2] The institute was the inspiration of Kwame Nkrumah and his African-centred vision for scholarship and science. The journal began its life as the institute's flagship *Research Review* in 1964 and was relaunched as CJAS in 2012. CJAS is peer reviewed and published twice a year, publishing on any topic in African Studies, including papers that discuss and re-evaluate earlier research. The journal is 'committed to promoting knowledge from an African-centred perspective'.

In an interview, the editor-in-chief, Professor Akosua Adomako Ampofo, reiterated this mission. 'The point [of the journal] was to have pan-African conversations across Africa and to include global Africa ... the journal has always been a political project ... it is important to keep that space ... to fight for it to be better acknowledged.' Until 2021, there was an editorial committee of six, four based at the University of Ghana at the Institute of African Studies, one at the University of Cape Town, and one at Loyola University in the USA. Three additional members – based at KNUST, Wits (Witwatersrand) University and York University – were added in 2021. The editorial coordinator, translator, and two publication assistants are all based at the Institute of African Studies. Akosua explained that when she first became involved there were only two editors, and before that there was only one editor, so the work became overwhelming. The editorial team are not paid; the editor describes it as 'just part of the work we do'. The Institute of African Studies provides office space and support for the journal, which is in turn supported by the Carnegie Corporation philanthropy and its BANGA-Africa (Building A New Generation of Academics in Africa) project.

Each issue contains between five and nine articles from across the social sciences and humanities, including book reviews and

---

2   https://www.ajol.info/index.php/contjas

conversations. A recent issue (vol. 6, no. 2) was dedicated to questions of restitution and repatriation of illegally acquired objects in European museums. The majority of the authors are Ghanaian or have a Ghanaian affiliation. In 2019, with many academics increasingly unable to afford a subscription or to access journal articles, CJAS became open access. A paywall remains in place for issues published between 2013 and 2018. According to the editor, the move to open access reflected the changing publishing landscape, and increasing expectations. Akosua felt that the journal had more respect before the arrival of citation indexes and their stratification of journal status. She noted how, in the past, people would have published in CJAS from all over the world. The journal has also been involved in digitising back issues, but it has proven difficult to find all the back issues, and the committee has to decide whether to make all back issues open access.

Despite being open access, CJAS does not charge APCs, given that most Ghanaian researchers do not have research funding, and that the introduction of APCs would likely limit the types of disciplinary knowledge that were published, since not all research is equally funded. The decision not to introduce APCs reflects the journal's mission but does mean that the journal needs other sources of funding.

CJAS is not indexed in Scopus, DOAJ, or the other global citation indexes, and as a result the editors describe the struggle to attract sufficient original and high-quality work. The journal receives many submissions from Nigerian universities, but these are of variable standards, or may have already been published in other places. Their editorial strategy is to attract established scholars, who are no longer dependent on publishing in Scopus-accredited journals for career progression.

Like other journals, CJAS finds it hard to attract reviewers. All CJAS submissions are reviewed twice before they are accepted but delays in receiving reviews have led to frustration amongst authors. The option of paying reviewers has been discussed but dismissed by the editorial board as it risked commodifying the publishing process. According to the editor, this decision may be revisited.

Ghana Journal of Development Studies (GJDS)

The Ghana Journal of Development Studies (GJDS) was founded in 2004 as the official journal of the Faculty of Integrated Development Studies at UDS by Professor David Millar and Professor Agnes Atia Apusigah. It continues to be hosted by UDS and published on the AJOL platform.[3] It is a multidisciplinary, peer-reviewed journal with a development focus. The journal publishes empirical research and theoretical reflections on development policy, programming, and projects, accepting papers from a range of disciplinary areas. The focus on development issues has 'an emphasis on, but is not exclusive to, the Ghanaian as well as African settings'.

The journal is indexed with IBSS and EBSCO. Since 2013, the editorial chair has been Dr Africanus Diedong, a senior lecturer at UDS, supported by three other editors. The current editorial board of nine includes the VC of UDS, several UDS professors, and several senior UK-based and US-based academics. The founding editors are still members of the editorial board.

Two volumes have been published each year since 2004, initially with between seven and ten articles in each. This number has increased since the journal went online in 2015. When the current editor took over, the journal was only producing hard copies, and there was a backlog of unpublished papers. They were spending a lot of money to produce the journal, but the distribution was weak, which made it difficult to financially break even. By moving online and collaborating with other journals who were able to host them, they received higher visibility.

The scope of the journal is deliberately broad, as the most recent issue illustrates. The five articles include papers on mining safety, landownership, the use of sand in building construction, local government decentralisation, and entrance charges to city parks.

The journal receives as many as 40 submissions per issue, although usually only five to eight are published, enabling a focus on quality. The journal is the most selective of our sample. All papers are double-

---

3   https://www.ajol.info/index.php/gjds

blind reviewed. Dr Diedong notes that he does not accept papers simply because they come from UDS faculty. When a paper is rejected, the editors encourage authors to revise and resubmit their work. Dr Diedong refers to this as an issue of 'professional ethics'. According to Dr Diedong, they have enough submissions to publish four editions a year, however, due to structural constraints 'we need to make sure we don't overstep'. He worries that if the journal responded to the many requests for special editions, these might fall below their normal standards.

One of the key 'structural constraints' for the journal is the challenge of recruiting peer reviewers. GJDS provides a token payment to peer reviewers, although some professors refuse to take payment. Dr Diedong is also careful in choosing the reviewers, making sure that they have expertise, as well as a willingness to contribute. Deadlines are also important. Reviewers are given two months to peer review papers, and GJDS is strict in regard to the time frame; if someone is not able to deliver their review on time, the journal has a backup plan. 'We try to insure we don't delay,' explains Dr Diedong, 'so if there is a delay it's from AJOL'.

A key editorial challenge comes in ensuring that authors implement the recommended edits. 'Authors can be sloppy,' reflects Diedong, and editors can go back and forth two or three times with 'notorious' authors who do not want to do what the editors think is right. This lengthens the publishing timeline, and editorial labour.

One of the reasons that GJDS receives so many submissions, according to Dr Diedong, is that the journal is recognised by UDS academic promotion panels. 'There are a number of professors who have been promoted because of publications in our journals,' boasts Dr Diedong, 'so most academics want to have one publication in our journal'. He notes a tension between national and international journals. Although he aspires to internationalise the editorial board – given that international board membership is important for the perception of quality – he asserts the importance of publishing in local journals that are 'credible and good'. GJDS contributes to that important mission.

A key route to developing reputation is through accreditation in international indexes. This is something that GJDS authors have been requesting, and it is a long-term ambition for GJDS. Dr Diedong describes how difficult it is to be awarded a JPPS star, even though he has made a huge effort not to miss any editions: 'The struggles to make journals work in our context are very challenging.' Networking with other editors allows the sharing of good practice, and publishing workshops run by the British Academy have been useful.

Whilst the journal website does not mention APCs, authors are asked to 'pay a little amount to help the process'. The publishing workflow (including design and layout) is currently outsourced to a publisher at KNUST, but Diedong's ambition is for UDS to develop the technical capacity to carry out this work. These APCs do not fully cover the cost of the journal, but they do allow the journal to be published open access to the academic community. For Ghanaian authors, the charges are 300 Cedi (USD 51) and for foreign authors USD 150. While most of the authors are Ghanaian, the journal does attract authors from across the region. Dr Diedong noted that the journal is helpful 'not only for our institution, but also for academics in Ghana and beyond'.

Ghana Journal of Horticulture (JHORT)

The *Ghana Journal of Horticulture* (JHORT) – founded in 2002 – is an open-access journal published by the Ghana Institute of Horticulturists (GhIH).[4] It publishes papers relating to a range of applied agricultural fields, including fruit and vegetable production, floriculture, crop physiology, crop protection, agricultural economics and biotechnology. The institute is a professional body whose membership includes producers, processors, marketers, exporters, researchers, extension officers, government institutions, polytechnics, universities and NGOs. It aims to support horticultural producers, handlers, and exporters through information sharing and research. In 2020 they hosted their 20th Annual Conference at the University of Development Studies.

---

4   http://www.journal.ghih.org/index.php?journal=ghih

The institute supports the work of JHORT financially, but the three editors – who hold academic posts at KNUST and UDS – are not paid. Evidence of professional service is expected in applications for promotion by Ghana's universities. One of the editorial board members – Prof. Francis Appiah – is also vice-president of the institute.

The journal website, hosted by GhIH, includes publications from the most recent four years of the journal. One issue is published annually, with between five and ten articles, all by Ghanaian researchers on a range of applied agricultural topics. In 2012 JHORT began publishing online, a move motivated – according to Prof. Appiah – by a general struggle faced by many 'local' journals. Many academics sought international journals which would help their research to circulate, and their careers to progress. Even though horticultural issues are usually of interest to a specific local audience, academics 'want to kill two birds with one stone', namely, to share their research and achieve a high impact factor publication. Local journals, especially those only printing hard copies, could not compete in this new globalised system, and were therefore not receiving sufficient submissions.

The journal received technical support from GhIH to move online. Until 2018 the papers published annually in JHORT came from the institute's annual scientific conference, but the journal aims in future to compile these papers as a special issue, and for the standard volume to address more 'cross-cutting' issues. Typically, the journal publishes only Ghanaian researchers, but the editor is keen to develop a more international profile. Prof. Appiah has explored taking the journal to a commercial publisher, and JHORT has been in talks with Academic Journals, the Nigerian-based entrepreneurial publisher of a suite of more than 100 open-access science journals.

International Journal of Pedagogy, Policy and ICT in Education (IJOPPIE)

The *International Journal of Pedagogy, Policy and ICT in Education* (IJOPPIE) was set up in 2009 by Dr Naah Yemeh as an online journal. It aims to 'provide a platform for educational research dissemination in Africa, covering pedagogy, language policy, and ICT in education'. It publishes one issue a year open access on the AJOL platform, usually with between five to seven articles on a range of educational topics, including work on higher education pedagogies. Until recently, most issues have had one or more contributions from the University of Education Winneba (UEW), Ghana, where the journal is based.

In 2009 Yemeh was a senior lecturer in applied linguistics at UEW and held quality assurance responsibilities in the faculty. Committed to making books more widely available in schools, he had recently set up a publishing company called AskAfrica Books and Co. After attending a workshop on journal publishing, he decided to also launch an academic journal to provide publishing opportunities for his university faculty. With no financial support forthcoming from his faculty his company provided initial support. He continues to edit the journal, and it is now published on the AJOL platform.[5]

With no organisational sponsorship, the journal's finances relied from the beginning on authors paying APCs to cover the costs of reviewing and printing. 'We encourage reviewers by giving them a token amount'. This also covered the printing costs, as well as mailing and distribution. Dr Yemeh defended the move, saying that 'once people value it, they will pay; publishing is something that is close to the hearts of many intellectuals because they need it for promotion'. Initially non-Ghanaian researchers paid USD 100. This went up to USD 200 but as of late-2022, was reduced again to USD 50.

Dr Yemeh described his inclusive vision for the journal. 'It started as a project at the faculty of languages but then of course we are in a university of education, so I thought of not leaving out the pedagogy. And then people were getting more interested in ICT.' He went on to note how some colleagues publish in French, and so the journal also publishes work in French.

He made the decision to publish open access on the AJOL platform after attending workshops run by AJOL in Accra. Dr Yemeh admitted to being uncertain about going OA but recognised that he would be

---

5   https://www.ajol.info/index.php/ijp/index

able to cover the costs of going open access through increasing APCs charged to international contributors. The journal has published several Nigerian authors, including those who have spent time at the University of Education Winneba whilst on sabbatical who had spread word of the journal. The journal continues to produce print copies, partly because some US authors 'have not fully migrated to digital', and they also sometimes must print articles for reviewers to read. Asked about using the OJS journal workflow software, he replied 'we know of OJS, but we are not using it yet'.

Initially the journal came out twice a year, with a 90% acceptance rate – those rejected are encouraged to resubmit. Yemeh's ambition is to increase the number of submissions and publish two issues a year partly through issuing calls for special issues. He noted how in 2020, 'we are supposed to come out in the first quarter, but the pandemic has interrupted us'. Despite actively promoting the journal, IJOPPIE is facing declining submissions, and Yemeh suggests that this is because he is no longer employed at Winneba: 'When I was a lecturer I could talk to fellow lecturers and I could use the university as a publicity forum, and now that I am no more with them, we are getting more from Nigeria than Ghana.' On the other hand, he noted that some had said they had been promoted because of their publication in IJOPPIE.

Yemeh noted that even the low APCs charged present a financial challenge to authors: 'People have told us that they know more renowned journals that are not charging, so I ask why they are not going to them? But they still submit their papers to us.' He acknowledged that his university promotion criteria required at least one international publication, but argued that the 'international publishing houses are dealing with issues very different from those we are dealing with in Ghana, so it's not easy for them to immediately accept your paper'.

Yemeh admitted to the challenge of those who 'want to publish quickly putting intense pressure on us'. He acknowledged how 'reviewers have their own challenges, and the best we can do is to remind them'. He also acknowledged that one author had recently insinuated that IJOPPIE was predatory. To 'reassure him of what was happening we sent him the reviews of his paper'. He admitted that the term 'was not in our vocabulary', and that he always relied on the expertise of subject experts in making decisions.

Asked about his ambitions for the journal, Yemeh felt that this depended on the sustainability of his publishing house: 'My idea is that in Africa we need to encourage reading, writing, researching. That is the objective of the publishing house and the journal is part of that. It's not about making profit.' The journal continues to rely on the support of AJOL's advice and training. Yemeh felt that AJOL workshops 'give us a chance to measure up against other journals and see what others are doing'. He was also hopeful that the journal would meet the requirements for a JPPS star.

Supporting Ghana's scholarly ecosystem: the role of AJOL

Journal case studies illustrate their different histories, with some getting strong institutional backing, and others reliant on the commitment and vision of individual editors. In the shadow of the global citation indexes and publishing infrastructures, their challenges are increasingly similar. It highlights how many have relied on the training, guidance and support offered by African Journals OnLine (AJOL), a non-profit company based in South Africa. All five now also host their journals on the AJOL platform.

AJOL began in 1998 as a donor-funded journal database project led by an Oxford-based NGO called INASP (International Network for the Availability of Scientific Publications). By 2000 AJOL hosted data on 50 English-language African-published journals in agricultural sciences, science and technology, health, and social sciences, providing abstracts and full-text documents. Murray (2009) documents this growth as well as the challenges AJOL faced in its early years.

As AJOL expanded its coverage and support, it found itself increasingly helping journals with the transition to digital publishing, and in giving editorial teams the technical expertise they needed to meet international publishing standards. It has relied on core funding from SIDA, the Swedish aid funder, and has been supported by US philanthropies. However, attempts to diversify its donor base have made little progress. Moves to a more sustainable business model – such as charging for training and journal hosting – are made difficult by the constrained resources of the journals it supports. According to Susan Murray, AJOL's director, a stronger financial commitment from African governments is key to AJOL's future sustainability. AJOL employs four full-time staff, and with a limited income stream the organisation struggles to keep up with growing demands from newly launched journals for accreditation and inclusion.

AJOL now describes itself as the 'world's largest and preeminent platform of African-published scholarly journals'. It aims to promote global access to African journals, increase African readership, strengthen journal capacity, and 'show-case credible and trusted African-published research journals'. In 2022 it hosted around 660 journals (of which approximately two-thirds are active), more than 15,000 issues, and 180,000 article abstracts. Most journals are based in anglophone Africa, and fewer than ten are published in French. There is growing demand for its services, and in 2020 a further 380 journals were on the waiting list to join AJOL. According to the director, assessment of new journals involves extensive 'cyber stalking' and 'background checks' on journals, their editorial boards, and their peer review processes. The site has millions of monthly downloads from nearly every country in the world, and more than half of the repeat users are from Africa. AJOL is heavily involved in training journal editors and academic capacity building, as our case studies attest. With donor-funding, AJOL also set up a Ghana open-access journal platform called GhanJOL, but this is no longer supported.

AJOL's original remit was to make African journals more globally visible, rather than to attempt to assure their quality. Increasingly they realised that researchers were citing a journal's inclusion in AJOL as a quality marker when applying for university promotion. As a result, AJOL decided to 'step up' its quality assurance role, and in 2015 developed a quality framework. The result, developed in collaboration with INASP, is the Journal Publishing Practices and Standards (JPPS) framework.[6]

---

6   https://www.journalquality.info/en/

The JPPS framework is designed as 'both carrot and stick', setting out detailed assessment criteria for journal inclusion, much as existing citation indexes do. Journals are given one of six levels: Inactive title, New title, No stars, One star, Two stars, and Three stars. The requirements for one-star accreditation include providing clear information about the journal, its editorial board, its instructions for authors, and having a track record of at least two years. Three-star accreditation requires meeting further publishing and archiving protocols, but is still far less onerous than the requirements made by an index such as Scopus. In 2022, around 160 AJOL journals had one star, 45 had two stars and no journals had three stars. The first and 'rather strict' round of JPPS assessments was carried out in 2018, and led to an enormous reaction, with journals now far more ready to provide clear guidance on their publishing policies. As of late 2020, another assessment was being planned. Sustaining any form of journal ranking system is time and resource intensive, and AJOL was not designed for this purpose.

AJOL has three priorities: supporting and developing nascent or weak journals, advising editors who have little publishing experience, and helping journals transition their editorial teams. Many AJOL-sponsored journals are run on a voluntary basis by highly dedicated individuals who give a lot of time, making editorial handovers difficult. The future of AJOL's own capacity to fulfil this role is uncertain, given that it does not wish to charge journals for accreditation or inclusion. It has suspended a few journals on the grounds of problematic publishing practices. These, according to Murray, included a publisher that grew rapidly, and whose journals gained in profile and impact factor, but then the 'editor-in-chief started a publishing company and opened a whole bunch of shell journals, offering very rapid turn-around of peer review'. As a non-profit, AJOL is committed to its public-good business model.

Despite its invaluable 'capacity-building' role, AJOL's challenge is knowing how to respond to the rise of commercial open-access academic publishing initiatives. Some AJOL stakeholders are wary of charging journals for its services, even though this would provide a sustainable income source for AJOL to support its provision of training, web-hosting and accreditation. For the same reason, AJOL does not recommend journals to rely on APCs as an open-access business model, because this potentially excludes submissions from students and those with the lowest incomes such as early career researchers, as well as those without research funding. Yet without an income stream, journals remain dependent on subsidies from scholarly societies or host universities. This 'diamond' open-access model is more realistic in well-resourced university systems, but not necessarily easy in many African countries. Meanwhile, AJOL encourages journals to develop relationships with their host universities, ensuring that libraries and research offices are aware of their existence, and maximising institutional backing and support.

Towards an African 'knowledge commons?

In his critique of the new politics of journal publishing, Striphas (2010) identifies five major trends that have reshaped the economics of the industry: alienation, proliferation, consolidation, pricing and digitisation. Since 2010, the dynamics of capital accumulation and speed of change have been even more acute, while academic boycotts (such as that of Elsevier) have had relatively little impact on the publishing economy as a whole.

Thornton and Ocasio (1999) track a gradual shift from the dominance of an 'editorial logic' to a 'market logic' in US academic publishing over the second half of the twentieth century. The first sees publishing as a scholarly profession, with legitimacy generated by an editor's reputation, and growth coming from their personal networks, with prestige more important than profit. The second sees publishing as a business, with the aim being to increase profits and market value. The values of most Ghanaian journals we review are largely still orientated to this earlier institutional logic, with editors motivated by professionalism and a sense of disciplinary service.

What does the future hold for these institutional journals? All five face the same dilemma: the largely unrecognised and unrewarded nature of editorial labour. Whether long-established or recently launched, editors described how they had to constantly work to attract high-quality submissions, ensure peer reviewers provided timely and useful comments, and meet the relentless deadlines of a publication schedule and make the finances work. None of this is unique to Ghana. Across Africa and much of the global South, under-resourced scholarly journals face similar challenges. Unlike their often wealthy scholarly associations and societies of Euro-America that own profitable journals that are published on their behalf, the Ghanaian scholars we spoke to are all curating academic knowledge on a shoe-string. Academics are already stretched, the work of peer review is rarely a top priority, and international visibility matters. In the face of the global consolidation of the publishing industry, the dominance of a few major international conglomerates (Mirowski 2019; Posada and Chen 2018), and a continuing shift from an 'editorial logic' to a 'commercial logic' (Thornton and Ocasio 1999), there are many struggles ahead.

One consequence of the new publishing temporality is that it reduces the desirability of long-established 'scholar-led' journals based in Ghana, which are often reliant on volunteer editors and non-existent budgets. Researchers instead gravitate towards more commercially orientated journals that promise an efficient approach to publishing.

Journal reputation is increasingly measured by its impact factor, which in turn is determined by inclusion in journal databases and citation indexes. A venerable Ghanaian journal that once had an enviable reputation amongst a disciplinary community of peers can gradually become invisible to a new generation of scholars attuned to impact factors and global visibility. Ghana has three journals listed in Elsevier's Scopus database – the *Ghana Medical Journal, African Review of Physics* and the *West African Journal of Applied Ecology*. The first is backed by the Ghana Medical Association, the second is published with the editorial backing of the Italian Centre of Theoretical Physics, and the third is long established, and financially supported by the University of Ghana. They are all in the third or fourth quartile of their fields, with low citation rates of less than one per paper. Only six Ghana-published journals are indexed in DOAJ, the world's main open-access journal index, including four published by two small commercial publishers in Accra. None of the five journals profiled in this chapter were indexed in either DOAJ or Scopus in 2020.

Meanwhile, the shift to digital publishing creates new technical and logistical challenges. Whilst open-source OJS (Open Journal Software) provides an off-the-peg model for journal production, there are many other skills that publishing requires, including use of editorial distribution, marketing, and publicity. These are services that commercially minded publishers, platforms and content aggregators can now provide. Developing an income stream by combining affordable APCs with the income from commercial journal distributors (such as Project Muse and JSTOR) requires professional knowledge and a publishing infrastructure unavailable to small publishers.

Some respondents were aware of these pressures on what they called 'local journals'. In the words of Kwaku, a UDS social science lecturer, 'African universities should develop local journals and try to accept publications from local people because we are familiar with our own issues, we need to indigenise knowledge'. He went on to highlight how international journals might 'doubt the authenticity' of the data, or that some of the 'research might not be applicable to them'. But his was a dissenting voice, and few spoke up for the importance of this local knowledge ecosystem. As Nolte (2019, 305) notes, there is a double burden of expectation placed on African scholars, both to publish in both 'local' and 'international' journals (in Nigerian parlance 'onshore' and 'offshore'), and to negotiate the 'different discourses and publishing paradigms' each require.

Can this diverse mosaic of institutional and university journals, often reliant on volunteers and a strong sense of academic service, continue in the face of the promises of rapid publishing offered by commercial open-access publishers or the reputational imprimatur provided by the global conglomerates such as Elsevier or Taylor and Francis? Is there an opportunity for university-hosted journals to develop more inclusive 'diamond' open-access models based on library funding, contributing to what Luescher and Van Schalkwyk (2018) call the 'logic of the knowledge commons'? Or will these institutional initiatives be overshadowed by independent publishers that are better resourced and more able to pursue a commercial and 'market-led' strategy? The rise of independent academic publishers across West Africa and beyond is the subject of the next chapter.

Chapter 8

Independent academic publishing in Anglophone Africa

The Nigerian publishing industry is very conservative, and it is influenced by a colonial mentality. The Nigerian universities will insist on the publication being in a London or Oxford press for their faculty to be promoted. This is the battle we have. I am trying to make them understand that there could be a local journal with an opportunity. If there is a requirement for publication, it doesn't have to be a traditional journal. (Editor, *Education and Entrepreneurship*)

Most people who have published in our journals have been promoted. So, we have contributed to making somebody, somebody. (Editor-in-chief, ADRRI journals)

Introduction

In 1982, the Institute of African Studies at the University of Ghana published volume 10, issue 1 of its flagship journal, *Research Review*. As the journal was launched in 1964, the tenth volume was meant to have come out in 1974. Political instability and economic crisis meant that the volume had been delayed by almost a decade. The front cover for the issue had already been printed, and rather than be wasted, it was reused, with the numerals 1974 blacked out and the revised 1982 publication date printed alongside. The journal editorial included a curt comment that timely publication had, 'for several reasons', not been possible. The travails of the intervening years did not need to be spelt out.

Many have documented the demise of Africa's commercial publishers during the 1970s and 1980s, and the consequences for the scholarly ecosystem. Paper shortages, distribution challenges and fragmented markets all took their toll. Many of the scholarly journals set up in the 1960s and 1970s closed, and university presses fell silent. The journals and publishers that remained struggled to cover the costs of printing and distribution, and relied heavily on the dedication of their editors and reviewers. Many writers and scholars resorted to self-publishing (Umezurike 201;, Nolte 2019).

There has been a slow re-emergence of independent Africa-based academic journal publishers over the last 20 years. The first green shoots of recovery were visible in the 1990s as higher education once again became a priority for African governments, the World Bank and international donors. The African Books Collective was launched as a self-help network for African publishers in 1989 and the donor-funded African Journals Online (AJOL) database began its work in 1998. During the 1990s, US philanthropy once again started funding Africa's research universities (Jaumont 2015) and a range of university 'capacity-building' initiatives (Mills 2004).

The millennium marked a digital watershed, when new software technologies and the internet seemed to disrupt every aspect of academic publishing. As part of a growing movement to 'open access' to scholarly knowledge, the first open-source publishing software – Open Journals Systems (OJS) – was launched in 2001, simplifying the editorial and publishing workflow. The potential to publish journals online transformed the economics of journal publishing, removing the costs of printing and distributing paper copies. These changes opened up the possibility of a model of community ownership of journals, a move championed by many in the open access movement. The internet also offered new sources of revenue, and entrepreneurial academics across Africa and beyond saw this as an opportunity to launch new online journals and create independent publishing houses. Yet Darko-

Ampem's 2004 review of six African university presses highlighted just how little they had adapted to these new conditions, and increasingly only focused on undergraduate textbooks (Darko-Ampem 2005). With very few exceptions, the state of African university presses continued to worsen, and Luescher and van Schalkywk (2018) found only 15 of 52 university presses still active. Of these, only one relatively new press – that of Wollega University in Ethiopia – was actively committed to promoting a 'knowledge commons' through university subsidy, commitment to sustainable open access, to supporting the local scholarly ecosystem, publishing a widely indexed, multidisciplinary journal, with several more journals planned.

This chapter profiles a spectrum of independent publishers from across anglophone Africa, analysing their emergence and position within different national and regional research ecosystems. Some are run as NGOs, others as companies. A few have developed a commercially successful publishing model; others sustain single journal 'brands'. They occupy very different positions in the African research and publishing ecosystem, depending on the academic fields and communities they serve. Nearly all have adopted an open-access publishing model, with journals charging article processing charges, in some cases supplemented by other income streams. Five are Africa-based. One is a pioneering non-profit Kenya-based agricultural journal, whilst the other four publish journals across a range of disciplines from South Africa, Ghana, and Nigeria. As a contrast, Hindawi provides a very different final case. Founded in Egypt but now based in London, Hindawi now has a global profile, a turnover of USD 30 million per year, and in January 2021 was acquired by Wiley.

Interviews with the founders of these presses inform this analysis. Each had their own 'start-up' story, creating their own niches in national, regional, and international publishing ecosystems. Along with struggles to gain accreditation, they reflect on the tensions of developing an international profile whilst also building capacity within their particular fields and host countries.

The chapter ends with a comparative analysis of their different business and editorial models, their models of attracting submissions, and gaining reputation within an international 'credibility economy'. It asks whether this diversification of options benefits African scholarship, the potential for a non-profit publishing commons in a resource-constrained environment, and explores the future of Africa's academic publishing economy with the growth of open science and the move to online journal platforms.

Jamal Mohammed and ADRRI

African journals are scarce on DOAJ, the Swedish-based Directory of Open Access Journals, and the main global directory for open-access journals. In 2020, only six Ghanaian OA journals were listed, along with 15 from Nigeria, six from Ethiopia, and seven from Kenya). Of the six Ghanaian journals, three were published by ADDRI (Africa Development and Resources Research Institute), a small NGO based in Koforidua, Eastern Ghana, founded by Jamal Mohammed, senior lecturer at Koforidua Technical University.

Jamal Mohammed began his academic career as a teacher in Ghana's Northern Region before doing a PhD at KNUST in economics, researching the micro-entrepreneurial practices of urban fuelwood sellers. After taking up an academic post he set up ADRRI as an NGO in Koforidua. It began by offering a range of development research and consultancy services, such as a 'community barometer' for people to report issues of concern.

Jamal launched the first ADRRI journal in 2014, with three further journals in 2015 and 2016. Jamal had been trained by African Journals Online (AJOL) as part of its GhanJol initiative, which aimed to create a portal for Ghana's open-access journals. He quickly picked up the requisite technical and organisational skills that publishing demanded. Initially using WordPress, he later moved to using OJS. He recognised the importance of 'carving out a niche' and a reputation for quality, transparency, and openness; all requirements set down by the indexing services. Whilst early issues were published monthly, he explained that he had now moved to a quarterly publishing cycle to allow more time for review.

Key to ADRRI's success was getting its journals indexed in the non-profit DOAJ. In 2022, however, the ADDRI journals were removed from DOAJ. DOAJ indexes journal abstracts and metadata from more than 12,000 OA journals across the world. Being indexed becomes a key marker of the journal's scientific legitimacy and quality. Any open-access journal can apply for inclusion, but the process is slow and vetting is thorough.

Jamal is editor-in-chief of four of ADRRI's journals, and the deputy editor is also an employee of ADRRI. Whilst reviewers are listed as members of the boards (some of whom are based in India), final decisions are made by Jamal and an internal editorial team. *ADRRI Arts and Sciences Journal* (which 'seeks to provoke scholarly writings and publication in academia and industry in a wide area of specialisation') publishes 3-6 articles in each issue on a wide range of topics, all of which are very applied and focus on Ghanaian issues. There is no sense of focus or dialogue. Its profile is very similar to *ADRRI Journal (Multidisciplinary)*. The two other journals, *ADRRI Agriculture and Food Sciences* and *ADRRI Journal of Engineering and Technology,* have a more specific subject focus, but publish more irregularly, and most issues have only one article.

The home page for ADDRI's journals gives a sense of the breadth of work they publish, including

All aspects of the environmental, labour economics, economics in general, gender studies, child rights, social, and cultural sustainability, including land resources, water resources, energy, agriculture, marine resources, ecology, environmental protection, health risks, education, human relations, labour, social policy, corporate responsibility, law, governance, urban planning, transportation, products and services, management, marketing & financial development, economic development, technological development, public policy formulation, engineering, water, trade, medicine, nutrition, management and marketing, poverty, political science, entrepreneurship, mathematics, statistics, actuarial science, sociology, procurement, supply chain, English, art, accounting, fashion and design, ceramics and so on.

ADRRI's journals are published using OJS (Open Journal Software) and Jamal employs five technical faculty and two content proof-readers. OJS provides users with citation data so they can monitor the impact of the journal. He makes sure that any reviewers listed on the journal's site are actively involved in reviewing, and he removes 'dormant' names. He admits the production quality is 'not perfect but we are working on it'. After three years of not charging any processing fees, the journals began charging USD 50 'donations' or 'subscriptions' for Ghanaian researchers (and double that for international authors), as the term APC is associated by many with 'predatory' publishing. They started by making these donations voluntary, but many only offered small sums. They regularly grant waivers, especially to the faculty of Koforidua Technical University. ADRRI do not actively solicit submissions but rely on word-of-mouth recommendations.

Jamal admitted to communicating with Jeffrey Beall in 2014 after an ADDRI journal was added to Beall's list. After showing Beall his publication processes, the journal was removed. 'We passed his mark and I felt the impact.' Jamal went on to note that, 'indexing is good … there should always be a watchman checking what we do'. Having DOAJ accreditation, even briefly, helped raise the profile of the publisher, but the future is now uncertain. Whilst perhaps 80% of submissions are from Ghana, a few submissions come across Africa and beyond. Jamal's ambition is to get his journals listed in Scopus, and to 'become a household name'. This will involve meeting demanding Scopus metrics and benchmarks, including the geographical diversity of authorship and the editorial board, and a five year publication record. There are also technical hoops to negotiate, including stable web-based archiving, and membership of Crossref, the publishing organisation that issues the unique numerical identifiers (called DOIs – digital object identifiers) that every published journal now has.

Jamal described how 'Ghanaian research' was different from work carried out in the Global North: 'The things we write are at the micro level compared to research in the UK and Europe; these problems are localised and specific'. This is evident in the diversity of topics covered within the journals. Being included in DOAJ did lead to further interest from authors, and in the last quarter of 2020, ADDRI received 80 submissions, with 26 published in the journals.

Jamal is also Director of Research at Koforidua Technical University and has put his commercial publishing experience to good use in strengthening the quality of the university's journal, the *International Journal of Technology and Management Research*. He recalls a meeting with one senior professor who announced at a workshop that, 'this journal is credible even if not in Elsevier'. His analysis showed that most ADRRI authors have been promoted, and so we 'have contributed to making somebody, somebody'. Like other editors interviewed for this project, Jamal was proud of his achievements, and 'slept soundly' knowing that he had contributed to knowledge production.

Imhotep Paul Alagidede and the *Ghanaian Journal of Economics* (GHE)

Imhotep Paul Alagidede is a Ghanaian-born professor of finance at the University of Witwatersrand (South Africa). Schooled in Ghana and at KNUST, he left to study for his PhD in Economics at Loughborough University (UK). After holding teaching posts in the UK, he moved to South Africa to build his academic career. In what is a common lament amongst African researchers, Paul had been frustrated by the lack of opportunities to publish African content in UK journals, with his work being rejected as too 'specialised'. He currently runs a consultancy company in Johannesburg as well as publishing the *Ghanaian Journal of Economics* from South Africa.

His first journal – the *African Review of Economics and Finance* (AREF) – was set up in 2009 whilst he was teaching at Stirling University in the UK. On taking up a lectureship at the University of the Witwatersrand in South Africa, Paul also founded AREF Consult, a Johannesburg-based consultancy company to support the journal and to provide consultancy advice, forecasting tools and training.

African Review of Economics and Finance styles itself as the 'leading peer-reviewed journal of African economics, economies, and finance'. It publishes two open-access issues a year, with between six and ten articles. Most speak to contemporary debates in African political economy, with a particular focus on South Africa, Eswatini, and the SADC region. AREF provides detailed download data on its site, makes no charge for publication, and promises to return reviewers' comments within six weeks of submission. Currently under the editorship of Dr Franklin Obeng-Odoom, a 2019 editorial reviewed the first ten years of the journal's commitment to publishing Afrocentric analysis, and its growing international reputation (Obeng-Odoom et al. 2019). Accredited by the South African DHET (Department of Higher Education and Training) and the Australian Business Dean's Council, the journal's finances depend on a subsidy from the University of Witwatersrand and on income generated by its annual conference and article downloads. It is now published by Porthologos Press, the publishing wing of the Nile Valley Mulitiversity.

Paul founded the *Ghanaian Journal of Economics* (GJE) a few years later in 2013, partly to ensure that AREF was not dominated by the Ghanaian researchers across Africa and in the diaspora. Published by AFEC in South Africa but with links to the department of Economics at the University of Ghana, he continues to act as editor-in-chief. The journal is dedicated to publishing 'cutting-edge' academic and policy research, and publishes one issue per year, with papers focusing on Ghanaian economics, finance, and development issues. The journal is hosted on Sabinet, a for-profit South African information services and library 'solutions' provider set up in the mid-1970s. Sabinet hosts more than 500 journals, as well as providing a range of other products for libraries, a news service, and legal databases. GJE's articles are not free to access, and universities can subscribe to either a specific journal or a collection. Others are charged USD 40 to access each journal article. Sabinet gives journals 80% of these sales revenues.

GJE does not charge APCs to its authors. Paul argues that 'APCs corrupt this process ... it becomes more about the bottom line. That's why we have these predatory journals'. The journal receives some financial support from the University of Witwatersrand and a share of the income from articles sold via Sabinet. The board has discussed whether South African authors – who receive a university subsidy for publishing – should be charged to publish with GJE, but so far this idea has been rejected. According to Paul, the journal receives approximately 100 submissions per year, of which up to ten are accepted. Ninety per cent of authors are Ghana-based, but 99% of reviewers are from outside Ghana. For Paul 'Ghanaian reviewers can be too slow, and often fussy, so we don't ask them'. He is frank about the importance of reviewing as a form of collaborative work, a contribution to the discipline, and a developmental exercise: 'When I was young, I rejected a lot of articles.'

When AREF hosted its annual conference in Ghana, Ghana's scholars had to be 'begged to come', because they wanted to use their conference grants to travel abroad rather than attend a 'local' conference. One of Paul's many ambitions is to relaunch the Ghanaian Association of Economics that fell into abeyance in the 1980s. However, he is aware that if he applies for a job in Ghana, 'you start at the bottom, so that's not something I want to do'.

As with AREF, there is a strong focus on mentorship in GJE, and the journal relies on young academics to conduct peer review. Papers on Ghanaian topics are often directed to GJE, even though Ghanaian-based authors would rather publish in AREF because of its perceived 'international' reputation. We asked Paul about his choice of title for the journal, and his response was forthright: 'I was very determined to keep the term' he explained. 'It is about the scientific merit of the field, we wanted to strengthen Ghanaian Economics: there is an American Economics Research journal so why not one for Ghana?'

Despite being published in South Africa, GJE has, to date, not been registered and accredited by the South African DHET. Although the journal is hosted by the University of Witwatersrand, it is perceived as having a Ghanaian focus. South African scholars who publish in GJE therefore do not receive extra funding for their publication.

Paul has also faced the challenge of ensuring GJE is accredited by other relevant indexes, such as the Australian Association of Business

Schools: 'I don't know what they want, but it makes us want to find out'. Whilst hesitant to talk about discrimination by these indexes, Paul was very clear about the importance of 'African-focused reviewing systems' and an 'Africa-centred model of quality' that supported the 'African research agenda', whilst keeping in mind the 'uniqueness of the challenges Africa faces'.

How do the two publishing initiatives compare? Whilst both rely on entrepreneurial founders, the journals published by ADRRI are at a much earlier stage than AREF, publishing work at a very different level, with different standards and a different audience. This reflects the journals' different constituencies and reputations. An international community of African scholars – including a large community of diaspora Ghanaians – publish in GJE and AREF. Both of these journals publish work in African political economy, ensuring a clear focus and remit. ADRRI's journals are much more inclusive, catering for Ghanaian researchers at Koforidua, especially those new to publishing and the expectations of an emerging research ecosystem.

There are several other examples of successful African academic publishing houses set up by diaspora-based African scholars. One is Abbey and Adonis publishers, established in London and incorporated as a UK company in 2003. It was founded by Professor Jideofor Adibe, professor of political science at Nasarawa State University (Nigeria), who also was the founding editor of its longest-running journal *African Renaissance,* and the founder of an online Nigerian news site called *The News Chronicle.*

Abbey and Adonis set out, in its own words, to 'address the problem of the high mortality rate of academic journals published by Africans, and to let African scholars set and own their research agendas'. As well as having published more than 160 books, it oversees a stable of subscription-only journals, with editors based at African universities. Espousing a strong pan-African vision, only three of the 16 journal editors are Nigerian, and none are based in Nigeria.

Eight Abbey and Adonis journals have been listed in the IBSS database and four are in Scopus (almost equal to all the Ghana-based journals currently in Scopus). Adonis and Abbey have been very successful in marketing their journals through a range of regional and global journal aggregators and subscription platforms, including Sabinet, JSTOR, ABDC and ProQuest.

The success of Adonis and Abbey at getting its journals into the Scopus index, and of ADRRI in being included within the DOAJ directory, is a reflection of the slow and painstaking work of reputation building, and underscores the gatekeeping role of the international indexes and databases. It contrasts with the difficulties GJE has faced with getting indexed by DHET and by some disciplinary indexing services. The comparison highlights the discipline- and country-specific nature of debates around journal authenticity and legitimacy, and the different gatekeeping roles played by indexes.

Ruth Oniang'o and the *African Journal of Food, Agriculture, Nutrition and Development* (AJFAND)

There are many different routes an ambitious editor or publisher can adopt in creating new research communities through journal publishing. One is to steadily build the reputation of a single journal, and the other is to nurture a stable of sister journals. The first is the path adopted by the Kenya-based *African Journal of Food, Agriculture, Nutrition and Development* (AJFAND) set up by Professor Ruth Oniang'o as a non-profit publishing initiative, and now a Scopus-listed journal.

On completing her PhD at the University of Nairobi in 1982, Ruth Oniang'o took up a professorship at Jomo Kenyatta University. She founded an NGO, the Rural Outreach Programme in 1992, in order to 'make an impact on the ground', as she put it, and to influence Kenyan policy debates around malnutrition. The idea to set up a journal came later. She realised her colleagues were not publishing, and also encountered 'problems in publishing my own work'. She began to wondered if Kenya-based work was just not seen as relevant to 'international audiences'. Inspired by a friend who had also started the *Asian Pacific Journal of Nutrition*, the first issue of AJFAND came out in 2001, initially in print only.

With a room in her house given over to a fledgling team of administrators and student interns, the demands of print publishing proved overwhelming. As she recalls: 'For the third issue, we stayed in office until midnight, and when the print came out there was a mistake in the title, and I thought I am not going to do this anymore.' Faced with a lack of resources for printing and distribution, AJFAND took a 'leap of faith' and became an open-access online journal in 2005 (Oniang'o 2005) with funding from a range of European sources, including the Nestlé foundation, GIZ and a Belgian nutrition programme. Initially it was hosted on the Bioline International platform and benefitted from Bioline's expertise in supporting journals in the Global South. Bioline International was a pioneering not-for-profit open science journal aggregator platform set up in 1993. The inspiration of a UK microbiologist called Barbara Kirsop, the platform was later supported by the Electronic Publishing Trust for Development, a UK registered charity focused on providing access to scientific research from the developing world (Canhos et al. 2001). Looking back, Ruth reflected on the *East African Medical Journal*, first established in 1923: 'They were sitting there and were being our father, and we went online before them.'

Today, AJFAND is a peer-reviewed, open-source journal published in Kenya by the Africa Scholarly Science Communications Trust (ASSCAT), a not-for-profit established by Ruth in 2009. The administrative costs of the journal are partly covered by grants awarded to the Trust for consultancy research around food policy work. Ruth currently chairs Kenya's Food Security and Nutrition Taskforce, helping to develop a national nutrition strategy. She also sits on a range of high-profile international advisory boards.

AJFAND covers a wide range of scientific and development disciplines, including agriculture, food, nutrition, environmental management, and sustainable development, with a strong focus on research policy. It publishes a diverse mix of original research and brings together information on agricultural technologies. AJFAND is one of only six Kenyan journals to be indexed in Scopus, finally achieving accreditation in 2016, but not before Ruth was forced to travel to the US to meet an Elsevier representative to push for inclusion. She rebuffs suggestions that 'African' in the title was part of the problem, saying to her students 'aren't you proud to be African?'.

Starting out with 14 articles in the inaugural 2001 issue, AJFAND expanded to publishing six or more issues a year (the record was 11 issues in 2011), with between 15 and 20 original research articles in each (one issue included 29 articles). In 2020, 97 articles were published in six issues. Most authors are not Kenya-based, and AJFAND is open to both African and non-African contributors. Ruth takes pride in the success of her authors, seeing the journal as 'her baby'.

The initial business model relied heavily on volunteer labour and student interns. In 2015 AJFAND began to charge an APC of USD 500, with waivers and reductions for those unable to afford the full fees. In some cases, students publish with more established internationally based scholars. She describes how she has resisted offers from UK and US publishers. For Ruth it is a point of pride that AJFAND is managed from Africa and supports the building of African research capacity within the field of nutrition studies. The journal continues to offer unpaid internships to students in nutrition, mentoring their first publications, profiling them in the journal, and encouraging their academic careers. This sentiment is reflected on AJFAND's website and its emphasis on capacity strengthening through training, workshops, and student internships.

As editor-in-chief, Ruth acknowledges her reliance on a 'huge network' of more than 200 peer reviewers around the world, built up during a long and varied career as a nutrition activist and politician (she was a member of the Kenyan parliament for four years). In each issue two peer reviewers are publicly profiled as a way to acknowledge their work and contribution. The journal's editorial board consists of 23 academics, most based in Africa, and five in Kenya. She describes herself as 'captain of the ship' and is very reliant on her 'crew', from the journal administrator down to 'technical reviewers' and copy-editing faculty. She estimates that around 40% of the articles do not make it through the review process and admits to personally checking 80 to 100 papers each year before they are published. When authors complain that the peer-review process takes too long, Ruth advises them to stick with the process, and reassures them that they will be happy with the outcome. Authors who ignore suggestions have their papers rejected.

Despite its international recognition, worries about financial sustainability and reputation continue. Ruth is constantly seeking to develop ways to assure its quality. Recent initiatives include the purchase of DOI identifiers and the introduction of plagiarism checking. Her long-term ambition is to seek out a commercial partner willing to invest further funding. She has continued to sustain links with Professor Leslie Chan based at the University of Toronto, the founder of Bioline and a leading open science advocate (Chan and Costa 2005; Chan et al. 2011). Like many other publishing initiatives in the Global South, the journal has benefitted from the mentoring advice and quality assurance support offered by the Toronto Centre for Science and Development, and Chan's Knowledge Gap project.

Nyerhovwo Tonukari and Academic Journals

The career of the Nigerian biotechnology researcher Professor Nyerhovwo Tonukari illustrates the potential for commercial publishers. Starting out with one initial journal in 2002 – the *African Journal of Biotechnology* – he set up a company called Academic Journals that today publishes more than 120 journals (Tonukari 2004, 2018). In the interview Tonukari recalls how the library at his Nigerian secondary school became his second home, and that his undergraduate lecturers at Maiduguri would rely on him to find books for them, and how as a master's student at Ibadan he would travel 80 miles to Lagos in order to access journal abstracts from the British Consulate. Enrolling at Michigan State University to pursue his PhD in 1996, he was particularly shocked at the lack of African journals (personal communication 2020). Aware of the emergence of e-publishing at that time, Nyerhovwo learnt to build a website and began to think about starting a journal. Appointed to a postdoctoral position in animal vaccine research in Nairobi, he reached out to all his contacts, and asked them to submit articles.

He launched the *African Journal of Biotechnology* in 2002 as an open-access journal that promised 'rapid (monthly) publication of papers on biotechnology and applied molecular biology' (Tonukari 2004, 124). At this early point, it defined its 'greatest appeal' as this 'speed of publication', aiming to 'provide the most rapid turnaround possible for reviewing and publishing' (Smart et al. 2005, 334). At that point few publishers had experimented with online-only open-access publishing, and the formula was appealing to African researchers. The founder's pan-African vision was to promote 'research and researchers from Africa and to make published articles from Africa free and easily accessible to the global research community'.

On his return to Nigeria, Nyerhovwo continued to publish the journal, initially from the garage of his home in Abraka, Nigeria. Like most start-ups, it relied on free labour and time. Working together with his wife and a small team, they worked long days to market the journal, attract submissions, and manage the editorial workflow. The journal was published on its own website, but also initially hosted on the pioneering Bioline International journal portal, as well as being promoted by INASP (Tonukari 2004, 125).

African Journal of Biotechnology published 145 articles in 12 issues during 2003, of which around a third were by Nigerian academics, 10% from US scholars, 10% by Egyptian researchers, and the rest from around 15 other countries (including Germany, Senegal, South Africa and Japan). With an international editorial board, and around 10,000 page views a month, the journal was already highly successful. In 2005, the journal published 284 articles in a further 12 issues. The company launched six further life-science journals in 2006, and then continued to expand rapidly, adopting new software. Responding to growing demand from authors, in one year alone (2009) it launched 50 journals. By 2011 Academic Journals was employing 120 staff and publishing 107 journals.

Nyerhovwo introduced in-house manuscript management software and automated online payment systems to manage this growth and introduce administrative efficiencies, as well as building a publishing portal. Then came the company's inclusion on a blog list of 'predatory open access publishers' maintained by the University of Colorado data librarian, Jeffrey Beall (2011). Rapid expansion led Beall to accuse the company of taking shortcuts with editorial quality. This had a major impact, and many faculty were laid off as submissions suddenly declined. Despite making a detailed appeal, Beall refused to remove the company from his list.

To date, Academic Journals continues to rebuff the accusation that it is engaged in predatory publishing. Its website is very open about its Beall's listing and its 2014 appeal. A statement from the publisher questions the sincerity of the list and suggests that it is biased against 'open-access' publications. Instead, it calls for a 'fair, transparent and rigorous evaluation of all our activities'. The journal marketing no longer makes mention of rapid publication, but instead describes its role as 'accelerating the dissemination of knowledge'.

Academic Journals has a well-designed journal platform, and of the approximately 120 journals it currently publishes, around half are in the life sciences. Twenty-three have the word 'international' and 20 feature 'African' in the title, highlighting the pan-African ambition and envisioned readership of the journals. Most of the remaining 76 are focused on particular areas of science, such as the *Journal of Plant Breeding and Crop Science*. The publisher's 'author-pays' business model relies on payment of a 'handling fee' (or APC) of around USD 500 once an article is accepted for publication. Full or partial waivers are generally granted to authors from low-income countries. Submissions and downloads continue to grow, and in recent years the company has acquired new journals associated with Nigerian institutions and associations. The company is also in talks to acquire other existing Ghanaian journals.

The journals attract submissions from across the world. Of the roughly 4,300 submissions received by the *African Journal of Agricultural Research* over five years, only 10% were from Nigeria; 25% were from Ethiopia, 25% were from Brazil and around 20% were from the rest of Africa. The website provides article read and download data. The company estimates that around 70% of their articles are cited, that the first Academic Journals journal now has 160,000 citations, and that 4.5 million articles were downloaded from the site in 2019. Google Scholar data shows that one article published in the *African Journal of Biotechnology* in 2005 entitled 'Phytochemical constituents of some Nigerian medicinal plants' (Edeoga et al. 2005) has been cited more than 3,100 times. Meanwhile, the journal has now published more than 12,000 articles. The University of Ghana library includes Academic Journals in its list of journal portals. It continues to add new journals to its portfolio, including several published by Nigerian professional associations. The *African Journal of Medical and Health Sciences* (AJMHS) was added in 2017, while the *Journal of the Nigeria Society of Physiotherapy* (JNSP) was added in 2020.

Most serials in the Academic Journals stable are focused on the sciences and medicine, but around 15 are in the applied social sciences (with a focus on marketing and management), along with ten in the arts and education. Examples include the *International Journal of Sociology and Anthropology*, *Education Research and Reviews* and the *International Journal of Education Administration and Policy Studies*. At least 50% of submissions are from Africa-based researchers. In some cases, these journals publish empirical research on a wide range of topics that are sometimes only tangentially connected to the disciplinary titles. For most academic journals there is no one named editor, but rather a relatively large editorial board who read submissions and make recommendations to the editorial advisors based in the company's central administration.

Pierre de Villiers and AOSIS

Pierre de Villiers founded AOSIS in 1999 to develop e-learning continual professional development (CPD) modules for South African doctors. As a professor of family medicine with a background in private practice, he saw opportunities for professional development materials online. He was also editor of the *South African Journal of Family Practice* that was sent as a membership benefit to GPs. Funded primarily by pharmaceutical adverts, the journal's research profile was weak, and few GPs read the journal. Seizing the opportunities offered by digital open- access publishing, he used OJS software to publish an online issue of the journal which could be downloaded for free. The site and its bronze OA model attracted the attention of INASP, and Pierre was invited to speak to a large gathering of other journal editors at the Academy of Science of South Africa (ASSAf).

This led to a series of enquiries from other editors who wanted to be relieved of publishing tasks, and in 2008, the scholarly publishing arm of AOSIS was launched. *Koedoe: African Protected Area Conservation and Science* was its first acquisition. Originally founded in 1958 and previously published by the government park service, AOSIS took the journal open access. The journal continued to thrive, and in 2013 it was given a Clarivate JCI impact factor, with 196,000 article downloads in 2019 (Foxcroft 2020). AOSIS began to seek out other such journals, as well as new and emerging disciplinary 'niches', and always works closely with journal editors. In 2022, AOSIS published 47 open-access journals as well as open-access books and CPD provision for the health professions. Several, including three theology journals, publish in English and Afrikaans, sustaining a multilingual profile.

Initially, each journal's institutional sponsor covered the publishing costs, but quickly all AOSIS journals moved to charging APCs. This decision made the most of the subsidy culture within the South African research ecosystem, where since 1986 universities receive DHET (Department of Higher Education and Training) funding for each article published in accredited journals. As a consequence, many South African universities offer faculty financial incentives for publishing in these outlets. This creates a publishing culture and ensures there is funding in the system to cover APCs. Some universities pay this subvention directly to authors, but others, including UCT and Wits, direct these funds into research support. On average AOSIS charges between ZAR 700 and ZAR 1900 per page (USD 45 and USD 125) for journals accredited by DHET or other DHET-approved journal indexes. In the period 2005-2017, 133 AOSIS publications were submitted to DHET for funding. Whilst this is only 10% of those published by Taylor and Francis, it is comparable to the 187 published by Unisa, the largest South African university press, set up in 1956.

Over the years, DHET has also sought to monitor attempts by South

African academics to 'game' the subsidy system through individual journals 'over-publishing' their editors and certain authors (Biagioli and Lippman 2020). Tomaselli (2019) vividly depicts the 'perverse incentive' and distorted 'rent-seeking' that this subsidy system creates, arguing that this commodifies research and turns journals into 'cash cows' for publishers. Regular and detailed evaluations of the quality of the South African science system (e.g. ASSAf 2019; Mouton et al. 2019; Mouton and Valentine 2017) as well as disciplinary level evaluations (Assaf 2020) scrutinise publishing practices and identify journals that are not suitable to be accredited by DHET.

In his mea-culpa admission to publishing articles in journals that were subsequently delisted by DHET and accused of being predatory (Naidu and Dell 2019), Maistry (2019) points to the complicity and culpability of universities and regulators in what he called the 'neoliberal university'. Le Grange (2019) complicates this story even further, showing how the publisher in question (KRE – Kamla Raj Enterprises) was seen as sufficiently reputable for the Taylor and Francis publishing group to enter into a publishing relationship with it in 2017. Le Grange argues that attempting to classify journals is a category error, and that the focus should be on the quality of the contents, not the 'container'. He also points to the inadequacies of peer review, and the ethical prerogative to do research that 'enhances life … rather than ensuring that research is metrically accurate' (Le Grange 2019, 310).

Key to the AOSIS financial model is journal accreditation, and this takes a minimum of four years. Each year applications to the South African DHET are declined, and the assessment process is not always transparent. In some cases, it is easier for the journal to seek accreditation with Scopus or WoS than with DHET. The model depends on ensuring support for the academic editors, avoiding publication delays, making sure that copy-editing, and proofreading are done to international standards, and on 'not trying to make excess profits'. They aim for a net profit margin of 10–20%.

Given the pressure on South African academics to publish in accredited journals, newer AOSIS journals without accreditation make no charge, as a way of attracting submissions and encouraging new journals. Support for new initiatives is seen as an upfront investment, given that costs are initially covered by the publisher. As Pierre pointed out in an interview, 'We have to carry the journal for at least four to five years: it is a very solid steady business, but it's a long-term business.' Pierre describes the editors as 'the engines of the journal', but that this cannot be a 'one-man show'. Instead, it has to be a team effort, creating a sense of partnership.

Pierre positions AOSIS not as a South African publisher, but as an African publisher with 'a mission to take African knowledge to the world'. This discourse of inclusion and African-centredness is attractive. In some journals a significant proportion of authors are affiliated to universities in other African countries in the region. Often these authors find the APCs prohibitive, and the company either grants APC waivers to researchers without institutional support or encourages them to collaborate with South African academics who can access university support. AOSIS sees its biggest competitor as the university-subsidised Unisa Press, which publishes a similar number of journals. However, AOSIS claims to be more able to 'scale up', both because of its independence and the economics of its business model.

The *Journal for Transdisciplinary Research* (otherwise known as TD) is an AOSIS-published journal set up by Johannes Tempelhof, an historian with a range of interdisciplinary interests. It was initially funded by his university but struggled to gain acceptance from his colleagues. After getting accredited by DHET, its reputation improved, especially amongst academics who felt marginalised in their fields. It fosters an 'open-ended' approach to looking at how sciences interact, and how different disciplinary methodologies could be put into dialogue. As Johannes puts it, 'TD is a window of opportunity to explore fields of knowledge, getting people without voice to have a voice ... empowering people at the grassroots.' Initially published in print, and then through Sabinet, which brought in some royalty income, TD joined AOSIS in 2017. It has one edition every year. Articles are published online once accepted, with around 16 articles in each issue.

Like most of the editors we spoke to, Johannes is committed to building capacity in his field, and working with authors to strengthen their submissions. There is a lot of interest from scholars in the region, partly because, as he put it, 'African journals are often very slow to publish, but TD can publish in two months'. Despite 'more and more African scholars coming in who aspire to publish', he also admitted to the challenge of ensuring quality. Less than 20% of manuscripts get accepted, and Johannes feels he is 'the old chief in the village,' supporting this new journal to mature and guiding 'a new generation to emerge'. He sees the importance of the community in creating a 'sense of vitality' to attract scholars who are 'capable and can help with decolonising education in South Africa'.

Ahmed Hindawi, Nagwa Abdel-Mottaleb and the global rise of Hindawi

The publishing house Hindawi was launched in Cairo in 1997 by Ahmed Hindawi and Nagwa Abdel-Mottaleb, a husband-and-wife team of scientists. They had been studying in the US, and working in the field of high energy physics, Ahmed had become interested in the potential of the internet for publishing and archiving. Determined to 'disrupt the scholarly communications universe' (Poynder 2012) by taking journals online, they used Egypt's low labour costs and a highly educated workforce to undercut existing publishers and transform the economics of science and medical publishing. Developing its own manuscript management system and publication platform, Hindawi expanded rapidly. Growing initially through acquisitions and journal launches, in 2003, Hindawi started experimenting with open-access publishing, partly in response to library funding cuts, journal consolidation, and the growing use of 'Big Deals' by other publishers (Peters 2007). Feeling that 'they did an excellent job in managing relationships with thousands of authors, editors and reviewers', Hindawi realised that open access played to their strengths, rather than dealing with libraries and building a sales force. They gradually converted all their subscription journals to an open-access model and launched a series of new open access journals. It decided to end all subscription-based publishing programmes in 2006, selling its remaining subscription journals to Oxford University Press (OUP), and in 2007 all 100 of its journals were published open access (Peters 2007). But the aim was not simply to grow the number of journals, but also the number of articles. In interview (Poynder 2012), Hindawi described how his goals for the company had been to reach '10 by 10' (i.e. 10,000 articles by 2010) and then 10 by 20 (10% of all articles published worldwide by 2020).

Hindawi has continued to champion the principles of open-access publishing and helped set up OASPA (Open Access Scholarly Publishers Association) to set standards for the industry. In 2018 it left the influential STM association, feeling that the transformation to open access had stalled. Some of Hindawi's journals were listed as predatory by Beall, but after an appeal this decision was rescinded, with Beall saying that this was a 'borderline case'. In 2012, the publisher recorded profits of USD 3 million dollars on a turnover of 6 million, suggesting a profit margin of more than 50%. The association of low-quality publishing with its base in Cairo may explain the company's move to London in 2016 (though the publishing administration continues in Cairo), and its work to rehabilitate its credibility. Hindawi has actively promoted itself as an ethical publisher, and its head of research integrity regularly blogs about predatory publishing and the importance of standards (Hodgkinson 2012, 2018). Hindawi now has a stable of more than 200 journals, and an annual turnover of almost USD 30 million, placing it in the global 'top-ten' of academic publishers by number of journals published (Johnson et al. 2018). In December 2020 it was acquired by Wiley, one of the 'big five', for USD 300 million.

Nearly all Hindawi's journals are in science, technology, and medicine. One of the few exceptions is *Education Research International* (ERI), a journal that 'considers scholarly, research-based articles on all aspects of education, aimed at facilitating the global exchange of education theory'. Its home page signals an acceptance rate of 17%, a time to decision of 45 days and an APC of USD 1,025. Articles are published online when ready and referenced as an annual volume (e.g. Volume 2013, Volume 2017, etc.), allowing rapid turnaround. Like all Hindawi journals, ERI is indexed in all the major indexing services.

Hindawi – like Academic Journals and other commercial open-access publishers – has moved away from an editor-led approach, and instead distributes responsibilities to large editorial boards. ERI has what seems to be a large editorial board with to around 50 editors, and no editor-in-chief. In Hindawi terms this is a small team: other Hindawi journals have up to 300 editors. Researchers can put their names forward to join editorial boards. Individual academic editors are designated for each paper, receive peer-review reports, and then make accept/reject decisions (Schneider 2016). Editors are also named at the top of the published article. Guest editors are invited to edit special issues as another way of recruiting authors. Hindawi's approach to proactively soliciting submissions and guest-edited special issues is a way for publishers to increase journal revenue, and this approach has been taken to an extreme by MDPI (Crossetto 2021).

ERI editors are based all over the world, including six in Taiwan and four in Spain. In 2022, ERI had only one Africa-based editor. Like many open-access journals, ERI has recently grown rapidly in size. From 2011 to 2017 it published around 30–35 articles a year. In 2022, it published 227 articles. In 2019, around half of the 30+ articles were from authors with affiliations in the US and Europe, and the other half were from other parts of the world (including researchers based in Kenya, Bangladesh, Ethiopia, Tanzania, India and Iran). A huge variety of topics are covered, from cultural attitudes, to infant mortality in Nigeria, to smartphone addiction among Mexican students. Authors from low-income countries (including all of sub-Saharan Africa) can obtain a 100% APC waiver, which explains the diversity of authorship.

The model of a generic open-access rapid-review journal is relatively new in the social sciences. Most existing scholarly journals have tended to have a more specialised remit and focus, with a hands-on editorial team providing editorial direction. This new model of a very large and distributed editorship is increasingly being adopted by challenger open-access publishers such as MDPI and Frontiers (Schneider 2016) as well as by Sage and Informa. MDPI and Frontiers have both expanded massively in recent years. MDPI is an interesting comparator to Hindawi. It published 37,000 articles in 2017, and

235,000 in 2021 (Crosetto 2021). Of its 74 journals with an impact factor, some are highly regarded, others less so, but all publish huge numbers of special issues, on average 100 a year for each journal. The journal *Sustainability* has 14 section editors and 2073 editorial board members.

The model relies on the devolution of editorial responsibilities to a large editorial board who gain recognition for their work. The juxtaposition of Hindawi with the other Africa-based publishers in this chapter is in many ways unfair, given the very different scale of their operations. However, the trajectory of Hindawi (and those of MDPI and Frontiers) reveals the potential for commercially orientated open-access publishers to scale up their operations in response to the growing demand for publishing opportunities, and the willingness of many academics and institutions to pay article processing charges.

New infrastructures, new publishing ecologies

The six case studies highlight the different trajectories of independent academic publishing in Africa. Operating across a range of scales and geographies, all make the most of open access and online publishing technologies, with business models built primarily around APCs. Most supplement this income by charging for other editorial services, or offering professional development opportunities, consultancy work, and running conferences. The two final case studies highlight the global market opportunities for ambitious open-access publishers, and the potential consolidation of the African academic ecosystem.

The contrast between the fortunes of these independent and often commercially orientated publishers and Ghana's institutional journals reviewed in Chapter 6 is marked. Rather than relying on voluntary labour or operating in a 'cashless' environment (Murray and Clobridge 2014), all six have made journal publishing financially viable. Hindawi has gone furthest, going from start-up to a highly profitable global operation (and its acquisition by Wiley) in little over two decades.

Several of the publishers interviewed described their initial motivation as one of making African scholarship accessible to the world. They had experienced having their own work rejected by elite journals and grappled with the perception that African research was seen as irrelevant to the interests of the 'high-impact' journals of the Global North (Beigel 2014; Collyer 2016). Three companies (including ADDRI, Academic Journals and Hindawi) rapidly expanded their journal portfolio, but then faced bruising encounters with integrity watchdogs such as Beall, as their journals were accused of 'predatory' publishing practices. They countered and appealed these decisions, with varying levels of success. As a result, each now has a different position within the academic 'credibility economy' (Shapin 1995), shaping their subsequent trajectory.

A key difference between the six cases is the role played by editorial boards, and the role played by chief editors in defining a distinctive remit for the journal. This more 'traditional' approach to journal editing is exemplified by Ruth in her leadership of AJFAND, and by Paul in his work setting up the *Ghana Journal of Economics*. This is also the model adopted by AOSIS, which seeks to work closely with scholarly editorial teams. With ADRRI, Academic Journals, and Hindawi, editorial decisions in response to peer review are either devolved to large editorial teams (Hindawi and Academic Journals) or made centrally by a core group (ADRRI). In this model, the direction of the journal is less dependent on the passion and commitment of one editor. Whilst this prevents a journal becoming 'captured' by a particular set of scholarly positions, it also makes it more difficult for the journal to take on a curatorial role, steering conversation and debate within a field. The journal instead takes on a new role, acting more as a repository and accreditation process for publications.

What does the future hold for this dynamic ecosystem? A growing number of other commercial actors are increasingly involved in publishing African research. Medknow is an India-based medical publisher, now a subsidiary of the major multinational publisher Wolter Kluwers, and provides publishing services for more than 50 Egyptian and Nigerian medical journals. In 2018 Elsevier launched *Scientific African* in association with the Next Einstein Forum, a network associated with the African Institute of Mathematics and funded by a

German philanthropy. The journal combines the reputational credibility offered by a global publisher with a competitive APC of USD 200, attempting to undercut many Africa-based competitors (Gray 2016). In 2021 Nature launched the online magazine *Nature Africa,* as a way of promoting African research, whilst in 2022 the University Gaston Berger in Senegal launched *Global Africa*, with the financial support of the French government.

The African publishing ecosystem continues to evolve. The International Africa Institute has championed the importance of Africa's universities developing their own digital research repositories, so that journal pre-prints can be found even if journals founder (De Mutiss and Kitchen 2019; Molteno 2016). In the STEM subjects, new digital publishing platforms have been created, such as the African Academy of Science's *AAS Open Research*. It champions the principles of open science, where all the data associated with a piece of research can be deposited, and the peer-review process is also opened up to scrutiny. Digital archiving services (including institutional repositories and AfricArxiv) and publishing platforms make it easier for researchers to share their findings, whilst platforms such as ResearchGate and Academia.edu also open up knowledge and academic visibility. Does this mean that the future for the continent is one of greater bibliodiversity, with a more equitable science ecosystem built around a range of open-access journal platforms (Meagher 2021)? Or are the bleak predictions of a global research system dominated by a small oligopoly of commercial platforms more accurate (Chen et al. 2019; Larivière et al. 2015)? This is the question for the final chapters.

Chapter 9

Ghana's research cultures
and the global bibliometric economy

University rankings are what universities look at and they include research output in Northern citation indexes. It's bad for developing country research. (Susan Murray, interview, 28 May 2020)

The international citation indexes collect, organise, and analyse skewed proportions of the world's scholarly publications mainly from the North and make generalisations about the state and structure of global scientific knowledge, thus exerting undue control and discipline on global intellectual discourse. (Nwagwu 2010, 228)

Introduction

In June 2020, the University of Ghana hosted an Elsevier training webinar entitled 'Avoid predatory publishing using Scopus and Scival'. The email invitation described publishing as a 'treacherous' affair, with 'fraudulent' journals causing 'vast damage to researchers' careers and to science in general'. The aim of the presentation was to raise awareness of so-called 'predatory publishing' and to offer a solution: Scopus,

Elsevier's 'source-neutral' citation index. In a world of risk, uncertainty, and predators, here was a 'trusted source' of high-quality journals.

The Elsevier webinar depicted a frightening publishing underworld full of predatory websites, 'fake' journals, and dubious citation indexes. Participants were given clues on how to spot spam emails and generic 'stock' photos of fake editorial boards. The webinar then shifted to a much calmer and more technical discussion of Scopus itself, the independence of its academic board, the data required of any journal seeking accreditation, and its monitoring of 'outlier' journals. The message was clear. It was no longer sufficient to have academic expertise in a disciplinary field. Now one had to understand the technicalities of journal publishing, to become an expert in spotting 'fake' journal indexes, and to trust Elsevier's metrics and assessments of journal quality (Mills et al. 2021).

Sceptical voices filled the chat function. Participants were particularly critical of Scopus for its limited African journal coverage, and the implications of this for African scholarly journals. In 2022, of more than 26,000 active journals listed in Scopus, only around 40 are published from sub-saharan Africa (excluding South Africa), including 21 from Nigeria, four from Ghana, and five each from Kenya and Ethiopia. Encouraging Ghanaian researchers to prioritise publishing in Scopus journals has potentially profound implications for knowledge production and dissemination. Participants complained about the discrimination experienced when sending work to 'high-impact' international journals, whilst another wondered whether top journals were also being 'predatory' by charging APCs of as much as USD 5,000.

One post was particularly blunt. 'Don't you think that the difficulty of African authors to have their manuscripts accepted for publication in reputable journals outside the continent makes them prey to predatory journals?' The question distilled the dilemma many Ghanaian scholars and researchers face. Should they send their research to elite 'international' journals, despite sometimes exorbitant APCs and the risks of rejection? Or should they prioritise publishing in 'local' West African journals, ensuring their findings and knowledge are more available nationally and for their students and colleagues, but possibly face both delays and the lack of reputational rewards that accrue from publishing in 'high-impact' journals? Or should they aim for newer open access 'international' journals that offer an efficient service but whose reputation and credibility is difficult to assess?

These questions that Ghanaian researchers face have been constant themes in this volume. Emotions, pressure and scarcity have been foregrounded, as have mentorship, collaboration and support. They have little choice but to publish 'internationally' if they want to gain promotion and progress their careers. Yet in an academic culture defined by time and resource scarcity, this comes with emotional and personal costs, especially for those with caring responsibilities. If Ghanaian scholarly publishing decisions are made with an eye to promotion, the perceived status and importance of Ghanaian as opposed to 'international' journals inevitably has to be taken into account. Some are lucky: by dint of their institutional context and disciplinary background, or ability to make connections and find support, they develop internationally-orientated publishing profiles. Others find this much more challenging. All are having to play by the new rules of the global research game.

It is not just Ghana's researchers who feel under pressure. The book has shown how the fortunes and futures of the region's academic journals and university presses are also at stake. Whilst a rigid distinction between local 'scholar-led' journals (Moore 2017; Morrison 2016) and 'market-led' commercial presses (Thornton and Ocasio 1999) is unhelpful, it is hard to ignore the increasing dominance and influence of the five major global publishing conglomerates and information companies (Posada and Chen 2019) on research and knowledge ecosystems. The technical expectations set for inclusion in the major citation indexes get ever more onerous. To be included in Scopus, journals have to meet minimum benchmarks on diversity of authorship and editorial boards, readability of articles and abstracts, the editor's standing, and the cited-ness of articles within Scopus. Any existing journal that is unable to publish with sufficient regularity or at an appropriate standard can also lose its accreditation. Membership of an organisation such as COPE (Committee on Publication Ethics) or OASPA (Open Access Scholarly Publishing Association) is another marker of repute, but the costs are often prohibitively expensive for small African publishers.

In this Alice in Wonderland-style caucus race, the rules are never quite clear (see also Bell 2015). Many African journals, whether published by professional associations, universities or local publishers, find it hard to keep up. Ghana is not alone in putting very little funding into university-based research and development. Regional research ecosystems and citation networks are under threat, unable to keep up with the changing infrastructures, technologies and economics of open-access publishing. Meanwhile the demands placed on academic faculty multiply.

This final chapter tries to predict the future. Will a few global journal citation indexes, including Scopus and WoS, increasingly define and patrol academic credibility and reputation? There is a risk that they become not just arbiters of quality but also a form of gatekeeping and knowledge exclusion. If citations and impact metrics become the only academic currency accepted in Ghana's universities, what happens to other genres of academic writing and publishing?

This chapter starts with the metricisation of credibility, focusing particularly on Elsevier's research 'solutions'. Elsevier heavily markets Scopus to African universities. The expectation on researchers to publish in 'reputable' Scopus or Web of Science journals creates constant uncertainty for the many African journals not included in these indexes and risks undermining Ghana's scholarly journals and publishing cultures. Yet there are a range of alternative journal indexes, databases and altmetrics that provide complementary sources of scholarly credibility – from DOAJ to Google Scholar. One future is a diversification of measures and rankings, even if this means yet more instrumentalisation of scholarly output.

The discussion then turns to attempts to create an African citation index, describing how continent-wide collaborations on such an index have been beset by funding concerns and institutional rivalries. Alternative approaches to assessing and incentivising research include calls to use metrics more responsibly (DORA 2012), and ways of sustaining a rich research ecosystem and diversity of African scholarly publishing, through open-access journals and other forms of dissemination. The chapter ends by exploring how these goals might be achieved in practical terms, making suggestions for Ghanaian universities and for researchers themselves, amid global calls for a more sustainable approach to research and publishing. The book ends with a discussion of the current debates around the potential of community-based 'knowledge commons' approaches to open-access publishing, and how these might shape the future of African research cultures.

Citation indexes and the metricisation of credibility

Elsevier is one of five major international academic publishers and has been particularly active in promoting its data platforms, analytical tools and indexing services to African universities and research networks, as well as to other emerging markets in the Middle East and Central Asia. While it publishes 2,500 journals – second only to the Springer Nature group, and making up 18% of the world's scientific research – journal publishing is only a small part of the business. Increasingly important to Elsevier (and its parent group RELX) is its data analytics work, providing universities and managers with 'research intelligence' that can be gained from these publications data. SciVal is an analytical tool for universities to compare their research performances, whilst Scopus is one of two major journal citation and abstract databases, bringing together information from 26,000 journals.

Tools such as ScienceDirect (Elsevier's e-book platform), Scopus and Research4Life are all prominent on the University of Ghana library website. Elsevier offers countries affordable licences to these products, and has also developed a bespoke institutional repository 'solution'. Partnering with the World Bank, it has worked on a range of capacity building initiatives across the continent, analysing data and publishing reports (e.g. World Bank 2014). The World Bank African Centres of Excellence initiative (Stallinga 2019) requires its 25 centres to measure impact by the number of articles published in Scopus journals. The company's philanthropic arm, the Elsevier Foundation, has funded the African Journal Partnerships Programme, partnering ten African medical journals with six 'Northern' journals. It is a relationship that at once builds capacity and sustains the African journals' financial dependence on their Northern sponsors. Bespoke training webinars, writing workshops, and a public 'Elsevier Africa' YouTube channel with webinars and videos on every aspect of the publishing process are all part of the company's 'service' to African universities.

Sociologists of higher education have studied the growing power of the journal citation indexes and their metricised influence over academic life and scholarly values, first in the US and then internationally. The field of 'scientometrics' emerged as early as the 1970s; historians of science tracked the relentless growth in the number of scholarly journals (DeSolla Price 1961), whilst statisticians like Eugene Garfield patented his article citations to identify the most influential scholars and serials (Garfield 1972). Gradually, other European and US social scientists took notice. Anthropologists began to think about the way 'audit culture' was reshaping their discipline (Shore and Wright 2000; Strathern 2000), whilst sociologists wrote about the power of the 'h-factor' to redefine academic subjectivities (Burrows 2012). Scholars of science showed how measures inexorably became targets, and in turn could be 'gamed' (Ball 2007; Lippman and Biagioli 2020). Reflecting on what he calls the 'accelerated academy', Carrigan argues that 'anxiety thrives, demands intensify, and metrics are the informational thread which holds this tangled web together' (2015). The consolidation and 'vertical integration' of the top 'information services' companies mean that they not only own profitable publishing businesses, but also a range of other publishing tools, from bibliographic software to tools for ranking and measuring impact (Posada and Chen 2016). Data analytics create a further source of revenue as the companies sell research management data to universities, who in turn use it to guide their researchers to publish in journals that improve their rankings. Until recently, work on the African research economy has focused primarily on the factors preventing African researchers from contributing to a global knowledge commons. As Elsevier's tools are adopted across the continent, the rising metrics tide (Wilsdon 2015) reshapes academic subjectivities and professional values.

The argument throughout this book has been that the academic identities and everyday work of Ghanaian researchers are being steadily and systematically reshaped by this publishing 'audit culture' (Strathern 2000). Whilst Nigerian and Ghanaian academics have been encouraged to publish in 'international' journals since the late 1990s (Adomi and Mordi 2003; Manuh et al. 2007), this expectation has become more quantified and more explicit (Omobowale et al. 2013). Most of the interviewees in this book were worried about publishing, worried about publishing enough, and worried about publishing in the right place. This pressure is compounded by gender disparities, which fall disproportionately on women researchers. As Africa's existing scholarly journals struggle to sustain scholarly legitimacy and visibility, and ever more commercially orientated publishers emerge, the academic discourse about 'predatory publishing' adds further uncertainty and anxiety (Inouye and Mills 2021). The citation indexes promise to robustly patrol the boundary between 'fake' and 'real' journals (Mills et al. 2021), but in doing so undermine the fragile academic credibility of many African academic publishing initiatives.

The struggle to create an African citation index

In 2008, only 0.7% of publications in global indexes were from Africa. Ten years later, and amidst the huge global growth in science, this increased to 1% (Duermeijer et al. 2018). Yet Elsevier uses this data to claim that change is coming, and that Africa is the fastest growing scientific region in the world. But even if this does represent a 40% growth in scientific production, it is from a very low base. This growth is also patchy: mostly in North Africa (Algeria, Egypt, Tunisia and Morocco) along with Nigeria, Kenya and South Africa.

The importance of publication data for African academics demonstrates the validity of Goodhart's Law – that when a measure becomes a target, it ceases to be a good measure – and the institutional 'gaming' that results. Duermeijer et al. (2018) highlight how Covenant, a private Nigerian university in Ogun State, uses Elsevier's SciVal tool to analyse its research performance. Less than two decades old, Covenant is now ranked fourth in Nigeria for journal output, and between 401–500 in the Times Higher Education (THE) World University Rankings, ahead of Ibadan, once the country's premier research university. Covenant's researchers are expected to publish only in highly ranked Scopus journals, and these metrics are built into promotion criteria.

Scopus may be one of the best known of the global journal citation indexes, but there are many others. Each has a different remit and disciplinary coverage, leading to a tangled Venn diagram of alternative sources of verifiability and credibility (Bell and Mills 2020). Examples include SciELO, set up by a network of sixteen Latin American countries, along with South Africa, in 1997. Mexico hosts RedALyC whilst India also has the Indian Citation Index. There are many other journal aggregators and hosting services (such as Sabinet in South Africa) that provide a reputational imprimatur to their members. Publishing membership organisations also offer credibility and legitimacy, including COPE and OASPA, but both charge affiliation fees that many African journals cannot afford.

Promoting open access, the Swedish not-for-profit DOAJ hosts open-access journals that pass their accreditation process, as well as providing training materials and webinars. DOAJ offers a much more transparent and inclusive approach to journal approval than Scopus, and a suite of recently established Ghanaian journals published by ADRRI are listed on DOAJ. However, it still hosts relatively few African open-access journals.

The closest that Africa has got to an African accreditation kitemark is the Journal Publishing Practices and Standards (JPPS) framework, established by INASP to help journals understand the minimum quality standards they needto meet. The framework is promoted by African Journals OnLine (AJOL) – the not-for-profit academic publishing capacity-building NGO based in South Africa. JPPS sets out a tiered scale for African and other 'Southern' journal portals sponsored by INASP, such as NepalJOL. Journals are assessed against the JPPS criteria on a six-point scale: Inactive title, New title, No stars, One star, Two stars, and Three stars. That no African AJOL journal currently has three stars is indicative of the challenges that many publishers have in meeting the administrative demands of professional publishing: international editorial boards and authorship, a track record of regular publishing, archiving, indexing, DOI registration with CrossRef, and membership of COPE. AJOL continues to promote this kitemark, but it is expensive and time-consuming to assess journals on a regular basis, especially with no sustainable income stream for AJOL.

One response to the dominance of Scopus and Web of Science would be an African citation index. This has long been the ambition of the Nigerian information scientist Williams Nwagwu, who argues that an autonomous 'citation index could be used to leverage the limited publicity of African resources' (Nwagwu 2008, 11). Nwagwu is highly critical of the international citation indexes, in particular the way they 'homogenise, centralise and globalise scholarly performance criteria' (2010, 228), and their lack of 'deference to global diversity and complexity' (2010, 228). He led CODESRIA's initiative to develop such an initiative, calling for it to be modelled on the principle of 'Africanism, recognising and putting African knowledge into a global perspective' (2010, 238).

Initially launching this vision in 2006, CODESRIA sought donor funding and institutional backing for more than a decade. The hope was that Africa's universities and disciplinary associations would see the value of the initiative and provide seed-funding. But many of these associations are largely inactive or operate on a shoestring, and universities are little better placed. To date, CODESRIA's proposals for an index have also failed to attract the support of donors, national governments, or the African Development Bank.

The proposal also attracted controversy within the African academic publishing community. Some questioned whether creating yet another citation index – and an accompanying set of journal rankings – was the right approach. Indexes reinforce a focus on citation metrics, and inevitably stratify academic fields, with journal impact factors used to justify high journal APCs in a publishing prestige economy. The initiative attracted the attention of Elsevier, who initially attempted to persuade CODESRIA to append an African index to Scopus, but would have been reluctant to see another rival index emerge. Whilst such an index could help rebalance the credibility economy, international development donors are unlikely to prioritise funding an index rather than research.

Alternative indexes may yet emerge. One initiative has been promoted by the Society of African Journal Editors (SAJE). Professor Oniang'o (see Chapter 9) first proposed an association of editors society at a publishers' meeting in Nairobi in 2004 (Shehu and Ameh 2005) sponsored by a range of international donors. The association set itself the task of training editors, improving their editorial and managerial skills, and improving the promotion, marketing, and distribution of journals. Failing to attract longer-term funding, the initiative was relaunched in 2018 (Tonukari 2018). This time the aim was to 'enhance the global visibility of African journals'.

SAJE harvests metadata from more than 1,500 African journals, and uses Google Scholar citations to provide journal reports for members. It combines citation data from Google Scholar metrics and Microsoft Academics to create its own journal ranking scale, from A+ to unranked. Thirty African journals are ranked as A+ within this database. The SAJE website lists the profiles of over 200 members and journal editors, most – but not all – of whom come from Africa. Whilst its coverage is partial and the methodology open to challenge, it does represent one attempt at creating an African journal ranking system. Without institutional backing for an African citation index, alternative indexes based on Google Scholar or Crossref citations could become more influential. They highlight the struggle to garner African scholarly legitimacy and credibility in an increasingly 'metricised' global academy.

Towards responsible metrics

In 2012, a group of editors and publishers met at the American Society of Cell Biology in San Francisco to discuss the challenges of evaluating the output of scientific research. Their recommendations – now known as the Declaration on Research Assessment (or simply as DORA) – sought to challenge the dominance of journal metrics within international science. Developed in the 1970s by Garfield (1972), Journal Impact Factors (JIF) calculated the yearly average number of citations that articles published in the last two years in that journal received. It was originally intended as a means for US academic librarians to evaluate journals, rather than to judge the quality of individual researchers. The metric took on a life of its own, facilitating a new prestige economy. Initially in North America and then in Europe, impact factor metrics became proxies for quality in promotion procedures and funding decisions, driving journals to seek to 'game' the numbers (Biagioli and Lippman 2020). This ignored the fact that citations depended on the size and culture of the scholarly community, varied widely between articles, and depended on whether it was original research or a review article. Whilst it stood to reason not to judge the quality of an individual piece of work by the impact factor of the journal it was published in, this was exactly how these metrics were being used.

The 18 recommendations of the DORA manifesto proposed ways of de-emphasising publication metrics and finding other ways to assess research. The DORA manifesto rapidly garnered policy attention and signatories, such that 2000 institutions as well as almost 1,700 individuals have now signed the declaration, and journals have started removing impact factors from their mastheads. DORA has been followed up by several similar declarations, including the Leiden Manifesto for Research Metrics in 2015. It has generated a range of initiatives and forums to promote the 'responsible' use of metrics.

While UK and US research policy-makers are seeking to turn the 'metrics tide' (Wilsdon 2015), the impact of what Murray (2009) calls 'impact-factor fundamentalism' on African universities continues to grow. Several respondents mentioned their interest in getting work published in 'high impact factor' journals, and the excitement of getting work accepted. Richmond, a UDS applied sciences lecturer, knew exactly the impact factor of a pharmacy journal in which he had eventually published what he called 'very good' work after several rounds of review.

Understandably, many of Africa's research universities are unable to see beyond the incoming tide. They are ever more attentive to world university rankings published by Times Higher Education, QS and Shanghai Jiao Tong. The University of Ghana 2014–2024 strategic plan sets out its ambition to be a 'world-class research-intensive university'. It is currently ranked between 800–1,000 in the Times Higher ranking, well behind the University of Cape Town (UCT) (ranked 136) and University of Witwatersrand (194). In the ten-year HERANA project, UCT's research profile became the benchmark for seven other national 'flagship' universities across the continent (Cloete et al. 2018). Whilst this has raised the profile of research in Ghana's universities, it has come at a heavy cost for national journals, as research and publishing agendas are increasingly internationalised. University rankings are based partly on research output in Northern citation indexes, and so the playing field is far from level for Africa's researchers. AJOL emphasises these inequalities and consequences in their training workshops. As Murray points out, this 'opens people's eyes', as 'academics in higher education are taught to question every-thing but they don't question the invisible structure around how their research is shared' (Susan Murray, interview, 28 May 2020).

As Nolte (2019, 301) notes, the 'growing divisions between ostensibly 'local' (i.e. Africa-published) and 'international' scholarship have been naturalised in both African and non-African discourses, reconstituting non-Africans as experts on the continent in a manner that reproduces colonial and racial hierarchies.

Interviewees were full of ideas about how to solve this conundrum. Several highlighted how they wrote for a range of other sources – including Ghana's online news sites as well as other blogs. Donkor, a UG health sciences lecturer, questioned the emphasis placed on 'traditional outputs' and suggested 'diversifying the premium we put on academic output'. 'Why', he asked, 'do we compel publishing in a very heightened journal which ordinary people would never read in any way?' He talked about his own scientific journalism, and why he felt it was important to publish policy briefs and write for 'newspapers that many more people are going to be exposed to'.

Several researchers signalled their commitment to writing more journalistic pieces. Mensah, a UG social sciences lecturer, pointed out that, unlike his research articles, if he writes a piece in Ghana's online news site *Ghanaweb*, then 'there is a guarantee that you will get one hundred people reading within two weeks'. He went on to ask about 'the value of doing all this academic work if people do not read it?'

Changing the Ghanaian research funding ecosystem

In the mid-1990s, the Rawlings government introduced a monthly book and research allowance to be paid to Ghana's academics. Intended to bolster research activity and 'top-up' paltry salaries, it did not in itself incentivise publishing. Its reform has become highly politicised, and the powerful UTAG (University Teachers Association of Ghana) has repeatedly threatened strike actions in response to proposals to end the subsidy. Each time, the government has backed down.

In 2019, after several years of consultation, the government finally tabled a bill for a new National Research Fund, but the implementation of this USD 50 million fund has been repeatedly held up. Ghana does not have a national research or higher education policy (Fosci et al. 2019), and its 2017 Science, Technology and Innovation strategy is led by a ministry that has no direct remit for universities. This means that there is little coordination between the government-funded CSIR and the universities. Whilst Ghana does spend 0.4% of its GDP on research and development, most of this goes to the government research institutes. This leaves universities and international donors to act as research funders, limiting the scale of funding available, and making Ghana's academics dependent on external collaborations. As a national 'flagship', the University of Ghana does have an internal research fund of USD 200,000, a well-organised Office of Research, Innovation and Development, strong links to international donors, and is a member of the African Research Universities Association, but this makes it the exception rather than the rule.

This research has highlighted a range of challenges facing the sustainability of the Ghanaian knowledge ecosystem in a global science publishing system that makes articles in elite journals, citations, and 'impact' the only valuable currencies of scholarly reputation. None of this is unique to Ghana. Yet as long as Africa remains at the peripheries of disciplinary 'credibility economies' and funding ecosystems, Ghana's scholarly journals and research communities will also remain vulnerable to the metric-driven whims of the science publishing system.

One solution to turning back the metrics 'tide' would be for Ghana's universities to move away from specific numerical targets for promotion, adopting a more holistic assessment of research activity and performance. This would lessen the temptation for researchers to accumulate publications as fast as possible, to prioritise quantity over quality, or to choose journals based on their impact factors. Whilst the University of Ghana revised its promotion guidelines in 2019, developing an elaborate points-based analysis of different scholarly activities (including teaching, research and public service) at different career stages, the assessment still foregrounds publishing in 'reputable peer-reviewed' journals.

The importance of publishing in 'elite' journals varies by discipline. Such journals are often expensive, difficult for African researchers to access, or have few African readers. They may also publish little of relevance to the region, and have limited local academic impact. Instead, Ghana's universities could encourage researchers to prepare fewer, and potentially more influential, publications and outputs. There could be greater reward for reaching a pan-African audience through Africa-based open science publishing platforms, such as that hosted by the African Academy of Sciences. There could also be stronger institutional support for research repositories, so that everyone can read and access Ghanaian research. Academic promotion assessments could also be broadened to include evidence of commitment to dissemination and communicating findings, and of prioritising social and economic impact where possible.

Supporting Ghanaian research cultures

How might Ghana's policy-makers, universities and research leaders respond to this challenge? As interviewees' accounts have shown, university promotion and appointment criteria drive people's publishing practices. Numerical output is key because the numbers are so clearly defined in university regulations: six articles for promotion to senior lecturer, twelve to associate professor, etc. Whilst there are attempts to diversify these criteria, the numerical targets remain.

There are other ways in which Ghanaian research cultures can be made more supportive and inclusive. A key finding from this research is the importance of supporting new researchers at the earliest stages of their research and publishing journeys. The supervisor and academic mentor are vital guides. These relationships are often built around friendship and can be difficult to formalise, but many highlighted the value of informal and formal mentoring in their career development. Like carrying out high quality research, knowing which journals to choose, how to submit a strong article, and how to deal with peer-review, are all skills best learnt in dialogue with more experienced peers. Chapter 5 demonstrates the value of formal mentoring schemes, informal mentoring arrangements, and the support that comes from co-authoring and research collaboration. International research collaborations also present new challenges, and need more support and guidance from departments.

It is not just about academic mentoring. Librarians and library services are well placed to share information about choosing journals and getting publishing. UG interviewees mentioned how much support they were already getting, particularly through the libraries, as well as via faculty inductions, student seminars, and briefing emails. The situation in UDS seemed less clear. One UDS applied sciences lecturer felt that workshops on publishing were not being run frequently enough, whilst a UDS head of an applied sciences department felt that general faculty-level workshops 'did not cater to the specific needs of his department'.

Participants differed in the extent to which they felt training workshops on publishing would be helpful to them. Around a quarter of respondents expressed their keenness to stay up to date, while a smaller group felt workshops were not going to tell them anything they did not already know. The consensus seemed to be that they were most useful for early career researchers. In the words of Jonathan, a

UDS health sciences lecturer, it 'requires so much to understand the ins and outs of the whole process'. He went on to note that as there were 'always new things coming up', it was incumbent on Ghana's universities to be 'constantly equipping' people and 'bringing them up to speed with what is happening'.

Some UDS faculty questioned whether they needed 'more knowledge' or training workshops. Emmanuel instead argued for universities to cover publication fees as well as to properly fund 'the raw material needed to do good work' (Emmanuel, UDS applied sciences lecturer). As important as training is the role of African universities in developing locally resourced and supported publishing infrastructures as well as financial support for university journals, and lobbying international publishers to charge more affordable APCs.

Many of Ghana's scholarly journals rely on the funding and in-kind support of host universities and libraries. Ghana has a strong academic librarian association, well-placed to guide researchers to ensure they get all the support that institutions and libraries can provide. Many of Ghana's journals would not have survived without the expertise of AJOL. Yet AJOL has to compete with the services provided to journals by commercial publishers, and it will need the support of Africa's universities if it is to develop a more sustainable business model.

What will open access mean for African research?

Sometimes historians write the best guidebooks to the future. In his history of the academic journal, Csiszar (2019) explores how in the 19th century, the journal article became the dominant format for reporting scientific advances, and why it is assumed that it is still the best way to report on research. Csiszar points out that 'we are in the midst of an intense period of experimentation in genres, formats, and practices of evaluation in science' (Csiszar 2019, 2). He points to the contradictory pressures now placed on journals to be both 'permanent archive and breaking news, both a public repository and the exclusive dominion of experts, both a complete record and a painstakingly vetted selection' (2019, 2). These tensions are evidenced in the exponential growth in new spaces for publishing, pre-publishing, depositing, and archiving research knowledge, along with new ways of measuring impact and outcomes.

Predictions about the future for global scientific communication range widely. Some offer dystopian accounts of academic 'platform capitalism' (Mirowski 2018), with a few major corporations seeking to own the whole publishing infrastructure, much like Amazon. Others forecast an increasingly fragmented and hierarchical publishing geography dominated by Northern academic interests (Connell et al. 2016). Others are more utopian, pointing to the potential of open-access infrastructures to 'reassemble scholarly communications' (Eve and Gray 2020, 5). Evidence from Latin America points to the emergence of a 'local' mediating academic elite that act as brokers between international and national debates (Beigel 2018). In 2020, China declared a move away from a 'publish or perish' culture that financially incentivises publishing in the Science Citation Index journals, and instead promoting Chinese language journals (Li 2020). The future is most likely to be a combination of publishing models within a stratified global research ecosystem. Commercial open-access journals offer an appealing combination of professionalism, timeliness, cost and inclusion for many African researchers (Kienc 2017; Macleavy et al. 2020; Nobes and Harris 2019). At the same time, international journal brands – such as *Nature* and *Science* – with long and prestigious histories are likely to retain their global dominance.

The lobbying of the open access movement led in 2018 to a major global initiative called 'Plan S' promoting the case for all research to be published open access. Led by the interests of the natural and life sciences, Plan S envisaged that either 'read and publish' agreements with publishers or author payments would replace subscriptions as a source of journal funding. Yet the prohibitive costs associated with 'gold' open access are inappropriate for the under-resourced humanities and social sciences, and high APCs are beyond the reach of many African researchers. Meagher (2021, 340) points to the 'inequitable and often neo-colonial effects' of these for-profit models on Southern researchers, along with the political capture of the OA agenda by Northern corporate and state interests.

The publishing numbers game has led to a distorted emphasis on patrolling research integrity: exemplified by the discourse around 'predatory publishing' (Inouye and Mills 2021; Mills and Inouye 2020). New commercial open-access journals offer alternative possibilities, but the 'normalisation' of APCs leads to further commercialisation of the research-publishing nexus. Many of these new journals have been particularly targeted by Beall and other research 'watchdogs'.

Given these constraints, does open-access publishing offer a solution? Many in the open access movement see it as providing an unprecedented opportunity for African researchers to become part of a more inclusive, open, and transparent culture of global science (Chan et al. 2019; Weingart and Taubert 2018). Yet the politics of open access are contested (Bell 2017). Some foreground the principle of access rather than focus on practicalities and commercial viability, whilst others see the movement as being a cynical cover for commercial interests intent on controlling digital publishing platforms (Mirowski 2019). One result of 'Plan S' is that the major publishing companies, whilst initially promoting the author-pays model, are increasingly seeking to sign transformative 'read-and-publish' deals with national funding bodies. These funders pay publishers based on the number of times papers are accessed or published by their researchers, another way to sustain their commercial control and profits. Given that African states will not have the resources to fund such models, there is the risk that individual researchers will be left negotiating unsustainable APC payments. Alternatively, the major companies will be able to undercut local journals by offering APC waivers for researchers from Africa and across the Global South to publish open access, as exemplified by those being charged by Elsevier's *Scientific African* initiative. Either way, the existing commercial publishers and their control present major challenges for Africa's publishers.

The global open science community champions community-led digital publishing as the best way to challenge the dominance of commercial publishers (Eve and Gray 2020; Moore 2017; Morrison 2016). Despite the gains of the open access movement, the debate continues to be conducted from the perspective of Northern research funders. Currently dominant 'author-pays' open-access models are increasing the profits of commercial publishers whilst excluding many African researchers (Meagher 2021; Okune et al. 2021). Many 'elite' international science journals are now open access, and if not, their universities usually require faculty to deposit preprints in institutional repositories. So whilst it is now possible for researchers around the world to access this work, the debate remains largely focused on the consumption, rather than the production of knowledge. The open-access model does not address the larger question of how to create socio-technical infrastructures that foster inclusion and diversity in scholarly knowledge (Okune et al. 2021).

Critical of what they see as elite 'Northern' approaches to open access such as Plan S, and the influence of global publishing conglomerates, they look instead to Latin America for models of sustainable community-led journal portals, databases, and citation indexes such as SCiELo and REdalyc (Eve and Gray 2020). Others have moved away from advocating open access to talk of open science, or simply of ethical publishing. University-based institutional repositories would help make research knowledge and publications more widely available (De Mutiss and Kitchen 2019).

The academic publishing landscape remains complex and rapidly evolving, presenting researchers, publishers and editors with a confusing set of choices. It is likely that scientific mega-journals and global publishing platforms will coexist alongside a dynamic mosaic of smaller green, gold and diamond OA journals in the humanities and social sciences, hosted and funded by universities, scholarly societies, philanthropies as well as smaller publishing companies.

The diversity and health of this ecosystem will depend on making scholarly journals more financially sustainable and less reliant on volunteer labour. A number of journal pilots for 'diamond' open access (i.e. free for both author and reader) are underway in Europe and the US (Crow et al. 2019). Their future will depend partly on the altruism of well-resourced libraries continuing their subscriptions. Across Africa, this model looks less sustainable. Whilst some major journals may seek to increase their market share by charging lower APCs, there is also a role for commercial journal platforms that aggregate journals or act as distributors (such as SabiNet in South Africa, or JSTOR in the social sciences).

Whilst an African citation index may, for now, be unlikely, there is room for African journal publishing platforms that can successfully navigate these contradictions of commercial and public-good goals. One ideal would be to see more African university presses adopting what Luescher and Van Schalkwyk call a 'knowledge commons logic', adopting models of 'social capitalism' that sees 'publishing as a collective social innovation enterprise rather than a business' (2018, 290). This would mean more ownership of journals by the sector. Key to this will be better financing for Africa's universities and their research infrastructures, from libraries to institutional repositories to online journals. At the same time, funding for open science publishing may provide an important new venue for many African researchers.

Compared to its regional neighbours, Ghanaian academia sustains a range of journals published by national research institutes as well as by universities and commercial presses. Despite this, the threat of 'publish *and* perish' remains, along with the damaging affective consequences of rankings and metrics. Universities, in Ghana and across the West Africa region, along with their counterparts in the Global North, will need to champion more holistic and responsible approaches to assessing research, a broader range of academic career trajectories, and a diversified knowledge and publishing infrastructure.

Where next?

The technical infrastructures underpinning digital publishing are never neutral, but instead 'shape who and what is assembled around research, as well as what is attended to' (Gray 2020, 251). This makes it vital to 'highlight voices, worldviews and epistemologies that have been historically excluded from the system' (Albornoz et al. 2020, 66). One response to the dominance of the two global citation indexes is to develop African-centred databases and indexes. Examples include AfriArxiV, AJOL, ABC and a range of library portals. To date, attempts to build continent-wide research infrastructures have had mixed success, beset by funding concerns and institutional rivalries. Some are suspicious of promoting yet more rankings and metrics. There is a risk that well-meaning initiatives to strengthen African research capacity and publishing 'standards' could reinforce the power of Euro-American research metrics and commercial publishing infrastructures. Others look to alternative approaches for assessing research, or highlight calls to use metrics more responsibly (DORA 2012). Publishers are more optimistic, arguing that African scholarly journals can sustain a rich diversity of institutional, national and regional knowledge ecosystems (Okune et al. 2021).

Chapter 10

Conclusion:
Beyond bibliometric coloniality?

In May 2022 two white US scholars published a 'Keyword' article in the US journal *African Studies Review* (Mara and Thompson 2022). Entitled 'Autoethnography', they made the case for greater use for this approach to research and writing within the field of African Studies. The article insinuated that autoethnography made it easier for white people to study Africa, and could even help decolonise the field. News circulated fast on social media, and the story was picked up by higher education journalists (Flaherty 2022). More than 1,000 academics signed an open letter asking the journal to retract the paper. The editor's refusal to do so only fed the perception that elite African Studies journals were complicit in sustaining a colonial academic system and its intellectual framings of the continent.

How different this situation feels to that of post-independence Africa. As seen in Chapter 2, the 1960s and 1970s marked a vibrant period for African science and scholarship. Rich intellectual and publishing cultures developed in Ibadan, Lagos, Accra, Makerere and Dar es Salaam, with the launch of high profile literary journals such as *Transition, The New African* and *Black Orpheus*. Structural adjustment policies, political instability and the underfunding of research infrastructures have all weakened African science ecosystems.

The answer to the 'why publish' question for Ghanaian academic researchers was that personal motivations tended to matter less than institutional expectations. For most participants, publishing ensured career survival and advancement. It is not an option. Both universities have precise numerical targets in their promotion criteria. One respondent compared research to a factory production line, relentlessly churning out papers, echoing the critiques about the impact of 'audit culture' on British universities (Strathern 2000). Many were frank and open about institutional pressures to publish, even if relatively few complained about this relentless focus on numbers and metrics.

Participants also talked of research and teaching as being comple-mentary – that an active research and publishing record was key to being a good academic teacher. Others were ambitious to share knowledge, to make a difference to policy and practice beyond academia, or were somply motivated to carry out curiosity-driven research. Most were keen to publish *and* teach *and* share their knowledge.

Publishing rationales and choices varied by age, seniority, disciplinary culture, training and research biography. Senior faculty were the most likely to talk of the research vocation and its intrinsic rewards. A few avoided speaking about their own motivations but instead offered normative explanations of what good science and publishing 'should' look like. One or two insisted that promotion didn't matter to them. None of this is unique to Ghana, but their cumulative impact on one research ecosystem rewards careful research.

These individual rationales are best read in the context of the changing status and importance of research in Ghana's universities. Since 2014 UG has aspired to become a 'world-class' research-intensive university, increasing the focus on publication 'outputs'. Whilst UDS has a mandate to work with local communities, its researchers also find themselves under pressure to publish in 'reputable' journals. Researchers at the margins of international knowledge ecosystems are forced to choose between global reputation and local relevance (Nyamnjoh 2004), between English and their own languages (Casanave 1998), and between different credibility economies (Hyland 2015; Mills and Robinson 2021). This makes the publishing stakes much higher.

Institutional expectations translate into individual publication decisions and strategies: the all-important 'where?' and 'how?' questions.

Does one prioritise 'international' reputation and 'impact factors', or local relevance and accessibility? There is a growing pressure to choose 'international' publications rather than established 'local' journals hosted by national scholarly associations. Research supervision practices, mentoring cultures and team-based research all play into publishing decisions and experiences. The book has spotlighted the emotional, temporal and financial demands this places on researchers, and how these demands are gendered.

The expectation to research and publish consistently is now integral to Ghanaian academic life. Journal articles are the currency of this quantified transnational republic of letters. Vignettes and portraits reveal how researchers learn the publishing ropes of academic life, choosing journals and coping with lengthy rounds of peer-review. Everyone faces the same questions: how to balance speed with reputation, visibility with recognition, access with cost. A growing range of open-access journals and open science platforms adds yet more options and complexity.

For those with heavy teaching and administration responsibilities, as well as family and caring roles, finding time to research and publish was particularly hard. It was not just about the emotional demands, the career pressures, or the stigma of rejection. There was the added challenge of inadvertently publishing in the 'wrong' journals. The odds can feel stacked against authors based far from the editorial boards and peer-reviewers of Northern academic journals. Publishing means reconciling contrasting temporalities, rushing to apply for grants, waiting long months for editorial decisions and delays surrounding publication.

New publishing opportunities have been opened up by digitisation, online publishing and open-source publishing software. The lack of sustainable funding models and the constant struggle to sustain academic credibility mean that the continent's scholarly journals struggle to compete on an unequal playing field.

These inequalities are exacerbated by the growing influence of the major citation indexes, leading to what we have called bibliometric coloniality. Researchers across the globe increasingly rely on commercial indexes such as Clarivate's Web of Science and Elsevier's Scopus database to assess the credibility of scholarly journals. Citation data is replacing the 'trust' that disciplinary networks used to provide. This is rewiring the global research economy according to an algorithmic logic, cutting Africa out of its circuits.

The great majority of Africa's scholarly journals are not indexed in these global journal databases and citation indexes. With the exception of journals published from South Africa, only around 40 of the 26,000 active journals in the Scopus database are published in sub-Saharan Africa. Asubiaro (2021) suggests that only 4% of Nigeria's 294 biomedical journals are indexed in the major indexes. There is also little overlap between the African journals hosted on AJOL (African Journals Online) and Scopus. A global science system that relies on Scopus and Web of Science renders much African research and publishing invisible. The resulting 'metricisation' of publishing integrity through citations is slowly but surely devaluing the credibility and visibility of long-established African scholarly journals, reinforcing academic coloniality and epistemic exclusion.

Africa's university presses have also struggled. Some are dormant or have just become textbook printing presses (Van Schalkwyk and Luescher 2017). Yet strong local publishing cultures and research ecologies still survive. Many African university faculties host open access online journals, sustaining institutional research cultures and offering publishing opportunities for their staff. Some of these journals struggle and disappear after a few issues, but a few have sustained long publishing traditions, finding ways to attract and reward African authors and reviewers. These are often shoestring operations, with editorial teams working long hours for little pecuniary reward. In an academic timescape in which authors want to publish immediately, but reviewers have other priorities, questions of speed and quality loom large.

It is not just an unequal political economy that sustains this coloniality. There is also an unequal credibility economy at work. Commercial science publishing actors amplify an emotive and de-humanising discourse about so-called 'predatory' publishing. Journals such as *Nature* publish articles about the phenomenon. Elsevier has a

Youtube channel with videos teaching people how to spot 'predatory' journals. They all work to instil a fear of the academic fake (Mills et al. 2021). The discourse has often targeted Nigerian publishers. As one Nigerian editor put it: 'When somebody says the journal is something to do with Nigeria, those from Europe look at you twice even if you are telling them the truth.' This discourse explains African universities' growing reliance on the major citation indexes and their metricised measures of quality.

Can Africa escape bibliometric coloniality? One editor felt that Nigeria needed to 'adopt her own metrics and standards of indexing while still looking up to the international ones'. The hard work of diversifying the global research system involves challenging citation thinking. There are other ways of mapping African scientific ecosystems. Increasingly scholars are using Open data, assembled from data sources such as CrossRef, Academia.edu or ResearchGate to map African scholarly production (e.g. Asubiaro 2021; Harsh et al. 2021). It may be that African-centred open-source citation databases and indexes eventually sit alongside those of Scopus and Web of Science.

These developments shape the lives and work of Ghanaian academics and African scholarly publishers. Putting their experiences into dialogue, and drawing on insights from history and political economy, this book has described how they 'get by' in a global research economy. What are the portents for African-centred research ecosystems and academic publishing? The future of Africa's research ecosystems depends on strong and well-funded national research systems, bibliodiversity, multilingual publishing, and alternative circuits of academic credibility. For now, Ghanaian researchers and publishers labour in the shadow of global science. Calls to defend the diversity of African publishing ecosystems are muffled by an increasingly monocultural global research economy. The fate of Africa's journals, research infrastructures and academic careers hangs in the balance.

Appendix:
Research design and ethics

Academics are never happier than when talking about their latest article or research findings. They may know little about the finances or logistics of journal publishing, but most will have an opinion about the strengths and weaknesses of particular journals in their field. It is more difficult to ask about the quality of peer review and editorial standards in the journals they publish in. They might feel they were being asked to evaluate the quality of their own work. Yet this question seemed important for a project researching publishing practices. Talking to editors and publishers about the quality and credibility of their journals also demands sensitivity and tact. The team drew on anthropological principles of methodological relativism in carrying out this work (Mills 2003). This meant suspending *a priori* normative judgements about the legitimacy (or otherwise) of particular journals or the publishing profiles of researchers. Instead, the aim was to ask interviewees to talk about their publishing journeys and journal choices.

In doing research *on* research, the challenge is to understand the everyday experiences, practices and rationales of all the different actors involved in the production of academic knowledge, and the infrastructures that underpin this global science system. A holistic approach to conceptualisation, design and analysis enabled this inclusive remit. The result is an analysis of the changing global publishing economy and its infrastructures, of African academic publishing ecosystems, and of Ghanaian university research cultures. The aim was to put the voices and views of interviewees into dialogue with existing academic literature on these topics, situating their experiences in different institutional, geographical and economic contexts.

There is a growing literature on the unequal nature of many international research collaborations. It was important for us to make our partnership as equitable and ethical as possible. The research ethics clearance was obtained from both Oxford University and the University of Ghana, and the sensitivities of talking about publishing choices were discussed within the team. We then designed a programme of interviews with Ghanaian researchers after seeking the permission of faculty deans and heads of departments. Under Paulina's supervision, Samuel carried out interviews in Ghana just before Covid-19 hit. During 2020 and 2021, David, Natasha and Abigail carried out interviews with publishers and editors via Microsoft Teams, WhatsApp and Zoom.

The interview consent form offered full confidentiality and anonymity to all respondents. With the exception of Associate Professor Akosua Darkwah (who granted special permission to use her career biography in the opening vignette), all the Ghanaian university faculty interviewed have been given pseudonyms. To ensure that the research was accountable to the Ghanaian academic community, a first draft was sent to respondents for feedback. The project team also developed policy recommendations and practical guidance for early career scholars starting out on their research and publishing journeys. All the journal editors and publishers were happy to be named, and had the opportunity to comment on, and amend, the case studies we prepared.

References

Acker, S., and Haque, E. 2015. The struggle to make sense of doctoral study. *Higher Education Research & Development*, 34: 229-41.

Acquah, E.H.K., and Budu, J.M. 2017. The University of Ghana: a premier university in national development. In D. Teferra (Ed.), *Flagship universities in Africa*. Berlin: Springer.

Adomi, E.E., and Mordi, C. 2003. Publication in foreign journals and promotion of academics in Nigeria. *Learned Publishing,* 16(4): 259-63. DOI: 10.1087/095315103322421991.

Adriansen, H.K., and Møller Madsen, L. 2019. Capacity-building projects in African higher education. *Learning and Teaching,* 12(2): 1-23. DOI: 10.3167/latiss.2019.120202.

Afful, J. 2017. Enhancing doctoral research education through the institution of graduate writing courses in Ghanaian universities. *Legon Journal of the Humanities*, 28(2). DOI: 10.4314/ljh.v28i2.1

Agbodeka, F. 1998. *A history of the University of Ghana: half a century of higher education*. Accra: Woeli.

Akuffo, H. 2014. Doctoral education and institutional research capacity strengthening: an example at Makerere University in Uganda (2000–2013). *Higher Education Policy*, 27: 195-217.

Alabi, G., and Abdulai, M. 2016. Expectations and integration of early career academics into the teaching career: empirical evidence from Ghana. *Studies in Higher Education,* 41(10): 1754-71. DOI: 10.1080/03075079.2016.1221654.

Alabi, G., and Mohammed, I. 2018. *Research and PhD capacities in sub-Saharan Africa: Ghana report*. London: DAAD / British Council IHE.

Albornoz, D., Okune, A., and Chan, L. (2020). Can open scholarly practices redress epistemic injustice? In M. Eve and J. Gray (Eds.), *Reassembling scholarly communications: histories, infrastructures, and global politics of open access*. Cambridge, MA: MIT Press

Allman, D. 2019. Pseudo or perish: problematizing the 'predatory' in global health publishing. *Critical Public Health,* 29: 413-23.

Allman, J. 2008. Nuclear imperialism and the pan-African struggle for peace and freedom: Ghana, 1959–1962. *Souls,* 10(2): 83-102. DOI: 10.1080/10999940802115419.

———. 2013. Kwame Nkrumah. African Studies, and the politics of knowledge production in the Black Star of Africa. *The International Journal of African Historical Studies,* 46(2): 181-203.

———. 2019. #HerskovitsMustFall? A meditation on whiteness, African Studies, and the unfinished business of 1968. *African Studies Review,* 62: 6-39.

Altbach, P.G. 1975. Publishing and the intellectual system. *The Annals of the American Academy of Political and Social Science,* 421(1): 1-13.

Altbach, P. G. 1978. Scholarly publishing in the Third World. *Library Trends,* 26: 489-503

Altbach, P. G. 1993. Perspectives on publishing in Africa. *Publishing Research Quarterly,* 9: 44-62.

———. 2004. Globalisation and the university: Myths and realities in an unequal world. *Tertiary Education and Management,* 10(1): 3-25.

Altbach, P.G., and Rathgeber, E-M. 1980. *Publishing in the third world: trend report and bibliography.* Greenwood.

Altbach, P., and Teferra, D. (Eds.). 1998. *Knowledge dissemination in Africa: the role of scholarly journals.* Chestnut Hill, MA: Bellagio Publishing Network Research and Information Center.

———. 1999. *Publishing in African languages: challenges and prospects.* Chestnut Hill, MA: Bellagio Publishing Network Research and Information Center.

Analoui, F., and Danquah, J.K. 2017. *Critical capacity development.* Cham: Springer.

Anderson, M., Shaw, M.A., Steneck, N.H., Konkle, E., and Kamata, T. 2013. Research integrity and misconduct in the academic profession. In M. Paulsen (Ed.), *Higher education: handbook of theory and research.* Dordrecht: Springer.

Archibong, I.A., Effiom, D.O., Omoike, D., and Edet, A.O. 2010. Academic staff disposition to promotion criteria in Nigerian universities. *Journal of College Teaching and Learning,* 7(10).DOI: 10.19030/tlc.v7i10.153.

Ashby, E. 1964.

———. 1966. *Universities: British, Indian, African: a study in the ecology of Higher Education.* London: Wiedenfeld and Nicholson.

Academy of Science of South Africa (ASSAf), (2019). *Twelve years later: second ASSAf report on research publishing in and from South Africa.* DOI: 10.17159/assaf.2018/0030

———. 2020. *Report on grouped peer review of scholarly journals in education.* DOI: http://dx.doi.org/10.17159/assaf.2019/0062

Asubiaro, T. 2021. Sub-Saharan Africa's biomedical journal coverage in scholarly databases: a comparison of Web of Science, Scopus, EMBASE, PubMed, African Index Medicus and African Journals Online. *Sage Advance Preprint.* DOI: 10.17632/52pncd8zmy.1

Atiso, K., Kammer, J., and Bossaller, J. 2019. Predatory publishing and the Ghana experience: a call to action for information professionals. *IFLA Journal,* 45(4): 277-88. DOI: 10.1177/0340035219868816.

Atolani, O., Adeyemi, O.S., Agunbiade, F.O., Asaolu, O.S., Gayawan, E., Jai- yeola, T.G., Usikalu, M.R., and Unuabonah, E.I. 2019. *Globafricalisation and sustainable development: research and researchers' assessments, 'publish or perish', journal impact factor and other metrifications.* Sciendo .

Atuahene, F. 2011. Re-thinking the missing mission of higher education: an anatomy of the research challenge of African universities. *Journal of Asian and African Studies,* 46(4): 321-41. DOI: 10.1177/0021909611400017.

Awori, A.S. 1967. East African university must be Africanised to help create and safeguard an east African national heritage. *East Africa Journal,* 4(9): 15-22.

Baldwin, M.C. 2015. *Making nature: the history of a scientific journal.* Chicago: University of Chicago Press.

Ball, S. 2007. *Education plc: understanding private sector participation in public sector education.* London: Routledge

Bao, Y., Kehm, B.M., and Ma, Y. 2018. From product to process. The reform of doctoral education in Europe and China. *Studies in Higher Education,* 43: 524-41.

Barbour, M. 1984. The supply of books and articles about African countries. *African Affairs,* 83(330): 95-112.

Bayart, J.F. 2000. Africa in the world: a history of extraversion. *African Affairs,* 99: 217-67.

Beall, J. 2009. Bentham open. *The Charleston Advisor,* 11: 29-32.

———. 2010. Predatory open-access scholarly publishers. *The Charleston Advisor* 12: 10-17.

———. 2012. Predatory publishers are corrupting open access. *Nature News,* 489: 179. DOI: 10.1038/489179a.

———. 2013. The open-access movement is not really about open access. *TripleC,* 11: 589-97.

Beall, J. 2016. Ban predators from the scientific record. *Nature*, 534: 326-26

Beaudry, C., Mouton, J., and Prozesky, H. 2018. *The next generation of scientists in Africa*. Cape Town: African Minds.

Beigel, F. 2014. Publishing from the periphery: Structural heterogeneity and segmented circuits. The evaluation of scientific publications for tenure in Argentina's CONICET. *Current Sociology*, 62: 743-65.

Beigel, M.F. 2018. A world of circuits: the shift from impact to circulation. *AmeliCA*. http://amelica.org/index.php/en/2018/11/27/a-world-of-circuits-the-shift-from-impact-to-circulation/

Bell, K. 2015. Journal standards and their stories. Or, a trip down the rabbit hole. *Medical Anthropology Theory*, 2(3): 182-189

Bell, K. 2017. 'Predatory' open access journals as parody: exposing the limitations of 'legitimate' academic publishing. *TripleC*, 15(2): 651-62.

Bell, K. 2019. Communitas and the commons: The open access movement and the dynamics of restructuration in scholarly publishing, *Anthropology Today*, 35: 21-24.

Bell, K., and Mills, D. 2020. What we know about the academic journal landscape reflects global inequalities. *LSE Impact of Social Sciences Blog*. https://blogs.lse.ac.uk/impactofsocialsciences/2020/10/12/what-we-know-about-the-academic-journal-landscape-reflects-global-in- equalities/.

Bence, V., and Oppenheim, C. 2005. The evolution of the UK's research assessment exercise: publications, performance and perceptions. *Journal of Educational Administration and History*, 37(1): 137-155.

Bening, R.B. (2005). *University for Development Studies in the history of higher education in Ghana*. Accra: Hish Tawawah.

Berger, M. 2021. Bibliodiversity at the centre: decolonizing open access. *Development and Change*, 52: 383-404.

Biagioli, M., and Lippman, A. 2020. *Gaming the metrics: misconduct and manipulation in academic research*. Cambridge, MA: MIT Press.

Bodomo, A.B. 1999. Pushing onto Publishville: frustrations and fruits – managing the 'publish or perish' maxim at the University of Ghana, W. Africa. In P. Habomugisha (Ed.), *Now and in the next millennium 1990s– 3000 CE: assessing Africa's scholarly publishing needs and industry*. Kampala: JARP.

Boyer, E. 1990. *The scholarship of teaching: priorities for the professoriate*. Princeton: Carnegie Foundation for the Advancement of Teaching.

Brown, C.H. 1947. Scientific publishing in continental Europe: notes on its war and postwar status. *Science,* 106(2742): 54-8.

Burrows, R. 2012. Living with the h-index: metric assemblages in the contemporary academy. *The Sociological Review*, 60: 355-72.

Cabanac, G. 2018. What is the primordial reference for ...? — Redux. *Scientometrics,* 114(2): 481-8. DOI: 10.1007/s11192-017-2595-4.

Cabral, A., Njinya-Mujinya, L., and Habomugisha, P. 1998. Published or rejected? African intellectuals' scripts and foreign journals, publishers and editors. *Nordic Journal of African Studies,* 7: 83-94.

Cahn, R.W. 1994. The origins of Pergamon Press: Rosbaud and Maxwell. *European Review,* 2(1): 37-42. DOI: 10.1017/S1062798700000879.

Canagarajah, A.S. 2002. *A geopolitics of academic writing.* Pittsburgh, PA: University of Pittsburgh Press.

——— 2013. *Translingual practice: global Englishes and cosmopolitan relations:* Abingdon: Routledge.

Canhos, V, L. Chan, and B. Kirsop. 2001. Bioline Publications: how its evolution has mirrored the growth of the internet. *Learned Publishing,* 14: 41-48.

Cardoso, S., Tavares, O., Sin, C., and Carvalho, T. (Eds.). 2020. *Structural and institutional transformations in doctoral education.* Basingstoke: Palgrave Macmillan.

Carré, N. 2016. From local to global: new paths for publishing in Africa. *Wasafiri,* 31(4): 56-62.

Carrigan, M. 2015. Life in the accelerated academy: anxiety thrives, demands intensify and metrics hold the tangled web together. *LSE Impact of Social Sciences Blog.* http://blogs.lse.ac.uk/impactofsocialsciences/2015/04/07/life-in-the-accelerated-academy-carrigan/

Casanave, E. 1998. Transitions: the balancing act of bilingual academics. *Journal of Second Language Writing,* 12(1): 175-203.

Case, C.M. 1927. Scholarship in Sociology. *Sociology and Social Research,* 12: 323-40.

Chakava, H. 1993. Private enterprise publishing in Kenya: a long struggle for emancipation. *Logos,* 4: 130-35.

Chan, L., and Costa, S. 2005. Participation in the global knowledge commons: challenges and opportunities for research dissemination in developing countries. *New Library World,* 106(3/4): 141-63. DOI: 10.1108/03074800510587354.

Chan, L., Okune, A., Hillyer, R., Albornoz, D., and Posada, A. 2019. *Contextualizing openness: situating open science.* Ottawa: University of Ottawa Press and IDRC.

Chan, L., Kirsop, B., and Arunachalam, S. 2011. Towards open and equitable access to research and knowledge for development. *PLOS Med.,* 8(3). DOI: 10.1371/journal.pmed.1001016.

Chen, G., Posada, A., and Chan, L. 2019. Vertical integration in academic publishing: implications for knowledge inequality. In *Connecting the knowledge commons – From projects to sustainable infrastructure: The 22nd International Conference on Electronic Publishing – Revised Selected Papers*. Marseille: Open Edition Press.

Clark, B.R. 1994. The research-teaching-study nexus in modern systems of higher education. *Higher Education Policy*, 7: 11-17.

Clark, W. 2006. *Academic charisma and the origins of the research university*. Chicago: University of Chicago Press

Clegg, S. 2010. Time future: the dominant discourse of higher education. *Time & Society*, 19: 345-64.

Cloete, N., Bunting, I., and Van Schalkwyk, F. 2018. *Research universities in Africa*. Cape Town: African Minds.

Cloete, N., and Maassen, P. 2015. *Knowledge Production and contradictory functions in African higher education*. Cape Town: African Minds.

Cloete, N., Mouton, J., and Sheppard, C.. 2015. *Doctoral education in South Africa: policy, discourse and data*. Cape Town: African Minds.

Cobbinah, J., and Aryeh-Adjei, A. 2018. Academics with professional doctorate degrees in Ghanaian universities. *International Journal of Adult Vocational Education and Technology* 39: 24-34.

Collyer, F. M. 2016. Global patterns in the publishing of academic knowledge: Global North, Global South. *Current Sociology*, 66: 56-73.

Connell, R., Collyer, F., Maia, J., and Morrell, R. 2016. Toward a global sociology of knowledge: Post-colonial realities and intellectual practices, *International Sociology*, 32: 21-37.

Cox, B. 2002. The Pergamon phenomenon 1951–1991: Robert Maxwell and scientific publishing. *Learned Publishing*, 15(4):273-8.

Craggs, R., and Neate, H. 2019. What happens if we start from Nigeria? Diversifying histories of geography. *Annals of the American Association of Geographers*: 1-18. DOI: 10.1080/24694452.2019.1631748.

Crosetto, P. 2021. Is MDPI a predatory publisher? Paolo Crosetto Blog. 12 April 12. https://paolocrosetto.wordpress.com/2021/04/12/is-mdpi-a-predatory-publisher/

Crossick, G. 2015. *Monographs and open access: a report to HEFCE*. London: HEFCE.

Crow, R., Gallagher, R., and Naim, K. 2020. Subscribe to open: a practical approach for converting subscription journals to open access. *Learned Publishing* 33(2): 181-5. https://doi.org/10.1002/leap.1262.

Crowder, M. 1987. 'Us' and 'them': the International African Institute and the current crisis of identity in African Studies. *Africa*, 57(1):109-22. DOI: 10.2307/1160186.

Cruz, M, and Luke, D. 2020. Methodology and academic extractivism: The neo-colonialism of the British university. *Third World Thematics*, 5: 154-70.

Csiszar, A. 2019. *The scientific journal: authorship and the politics of knowledge in the nineteenth century*. Chicago: University of Chicago Press.

Curle, A. 1962. Nationalism and higher education in Ghana. *Higher Education Quarterly*, 16(3): 229-442.

Currey, J. 2010. A model for an African scholarly network press. In S. Ngobeni (Ed.), *Scholarly publishing in Africa: opportunities & impediments*. Cape Town: Africa Institute.

Curry, M.J., and Lillis, T.M. 2017. *Global academic publishing: policies, perspectives and pedagogies*. Bristol: Multilingual Matters.

Darko-Ampen, K. 2005. A university press publishing consortium for Africa: lessons from academic libraries. *Journal of Scholarly Publishing*, 36(2): 89-114.

Davis, C. 2005. The politics of postcolonial publishing: Oxford University Press's Three Crowns series 1962-1976. *Book History*, 8: 227-44.

DeSolla Price, D.J. 1961. *Science since Babylon*. New Haven, CT: Yale University Press.

De Mutiss, A., and Kitchen, S. 2016. African digital research repositories: survey report. International African Institute. https://www. internationalafricaninstitute.org/downloads/ AfricanDigitalResearchrepositories.pdf

De Wit, H., and Altbach, P. 2021. Internationalization in higher education: global trends and recommendations for its future. *Policy Reviews in Higher Education*, 5: 28-46.

Dodson, D., and Dodson, B. 1972. Publishing progress in Nigeria. *Scholarly Publishing*, 4: 62.

DORA (Declaration on Research Assessment). 2012. https://sfdora.org/

Droney, D. 2014. Ironies of laboratory working during Ghana's second age of optimism. *Cultural Anthropology* 29(2): 363-84.

Duermeijer, C., Amir, M., and Schoombee, L. 2018. Africa generates less than 1% of the world's research; data analytics can change that. In *Elsevier Connect*. Elsevier. https://www.elsevier.com/connect/africa- generates-less-than-1-of-the-worlds-research-data-analytics-can-change- that

Edeoga, H.O., Okwu, D.E., and Mbaebie, B.O.. 2005. Phytochemical constituents of some Nigerian medicinal plants. *African Journal of Biotechnology*, 4: 685-88.

Edwards, M.A., and Roy, S. 2017. Academic research in the 21st century: maintaining scientific integrity in a climate of perverse incentives and hypercompetition. *Environmental Engineering Science* 34(1): 51-61. DOI: 10.1089/ees.2016.0223.

Effah, P. 2018. Rethinking higher education governance in Ghana: reflections of a professional administrator. *CODESRIA Working Papers*. Dakar: CODESRIA.

Eriksson, S, and Gert, H. 2018. Time to stop talking about predatory journals. *Learned Publishing*, 31: 181-83.

Esposito, J. 2013. Parting company with Jeffrey Beall. *Scholarly Kitchen*. 16 December 2013. https://scholarlykitchen.sspnet.org/2013/12/16/parting-company-with-jeffrey-beall/

Eve, M., and Gray, J. (Eds.). 2020. *Reassembling scholarly communications: histories, infrastructures, and global politics of open Access*. Cambridge, MA: The MIT Press. https://doi.org/10.7551/mitpress/11885.003.0026

Faciolince, M., and Green, D. 2021. One door opens: Another door shuts? *Development and Change*, 52(2), 373-82. https://doi.org/10.1111/dech.12633

Fire, M., and Guestrin, C. 2019. Over-optimization of academic publishing metrics: observing Goodhart's Law in action. *GigaScience* 8(6). DOI: 10.1093/gigascience/giz053.

Flaherty, C. 2022. Retract or attack? *Inside Higher Ed*. 24 May 2022. https://www.insidehighered.com/news/2022/05/24/black-scholars-demand-retraction-autoethnography-article#.YrRVYg_dSfE.link

Fosci, M., Loffreda, L., Chamberlain, A., and Naidoo, N. 2019. *Assessing the needs of the research system in Ghana*. Report for the SRIA programme. London: DFID.

Foxcroft, L.C. 2020. *Koedoe*: Changing of the guard. *Koedoe*, 62:(1): a1645. DOI: 10.4102/koedoe.

Fyfe, A., Coate, K., Curry, S., Lawson, S., Moxham, N., and Røstvik, C.M. 2017. *Untangling academic publishing: a history of the relationship between commercial interests, academic prestige and the circulation of research*. University of St Andrews. https://doi.org/10.5281/zenodo.546100

Galloway, N, and Rose, H. 2015. *Introducing global Englishes*. Abingdon: Routledge

Ganu, K.M. 1999. Scholarly publishing in Ghana: the role of Ghana Universities Press. *Journal of Scholarly Publishing*, 30(3):111-23.

Garfield, E. 1955. Citation indexes for science: a new dimension in documentation through association of ideas. *Science* 122(3159): 108-11g. DOI: 10.1126/science.122.3159.108.

Garfield, E. 1972. Citation analysis as a tool in journal evaluation. *Science*, 178: 471-79.

———. 1996. What is the primordial reference for the phrase 'publish or perish'? *The Scientist* 10(12): 11.

Gordin, M. 2015. *Scientific Babel: how science was done before and after global English*. Chicago: University of Chicago Press

Gray, E. 2016. An Elsevier African megajournal proposal re-colonising the university in Africa? *Blog of the IP Unit: University of Cape Town*. https://ip-unit.org/2016/an-elsevier-african-megajournal-proposal-re-colonising-the-university-in-africa/

Gray, J. 2020. Infrastructural experiments and the politics of open access. In M. Eve and J. Gray (Eds.), *Reassembling scholarly communications: histories, infrastructures, and global politics of open access*. Cambridge, MA: MIT Press. https://doi.org/10.7551/mitpress/11885.003.0026

Grimwade, A.M. 2018. Eugene Garfield – 60 years of invention and innovation. *Frontiers in Research Metrics and Analytics*, 3(14). DOI: 10.3389/frma.2018.00014.

Guzman-Valenzuela, C., and R. Barnett. 2013. Marketing time: evolving timescapes in academia. *Studies in Higher Education*, 38: 1120-34.

Gyamera, G.O. 2019. The internationalisation agenda: a critical look at the conceptualisation and rationalisation of internationalisation in public universities in Ghana. *Compare: A Journal of Comparative and International Education*, 49(6): 924-42. DOI: 10.1080/03057925.2018.1474729.

Halvorsen, T., and Nossum, J. 2016. *North–South knowledge networks: towards equitable collaboration between academics, donors and universities*. Cape Town: African Minds.

Haraway, D. 1997. *Modest Witness@Second Millenium: FemaleMan meets Oncomouse*. London: Routledge.

Harsh, M., Bal, R., Weryha, A., Whatley, J., Onu, C.C., and Negro, L.M. 2021. Mapping computer science research in Africa: using academic networking sites for assessing research activity. *Scientometrics*, 126: 305-34.

Hartcup, G., and Lovell, B. 2000. *The effect of science on the Second World War*. Maidenhead, England: Palgrave Macmillan.

Hill, C., and Thabet, R. 2021. Publication challenges facing doctoral students: perspective and analysis from the UAE. *Quality in Higher Education*, 27: 324-37.

Hodgkinson, M. 2012. Lambert Academic Publishing (or how not to publish your thesis). Journalology Blog: https://journalology.blogspot.com/2012/09/lambert-academic-publishing-or-how-not.html

————. 2018. Curbing the cargo cults. Hindawi Blog. https://www.hindawi.com/post/curbing-the-cargo-cults/

Hopkins, B. 1960. The Science Association of Nigeria. *Nature* 186(4723): 442-3. DOI: 10.1038/186442a0.

Hountondji, P. J. 1990. Scientific dependence in Africa today. *Research in African Literatures*, 21: 5-15.

————. 1997. *Endogenous knowledge: research trails*. Dakar, Senegal: CODESRIA.

————. 2009. Knowledge of Africa, knowledge by Africans: two perspectives on African studies. *RCCS Annual Review. A selection from the Portuguese journal Revista Crítica de Ciências Sociais* (1).

Hyland, K. (2015). *Academic publishing: issues and challenges in the construction of knowledge*. Oxford: Oxford University Press.

Inouye, K., and Mills, D. 2021. Fear of the academic fake? Journal editorials and the amplification of the predatory publishing discourse. *Learned Publishing,* 34(3): 396-406. DOI: 10.1002/leap.1377

Irele, F. 1973. Introduction: the African publisher. In Tayo Akpata (ed.), *Publishing in Nigeria*. Benin City: Ethiope.

Ivancheva, M., Lynch, K., and Keating, K. 2019. Precarity, gender and care in the neoliberal academy. *Gender, Work & Organization*, 26: 448-62.

Jaumont, F. 2016. *Unequal partners: American foundations and higher education development in Africa*. New York: Palgrave Macmillan.

Johnson, R., Watkinson, A., and Mabe, M. 2018. *The STM report: An overview of scientific and scholarly publishing.* International Association of Scientific, Technical and Medical Publishers.

Kaburise, J. 2003. New variations on the African development university: the UDS experience. Regional Training Conference on Improving Tertiary Education in Sub-Saharan Africa: Things That Work! Accra, Ghana: ADEA.

Kamler, B. 2008. Rethinking doctoral publication practices: writing from and beyond the thesis. *Studies in Higher Education*, 33: 283-94.

Kamler, B., and Thomson, P. 2008. The failure of dissertation advice books: toward alternative pedagogies for doctoral writing. *Educational Researcher*, 37: 507-14.

————. 2014. *Helping doctoral students write: Pedagogies for supervision*. London: Routledge.

Kamwendo, G. 2014. Language policies of South African accredited journals in Humanities and Social Sciences: Are they speaking the language of transformation? *Alternation*, 21(2): 207-22.

Kień, W. 2017. Authors from the periphery countries choose open access more often. *Learned Publishing*, 30: 125-31.

Kingori, P. 2021. Unmuting conversations on fakes in African spaces. *Journal of African Cultural Studies*, 33: 239-50.

Kingori, P., and Gerrets, R. 2019. Why the pseudo matters to global health. *Critical Public Health* 29(4):379-89.

Kuhn, T. 1962. *The structure of scientific revolutions.* Chicago: University of Chicago.

Kwiek, M. 2018. *Changing European academics: a comparative study of social stratification, work patterns and research productivity*. London: Routledge.

Laar, A.K., Redman, B.K., Ferguson, K., and Caplan, A. 2020. Institutional approaches to research integrity in Ghana. *Science and Engineering Ethics,* 26(6): 3037-52.

Larivière, V., Haustein, S., and Mongeon, P. 2015. The oligopoly of academic publishers in the digital era. *PloSOne,* 10(6): e0127502.

Larson, C.R. 2001. *The ordeal of the African writer*. London: Zed.

Lebeau, Y., and Mills, D. 2008. From 'crisis' to 'transformation'? Shifting orthodoxies of African higher education policy and research. *Learning and Teaching: The international journal of higher education in the Social Sciences,* 1(1): 58-88.

Le Grange, L. 2019. On 'predatory' publishing: a reply to Maistry. *Journal of Education*, 75: 21-30.

Le Roux, E. 2015a. Discrimination in scholarly publishing. *Critical Arts,* 29(6): 703-704. DOI: 10.1080/02560046.2015.1151104

———. 2015b. Open minds and closed systems: an author profile of South Africa's university presses. *Critical Arts,* 29(6): 746-765. DOI: 10.1080/025600 46.2015.1151110

———. 2020. *Publishing against apartheid South Africa: A case study of Ravan Press*. Cambridge: Cambridge University Press.

Li, Y. 2016. Publish SCI papers or no degree: practices of Chinese doctoral supervisors in response to the publication pressure on science students. *Asia Pacific Journal of Education*, 36: 545-58.

Li, S.Q. 2020. The end of publish or perish? China's new policy on research evaluation. *Observations*, 1. DOI: 10.17617/2.3263127.

Lillis, T. 2012 Economies of signs in writing for academic publication: the case of English medium national journals. *JAC*, 32(3/4): 695-722.

Lillis, T. M., and Curry, M. 2010. *Academic writing in a global context: the politics and practices of publishing in English*. London: Routledge

Livsey, T. 2017. *Nigeria's university age: reframing decolonisation and development*. Basingstoke: Palgrave.

Lorenz-Meyer, D. 2018. The academic productivist regime: affective dynamics in the moral-political economy of publishing. *Science as Culture,* 27(2): 151-74.

Luescher, T.M., and Van Schalkwyk, F. 2018. African university presses and the institutional logic of the knowledge commons. *Learned Publishing,* 31(S1): 288-98.

Lynn, P.N., and Bellanova, R. 2017. Lost in quantification: scholars and the politics of bibliometrics. In M.J. Curry and T.M. Lillis (Eds.), *Global academic publishing.* Bristol: Multilingual Matters.

Mabokela, R.O., and Mlambo, Y.A. 2015. "The older women are men": navigating the academic terrain, perspectives from Ghana. *Higher Education,* 69(5): 759-78.

———. 2017. Women, leadership, and organizational culture in higher education: lessons learned from South Africa and Ghana. In H. Eggins (Ed.), *The changing role of women in higher education: academic and leadership issues.* Cham: Springer.

MacLeavy, J., Harris, R., and Johnston, R. 2020. The unintended consequences of open access publishing – and possible futures. *Geoforum,* 112, 9-12. https://doi.org/10.1016/j.geoforum.2019.12.010.

Madikizela-Madiya, N. 2022. Transforming higher education spaces through ethical research publication: a critique of the publish or perish aphorism. *Higher Education Research & Development:* 1-14.

Maistry, S.M. 2019. (Re)counting the high cost of predatory publishing and the effect of a neoliberal performativity culture. *Journal of Education* 75: 5-19.

Mama, A. 2011. The challenges of feminism: gender, ethics and responsible academic freedom in African Universities. *Journal of Higher Education in Africa/Revue de l'enseignement supérieur en Afrique* 9(1-2): 1-23.

Mamdani, M. 2007. *Scholars in the marketplace: the dilemmas of neo-liberal reform at Makerere University, 1989-2005.* Dakar: CODESRIA.

———. 2018. The African university. *London Review of Books,* 40: 14

Manuh, T., Gariba, S., and Budu, J. 2007. *Change and transformation in Ghana's publicly funded universities: a study of experiences, lessons & opportunities.* Oxford: James Currey.

Mara, K., and Thompson, K. (2022). African studies keyword: autoethnography. *African Studies Review,* 65(2), 372-398. doi:10.1017/asr.2022.58.

Marginson, S. 2018. The new geo-politics of higher education: global cooperation, national competition and social inequality in the World-Class University (WCU) sector. *Working Paper 34.* Oxford: CGHE

———. 2021. What drives global science? The four competing narratives. *Studies in Higher Education:* 1-19.

Marincola, E., and Thomas, K. 2020. Quality research in Africa and why it is important. *ACS Omega,* 5(38): 24155-7.

Mazrui, A. 1997. The World Bank: the language question and the future of African education. *Race & Class,* 38.3: 35-48.

Mbembe, A. 2001. *On the postcolony.* Berkeley: University of California.

Mbembe, J.A. 2016. Decolonizing the university: New directions. *Arts and Humanities in Higher Education,* 15(1): 29-45.

McAlpine, L., and Amundsen, C. 2017. *Identity-trajectories of early career researchers: unpacking the post-PhD experience.* London: Palgrave Macmillan.

McCauley, J.F. 2013. Africa's new big man rule? Pentecostalism and patronage in Ghana. *African Affairs* 112(446): 1-21.

McCowan, T. 2017. Higher education, unbundling, and the end of the university as we know it. *Oxford Review of Education,* 43(6): 733-48.

McCracken, J. 1993. African history in British universities: past, present and future. *African Affairs,* 92: 239-53.

McKinley, J., McIntosh, S., Milligan, L., and Mikołajewska, A. 2020. Eyes on the enterprise: problematising the concept of a teaching-research nexus in UK higher education. *Higher Education,* 81: 1023–41.

McLean Rathgeber, E-M. 1979. Nigeria's university presses: problems and prospects. *The African Book Publishing Record* 5 (1): 13-18.

Meadows, A.J. 1980. *Development of science publishing in Europe.* Amsterdam: Elsevier.

Meagher, K. 2021. Introduction: The politics of open access — Decolonizing research or corporate capture? *Development and Change,* 52(2): 340-358. DOI: 10.1111/dech.12630

Mêgnigbêto, E. 2013. International collaboration in scientific publishing: the case of West Africa (2001–2010). *Scientometrics,* 96(3): 761-83.

Memon, A. 2019. Revisiting the term predatory open access publishing. *Journal of Korean Medical Science,* 34(13): e99. 10.3346/jkms.2019.34.e99

Merton, R.K. 1973. *The sociology of science: theoretical and empirical investigations.* Chicago: University of Chicago Press.

Mills, D. 2003. Relativism and cultural studies. *Think: The Journal of the Royal Institute of Philosophy,* 1: 29-32.

———. 2004. The new African higher education? *African Affairs,* 103: 667-75.

———. 2020. The epistemic politics of 'academography': navigating competing representations of Africa's university futures. *Globalisation, Societies and Education,* 1-12.

Mills, D., and Branford, A. 2022. Getting by in a bibliometric economy: scholarly publishing and academic credibility in the Nigerian academy. *Africa.*

Mills, D., Branford, A., Inouye, K., Robinson, N., and Kingori, P. 2021. Fake journals and the fragility of authenticity: citation indexes, predatory publishing, and the African research ecosystem. *Journal of African Cultural Studies,* 33(3): 276-96. DOI: 10.1080/13696815.2020.1864304

Mills, D., and Inouye, K. 2020. Problematizing 'predatory publishing': A systematic review of factors shaping publishing motives, decisions, and experiences. *Learned Publishing,* 34: 89-104.

Mills, D., and Ratcliffe, R. 2012. After method: anthropology, education and the knowledge economy. *Qualitative Research,* 12: 147-64.

Mills, D., and Robinson, N. 2021. Democratising publishing or preying on researchers? Geographies of credibility and visibility in a global research economy. *Science as Culture.* DOI: 10.1080/09505431.2021.2005562.

Mirowski, P. 2018. The future(s) of open science. *Social Studies of Science,* 48: 171-203.

Mlambo, A. (Ed.). 2007. *African scholarly publishing essays.* Oxford: African Books Collective.

Molla, T., and Cuthbert, D. 2016. In pursuit of the African PhD: A critical survey of emergent policy issues in select Sub-Saharan African nations, Ethiopia, Ghana and South Africa. *Policy Futures in Education,* 14: 635-654.

Molteno, R. 2016. Digital repositories: making Africa's intelligentsia visible? *Bulletin of the National Library of South Africa,* 70(2): 167-182.

Montgomery, S. 2013. *Does science need a global language? English and the future of research.* Chicago: Chicago University Press.

Moore, S.A. 2017. A genealogy of open access: negotiations between openness and access to research, *Revue française des sciences de information et de la communication,* 11. DOI: 10.4000/rfsic.3220

———. 2019. Common struggles: Policy-based vs. scholar-led approaches to open access in the humanities. PhD thesis, King's College London.

———. 2021. Decolonizing open access in development research open access, Plan S and 'radically liberatory' forms of academic freedom. *Development and Change,* 52(6): 1513-1525.

Moosa, I.A. 2018. *Publish or perish: perceived benefits versus unintended consequences.* Cheltenham: Edward Elgar.

Morrison, H. 2016. Small scholar-led scholarly journals: can they survive and thrive in an open access future? *Learned Publishing,* 29: 83-88.

Moskaleva, O., and Akoev, M.A. 2019. Non-English language publications in citation indexes – quantity and quality. In *ISSI2019: 17th International Conference on Scientometrics and Infometrics.* University of Sapienza, Rome: ISSI.

Mouton, J. 2008. Africa's science decline: The challenge of building scientific institutions. *Harvard International Review* 30(3): 46-51.

Mouton, J., and Blanckenberg, J.P. 2018. African science: a bibliometric analysis. In C. Beaudry, J. Mouton, and H. Prozesky (Eds.), *The next generation of scientists in Africa*. Cape Town: African Minds.

Mouton, J, and Prozesky, H. 2018. Research publications. In C. Beaudry, J. Mouton and H. Prozesky (Eds.), *The next generation of scientists in Africa*. Cape Town: African Minds

Mouton, J., and Valentine, A. 2017. The extent of South African authored articles in predatory journals. *South African Journal of Science,* 113(7/8). https://sajs.co.za/article/view/3995.

Mouton, J., Redelinghuys, H., Spies, J., Blanckenberg, J., Lorenzen, L., Ford, K., Visagie, A., and Van Niekerk, M. 2019. *The quality of South Africa's research publications. Final report to DHET*. https://www0.sun.ac.za/crest/wp-content/uploads/2021/01/quality-of-south-africas-research-publications.pdf.

Muller, J. 2017. Academics as rent seekers: distorted incentives in higher education, with reference to the South African case. *International Journal of Educational Development,* 52: 58-67.

Muller, J. 2019. *The tyranny of metrics*. Princeton: Princeton University Press.

Murray, S. 2009. Moving Africa away from the global knowledge periphery: a case study of AJOL. *Africa Bibliography*, 2008: vii-xxiv.

Murray, S., and Clobridge, A. 2014. The current state of scholarly publishing in Africa: findings and analysis Sept 2014. AJOL: Cape Town. Available at: https://www.ajol.info/public/Scholarly-Journal-Publish- ing-in-Africa-Report-Final-v04c.pdf.

Nabyonga-Orem, J., Avoka Asamani, J., Nyirenda, T., and Abigailmbola, S. 2020. Article processing charges are stalling the progress of African researchers: a call for urgent reforms. *BMJ Global Health,* 5(9): e003650.

Naidu, E, and Dell, S. 2019. Predatory journals in the firing line. *Unviversity World News*, 31 May. www.universityworldnews.com/post.php?story=20190531111556458.

Ndlovu-Gatsheni, S.J. 2017. The emergence and trajectories of struggles for an 'African university': the case of unfinished business of African epistemic decolonisation. *Kronos,* 43(1): 51-77.

Nerad, M., and Evans, B. 2014. *Globalization and its impacts on the quality of PhD education*. Rotterdam: Sense.

Ngobeni, S. 2010. *Scholarly publishing in Africa: opportunities & impediments*. Cape Town: Africa Institute.

Nicholas, D., et al. 2017. Early career researchers and their publishing and authorship practices. *Learned Publishing,* 30(3): 205-217.

Nkrumah, K. 1963. The African genius: Speech delivered by Osagyefo Dr Kwame Nkrumah at the opening of the Institute of African Studies, 25 October 1963. Accra: Government Printer.

Nobes, A, and Harris, S.. 2019. Open access in low- and middle-income countries: attitudes and experiences of researchers. *Emerald Open Research*, 1. https://emeraldopenresearch.com/articles/1-17.

Nolte, I. 2019. The future of African Studies: what we can do to keep Africa at the heart of our research. *Journal of African Cultural Studies,* 31(3): 296-313.

Nwagwu, W. 2005. A bibliometric analysis of patterns of authorship in the biomedical literature of Nigeria. PhD thesis, University of Ibadan.

———. 2008. Online journals and visibility of science in Africa: a role for an African social science citation index. Putting African journals online: opportunities, implications and limits. In *Proceedings of the Third International Conference on Electronic Publishing and Dissemination*, 1-14. Dakar: CODESRIA.

———. 2010. Cybernating the academe: centralized scholarly ranking and visibility of scholars in the developing world. *Journal of Information Science,* 36(2): 228-41.

———. 2016. Open access in the developing regions: situating the altercations about predatory publishing. *Canadian Journal of Information and Library Science* 40(1): 58-80.

Nwagwu, W., and Makhubela, S. 2017. Status and performance of open access journals in Africa. *Mousaion*, 35: 1-27.

Nwagwu, W.E., and Ojemeni, O. 2015. Penetration of Nigerian predatory biomedical open access journals 2007–2012: a bibliometric study. *Learned Publishing,* 28(1): 23-34. DOI: 10.1087/20150105.

Nwali, L.O. 1991. Book publishing in Nigeria: problems and prospects. *Publishing Research Quarterly,* 7(4): 65-70. DOI: 10.1007/BF02678333.

Nyamnjoh, F. 2004. From publish or perish to publish and perish: What 'Africa's 100 best books' tell us about publishing Africa. *Journal of Asian and African Studies,* 39: 331-55.

Obeng-Odoom, F., Mensah, J., and Botha, F. 2019. *The African Review of Economics and Finance*: past, present, and future. *African Review of Economics and Finance*, 11, 3-17.

Odjidja, E.N. 2021. What is wrong with global health? So-called glorified data collectors in low-income regions. *The Lancet Global Health*, 9: e1365.

Ogot, B.A. 1965. East African Institute of Social and Cultural Affairs, Nairobi. *The Journal of Modern African Studies,* 3(2): 283-5. DOI: 10.1017/ S0022278X00023673.

Okune, A., Adebowale, S., Gray, E., Mumo, A., and Oniang'o, R. 2021. Conceptualizing, financing and infrastructuring: perspectives on open access in and from Africa. *Development and Change,* 52: 359-72.

Oluwasanami, E., McLean, E., and Zell, H.M. (Eds.). 1975. *Publishing in Africa in the seventies: proceedings of an international conference on publishing and book development held at the University of Ife, Ile-Ife, Nigeria, 16-20 December 1973.* Ile-Ife, Nigeria: University of Ife Press.

Omobowale, A.O., Sawadogo, N., Sawadodo-Compaoré, E.M.F.W., and Ugbem, C.E., 2013. Globalization and scholarly publishing in West Africa. *International Journal of Sociology,* 43(1): 8-26. DOI: 10.2753/IJS0020-7659430101.

Omobowale, A., Akanle, O., and Adeniran, A.I. 2014. Peripheral scholarship and the context of foreign paid publishing in Nigeria. *Current Sociology,* 62(5): 666-84. DOI: 10.1177/0011392113508127.

Oniang'o, R. 2005. Overcoming challenges: the case of the young scientists in Africa. *African Journal of Food, Agriculture, Nutrition and Development,* 5(2). https://www.ajfand.net/Volume5/No2/editorial.html#gsc.tab=0

Ophir, A., and Shapin, S. 1991. The place of knowledge: a methodological survey. *Science in Context,* 4: 3-22.

Parker, M., and Kingori, P. 2016. Good and bad research collaborations: researchers' views on science and ethics in global health research. *PloSOne,* 11(10).

Peters, P. 2007. Going all the way: how Hindawi became an open access publisher. *Learned Publishing* 20: 191-195.

Posada, A., and Chen, G. 2018. Inequality in knowledge production: the integration of academic infrastructure by big publishers. In *ELPUB 2018.* Toronto.

Powell, R. 2007. Geographies of science: histories, localities, practices, futures, *Progress in Human Geography,* 31: 309-29.

Power, M. 1997. *The audit society: rituals of verification.* Oxford: Oxford University Press.

Poynder, R., 2012. The OA Interviews: Ahmed Hindawi, founder of Hindawi Publishing Corporation. https://poynder.blogspot.com/2012/09/the-oa-interviews-ahmed-hindawi-founder.html

Prah, M. 2002. Gender issues in Ghanaian tertiary institutions: women academics and administrators at Cape Coast University. *Ghana Studies,* 5: 83-122.

Price, A.R. 2013. Research misconduct and its federal regulation: the origin and history of the Office of Research Integrity—with personal views by ORI's former associate director for investigative oversight. *Accountability in Research,* 20(5-6): 291-319.

Rabkin, Y.M., Eisemon, T.O., Lafitte-Houssat, J-J., and McLean Rathgeber, E. 1979. Citation visibility of Africa's science. *Social Studies of Science,* 9(4): 499-506.

Raddon, A. 2007. Timescapes of flexibility and insecurity: Exploring the context of distance learners. *Time & Society,* 16: 61-82.

Raju, R., Claassen, J., Madini, N., and Suliaman, T. 2020. Social justice and inclusivity: drivers for the dissemination of African scholarship. In M. Eve and J. Gray (Eds.), *Reassembling scholarly communications: histories, infrastructures, and global politics of open access.* Cambridge, MA: MIT Press.

Readings, B. 1996. *The university in ruins.* Cambridge, MA: Harvard University Press.

Rodriguez-Medina, Leandro, Ferpozzi, H., Layna, J., Valdez, E.M., and Kreimer, P. (2019). International ties at peripheral sites: co-producing social processes and scientific knowledge in Latin America. *Science as Culture,* 28(4), 562-588. DOI: 10.1080/09505431.2019.1629409

Rohwer, A., Wager, E., Young, T., and Garner, P. 2018. Plagiarism in research: a survey of African medical journals. *BMJ Open* 8(11): e024777.

Sarr, F. 2022. Rebuilding knowledge in African countries. *Global Africa,* 1: 68-77.

Serra, G. 2015. From scattered data to ideological education: economics, statistics and the state in Ghana, 1948-1966. PhD thesis, London School of Economics and Political Science.

Schneider, L. 2016. OA publishers Hindawi vs. Frontiers: similar, yet different. *For Better Science.* https://forbetterscience.com/2016/02/15/oa-publishers-hindawi-vs-frontiers-similar-yet-different/

Shapin, S. 1994. *A social history of truth: civility and science in seventeenth-century England.* Chicago; London: University of Chicago Press.

Sharp, J.O. 2019. Practicing subalternity? Nyerere's Tanzania, the Dar School, and postcolonial geopolitical imaginations. In T. Jazeel and S. Legg (eds), *Subaltern geographies.* Athens, GA: University of Georgia Press.

Sheail, P. 2018. Temporal flexibility in the digital university: full-time, part-time, flexitime. *Distance Education,* 39: 462-79.

Shehu, B., and Ameh, E.. 2005. Editorial: The Society of African Journal Editors. *Annals of African Medicine,* 4.

Shields, R., and Watermeyer, R. 2020. Competing institutional logics in universities in the United Kingdom: schism in the church of reason. *Studies in Higher Education,* 45: 3-17.

Shils, E. 1972. *The intellectuals and the powers and other essays. Selected papers of Edward Shils*. Chicago: University of Chicago Press.

Shils, E., and Altbach, P.G. 2017. *The order of learning: essays on the contemporary university*. London: Routledge.

Shipley, J.W. 2017. Parody after identity: digital music and the politics of uncertainty in West Africa. *American Ethnologist*, 44: 249-62.

Shore, C., and Wright, S. 2000. Audit culture and anthropology. *Journal of the Royal Anthropological Institute*, 6: 523-26.

Sichermann, C. 2005. *Becoming an African university: Makerere 1922–2000*. Trenton, NJ: Africa World Press.

Sidaway, J.D. 2016. Scholarly publishing landscapes: a geographical perspective. *Area,* 48(3): 389-92.

Slaughter, S., and Rhoades, G.. 2004. *Academic capitalism and the new economy: markets, state and higher education*. Baltimore: Johns Hopkins University Press.

Smart, P., Pearce, C., and Tonukari, N. 2005. E-publishing in developing economies. *Canadian Journal of Communication,* 29: 329-41.

Smith, K. 1975. Who controls book publishing in anglophone middle Africa? *The Annals of the American Academy of Political and Social Science,* 421: 140-50.

Southall, R.J., and Kaufert, J.M. 1974. Converging models of university development: Ghana and East Africa. *Canadian Journal of African Studies,* 8(3): 607-628.

Ssentongo, J.S. 2020. 'Which journal is that?' Politics of academic promotion in Uganda and the predicament of African publication outlets. *Critical African Studies*, 12: 283-301.

Ssentongo, J.S., and Draru, M.C. 2018. Justice and the dynamics of research and publication: interrogating the performance of "publish or perish". In J.S. Ssentongo (Ed.), *Decolonisation pathways: postcoloniality, globalisation, and African development* (Uganda Martyrs University Book Series). Kampala: Uganda Martyrs University.

Stallinga, J. 2019. Elsevier: supporting higher education, science, technology and global competitiveness globally by partnering with the World Bank. In *Netherlands for the World Bank*. World Bank Group.

Strathern, M. 2000. *Audit cultures: anthropological studies in accountability, ethics and the academy*. London: Routledge.

Striphas, T. 2010. Acknowledged goods: Cultural studies and the politics of academic journal publishing. *Communication and Critical/Cultural Studies*, 7: 3-25.

Tarkang, E.E., and Bain, L. 2019. The bane of publishing a research article in international journals by African researchers, the peer-review process and the contentious issue of predatory journals: a commentary. *Pan African Medical Journal,* 32: 119.

Teferra, D. 2019. The publish-and-perish epidemic – Counting the costs. In *World University News.* 30 March. https://www.universityworldnews.com/post. php?story=20190326061756889

Teferra, D., and Altbach, P.G. 2003. *African higher education: an international reference handbook.* Bloomington, IN: Indiana University Press.

Thomas, M.A.M. 2018. Research capacity and dissemination among academics in Tanzania: examining knowledge production and the perceived binary of 'local' and 'international' journals. *Compare: A Journal of Comparative and International Education,* 48: 281-98.

Thornton, P., and Ocasio, W. 1999. Institutional logics and the historical contingency of power in organizations: executive succession in the higher education publishing industry, 1958–1990. *American Journal of Sociology,* 105: 801-42.

Tijssen, R.J.W., Mouton, J., Van Leeuwen, T.N., and Boshoff, N. 2006. How relevant are local scholarly journals in global science? A case study of South Africa. *Research Evaluation,* 15(3): 163-74. DOI: 10.3152/147154406781775904.

Tomaselli, K. 2015. Practices in scholarly publishing: making sense of rejection. *Critical Arts,* 29(6): 713-724.

___ ___ ___. 2018. Perverse incentives and the political economy of South African academic journal publishing, *South African Journal of Science,* 114: 1-6.

___ ___ ___. 2019. Indeterminacy, indigeneity, peer Review and the mind– body problem. *Junctures,* 20: 87-102.

___ ___ ___. 2020. Humanities, citations and currency: hierarchies of value and enabled recolonisation. *Critical Arts,* 33(7): 1-14. DOI: 10.1080/02560046.2019.1690534.

Tomaselli, K., Muller, J., and Shepperson, A. 1996. Negotiations, transitions and uncertainty principles: critical arts in the worlds of the post. *Critical Arts,* 10(2): i-xxii.

Tonukari, N.J. 2004. Research communications in the 21st century. *African Journal of Biotechnology* 3: 123-26.

Tonukari, N.J. 2018. The revival of the Society of African Journal Editors (SAJE), *African Journal of Food, Agriculture, Nutrition and Development,* 18(2). https://www.ajfand.net/Volume18/No2/saje.html#gsc.tab=0

Tousignant, N. 2018. *Edges of exposure: toxicology and the problem of capacity in postcolonial Senegal*. Durham: Duke University Press.

Tsikata, D. 2007. Gender, institutional cultures and the career trajectories of faculty of the University of Ghana. *Feminist Africa* 8: 26-41.

Umezurike, U.P. 2019. Self-publishing in the era of military rule in Nigeria, 1985–1999. *Journal of African Cultural Studies 32*: 1-19.

UDS (University of Development Studies). 2018. Administrative manual. UDS Tamale, Ghana.

UG (University of Ghana). 2014. *UG Strategic Plan (2014-2024)*. http://www.ug.edu.gh/publicaffairs/ug-strategic-plan-2014-2024

UG. 2019. Guidelines for implementation of policy on promotion of academic faculty. University of Ghana, Accra.

Van den Berghe, P. 1973. *Power and privilege at an African university*. London: Routledge and Kegan Paul.

Van Schalkwyk, F. 2020. Normative drift and self-correction in scholarly book publishing: The case of Makerere University. *Learned Publishing* 33(3): 259-68.

Van Schalkwyk, F., and Luescher, T.M. 2017. *The African university press*. Cape Town: African Minds.

Vigne, R., and Currey, J. 2014. The new African 1962-1969: South Africa in particular and Africa in general. *English in Africa* 41(1): 55-73.

Von Humboldt, W. 1970. University reform in Germany: reports and documents. *Minerva* 8: 242 -50.

Vostal, F. 2016. *Accelerating academia: the changing structure of academic time*. New York: Palgrave

———. 2019. Slowing down modernity: A critique. *Time & Society*, 28: 1039- 60.

———. (Ed.). 2021. *Inquiring into academic timescapes*. Emerald.

Vurayai, S., and Ndofirepi, A.P. 2020. 'Publish or perish': implications for novice African university scholars in the neoliberal era. *African Identities*, 1-14. 10.1080/14725843.2020.1813084

Waters, L. 2004. *Enemies of promise: publishing, perishing, and the eclipse of scholarship*. Chicago: Prickly Paradigm.

Weber, M. 1948. Science as a vocation. In H. Gerth and C.W. Mills (eds), *From Max Weber: essays in Sociology*. London: Routledge and Kegan Paul.

Weingart, P., and Taubert, N. 2017. *The future of scholarly publishing: open access and the economics of digitisation*. Cape Town: African Minds.

Weingart, P., Joubert, M, and Connoway, K. 2021. Public engagement with science—origins, motives and impact in academic literature and science policy. *PloSOne* 16. https://doi.org/10.1371/journal. pone.0254201

Wendland, C.L. 2010. A *heart for the work: journeys through an African medical school*. Chicago: University of Chicago Press.

White, E., and King, L. 2020. Shaping scholarly communication guidance channels to meet the research needs and skills of doctoral students at Kwame Nkrumah University of Science and Technology. *The Journal of Academic Librarianship,* 46(1): 102081. DOI: 10.1016/j.acalib.2019.102081

Wilsdon, J. 2015. *The metric tide: report of the independent review of the role of metrics in research assessment and management*. London: HEFCE.

Wilson, L. 1942. *The academic man: a study in the sociology of a profession*. New York: Transaction.

World Bank. 2014. *A decade of development in sub-Saharan African science, technology, engineering and mathematics research*. Washington, D.C.: World Bank.

Xu, X. 2019. 'China 'goes out' in a centre–periphery world: incentivizing international publications in the humanities and social sciences. *Higher Education,* 80: 157-172

Xu, L., and Grant, B. 2020. Doctoral publishing and academic identity work: two cases. *Higher Education Research & Development*, 39: 1502-1515.

Yanney-Wilson, J. 1961. Ghana Science Association. *Nature* 190(4781): 1064-1065. DOI: 10.1038/1901064a0.

———. 1962. The Ghana Science Association. *Nature* 195(4846): 1055-1056. DOI: 10.1038/1951055a0.

Yudkevich, M, De Wit, H., and Altbach, P. 2019. *Trends and issues in doctoral education worldwide: an international research inquiry.* New Delhi: Sage.

Zeleza, P. 1997. *Manufacturing African Studies and crises*. Dakar, Senegal: CODESRIA.

———. 2009. African Studies and universities since independence. *Transition,* (101): 110-35.

Zell, H. M. 1977. *The African book world & press: a directory*. Oxford: Hans Zell.

———. 1984. *Publishing & book development in Africa: A bibliography*. Paris: UNESCO.

———. 1998. *A handbook of good practice in journal publishing*. London: International African Institute.

———. 2017. The African university press – a gloomy picture. *University World News*. https://www.universityworldnews.com/post. php?story=20170922175606239.

———. 2019. Indigenous publishing in sub-Saharan Africa: A chronology and some landmarks. *African Research & Documentation: Journal of SCOLMA (The UK Libraries and Archives Group on Africa)* (136): 36-61.

Glossary of terms

Bibliographic database: An organised digital collection of references to published academic literature, usually including journal articles, conference proceedings, reports, books, etc. They usually contain detailed 'metadata' in the form of keywords, subject classification terms, or abstracts. A bibliographic database may be general in scope or cover a specific academic discipline.

Citation index: This is an index of citations between publications, allowing the user to easily establish which later documents cite which earlier documents. In 1960, Eugene Garfield's Institute for Scientific Information (ISI) introduced the first citation index for papers published in academic journals. The two main general commercially-owned and subscription-based citation indexes are *Scopus*, owned by Elsevier and *Web of Science* (WoS), owned by Clarivate Analytic. Scopus now includes the Latin American SciELO citation index. There are other open-access subject-based citation indexes, such as PubMed. There is currently no Africa-focused citation index.

h-index: The h-index is an author-level measurement, defined as the maximum value of h such that a given author/journal has published at least h papers that have each been cited at least h times. The index provides a more nuanced measure of influence than the total number of citations or publications.

Journal Impact Factor: This is a numerical measure of the yearly average number of citations that articles published in the last two years in a given journal received. It is used to measure the perceived importance of a journal within its field; journals with higher impact factors are deemed to be more prestigious and, perhaps more contentious, of higher quality.

Metrics: Any quantitative measure, used in this context in relation to publishing. Journals, articles and authors now all have 'metrics'. These would include the number of citations an article receives, a journal's impact factor, or a scholar's list of publications. Some would argue that the 'metricisation' of the academy is profoundly changing the nature of academic practice.

Open access: This term was popularised by the signatories to the 2002 Budapest Open Access Initiative (BOAI), who called for a 'new generation' of journals that did not invoke copyright to restrict access, but rather used copyright to promote permanent open access. They also called for self-archiving, and for new 'cost-recovery' and financing models for journals.

www.ingramcontent.com/pod-product-compliance
Lightning Source LLC
Chambersburg PA
CBHW052010030426
42334CB00029BA/3166